Some of
My Best
Friends
Are . . .

For Heather
Best wishes
Yasmin
Alibhai-
Brown

Some of My Best Friends Are . . .

Collected journalism

1989–2004

Yasmin Alibhai-Brown

POLITICO'S

First published in Great Britain 2004 by
Politico's Publishing, an imprint of
Methuen Publishing Limited
215 Vauxhall Bridge Road
London SW1V 1EJ

10 9 8 7 6 5 4 3 2 1

A CIP catalogue record for this book is available from the British Library.

ISBN 1 84275 107 7

Printed and bound in Great Britain by Mackays of Chatham plc, Chatham, Kent

Contents

Contents

Contents

Introduction

This book will not please Richard Marriott who wrote to me in the spring of 2004: 'Ms Brown, you are not representative of mainstream white opinion. You are out on a limb so long it is in danger of collapsing. You like to portray yourself as a fluffy bunny earth mother, whereas in reality you are as full of hate and as extreme as any member of the Ku Klux Klan. You hate and despise your adopted country – by returning your undeserved Honour you were spitting on this country and its people.' Mr Marriot's wife is black Jamaican, he says and these are her views too.

He joins the thousands round the world who regularly correspond with newspapers columnists. The internet is both a blessing and a curse for us.

Hours after my weekly column in the *Independent* appears, hundreds of missives, good, bad and ugly fly in. Each week produces a fresh crop of objectors and others who applaud or intelligently question. Readers have made me think, laugh, cry, scream and sometimes shiver fearfully through sleepless nights. It may just be because I am, at present, apparently one of only two non-white regular newspaper columnists in Europe. Like any respectable nerd, I used to count the positives and negatives and frequently fall into pathological anxiety. Not any more. Although it is enraging to hear from racists, Muslim Stalinists, unwavering ideologues and mean nationalists, it is important they do write in and I am getting tougher so it hurts less. These conversations are an essential part of the job which I love.

As I cannot ever be depended on to follow a certain line – for example, always pro-Labour, anti-racist, pro-feminist, pro-Islam, I also get many accusations of gross betrayal by various campaigners who believe I should be unquestioningly loyal. I am still getting such letters from overexcited sisters who objected violently when I wrote about how I was trying to become a less choleric wife to my husband after reading the book *The Surrendered Wife* by Laura Doyle. The offending column is in this collection. Funny how Nigella Lawson is admired when she suggests many ways to please a man (they tell me it is 'ironic') but not the rest of us mere mortals. I have got back into bad old habits again, by the way. So they can take that article off the Backlash Feminism course list.

If I discount the demonic haters and killers – of whom more later- my least favourite emailer this year was Ted (the second year running) who writes in with alarming frequency to tell me to shove off to where I came from, that I am a disgrace to the United Kingdom of Great Britain (sic) Ted, you are American from Austin, Texas. It is one thing to be invited to leave this island by the fans of Norman Tebbit but what gives you the authority? Have you really come to believe that we are now just another one of your many states?

Then there's Edward who longs to rip my clothes off and do me over: 'You Pakis with your shaved off clits need to be fucked sense-less by English patriots and thrown to the sharks, like in those James Bond Films.' There's no stopping Sharon or Michael either, oh no. Not since I wrote I was going to boycott Israeli goods (latest: check the labels of all the herbs in supermarkets) these two have been bombarding me with 'evidence' of only Palestinian barbarisms, never those perpetrated by Sharon and his army. One hundred and eighty-seven apoplectic Australians wrote in after I criticised Australian political attitudes following the bomb in Bali. They were the most easy-going people in the world, how dare a bloody Muslim say otherwise? Egocentric Americans continue furiously to demand a blind and unconditional approval of their nation. I must mention the O'Dwyers and Maureen and Milo (who likes to call me a 'trashy girlie') who are hysterically opposed to black immigration and repelled by my uppitiness. But Ted was the outright winner.

Among the most favourite were the readers who surprised.

Ali Santos, a Muslim convert in Argentina, shared his love for his adopted beliefs. A Middle Eastern prince (who has much to lose should this ever happen) expressed dangerous approval for the need for human rights values especially in Islamic countries. A confused ex-BNP supporter said he was madly in love with Lisa, jet black and a Zimbabwean asylum-seeker he met on a packed coach to Manchester. He had his wallet nicked; she gave him a fiver and they have been seeing each other ever since. She has no idea what the BNP is and he doesn't want her to find out. What do I think? Over two hundred black Britons agreed with the column which argued that peer group pressure was as damaging as racism to black men and boys. It was, however, denounced as 'rubbish' by one prominent black leader. Lucy, a white City broker wrote in to say she was mentoring a young black boy for the very reasons I brought up in the column. By far the highest number of approving letters arrive when I criticise the rampantly sexualised culture surrounding our children. I only wish those in charge of our public culture would take some notice.

Readers fearlessly put me right on facts, new developments and media assumptions. I was unfair and plain wrong when I said that Zadie Smith had moved to the US because she was a prima donna who couldn't stand any criticism. I made a foolish error by not checking when I claimed the surgeon Magdi Yacoub was a Muslim. Jonathan, a civil servant, provided useful information to show that the government is not slavishly following the agenda of the right-wing papers on immigration policies. Asad asked quite rightly why he should, as a Muslim, always be expected to denounce what other Muslims do. Are Catholics being asked to distance themselves from paedophilia?

And I was reminded, by his distraught friends, of Ross Parker, the poor white teenager who was murdered in a racist attack in Peterborough by three young men of Muslim origin. He was attacked with a CS spray, a hammer and a foot-long knife. His story was not on the front page of too many newspapers. There was no demonstration. I did not write on him. I failed.

It is always hard, this when you have spent your life fighting white racism. When news broke of the horrible murder of two-year-old Ainlee, a young girl murdered by her parents, people she was born to trust, I prayed the killers weren't black. They were. A gang jailed for carjackings and violence later that same week was black and three other Muslim men were convicted for the murder of a father of two young children after he tried to stop them stealing a car.

These dastardly acts are not worse because they are committed by black or Asian people but nor are they automatically more understandable because of racism. I will and do fight against injustice and inequality and the power merchants who apply low ethical standards when victims are people of colour. But the rot within also destroys too many communities.

These days, however, a few honest and brave individuals from these communities are beginning to speak out on the destructive effects of such problems which are kept well away from open public scrutiny and debate. (If you never wash your dirty linen in public the stench and dirt overpower everything.) I am particularly encouraged that the vast majority of Muslim correspondents agree that we need to reform ourselves. But we have ruthless enemies, fanatics who write emails like this Shahin, who distributes lofty thoughts like this:

Moderates like Yasmin Alibhai-Brown are our eternal enemies. Allah hates these people... her face is like a dog's backside, she denounces true Muslims who have taken the trouble to fight for true Islam. Wake up ms Apostate Brown. Allah shows us how to recognise these traitors. Alibhai-Brown has even supported the adulteress in Nigeria when all true Muslims know fornicators must be punished. She supports sodomites, she has Jewish and Christian friends. The only reward for these people will be death, crucifixion. We must undermine and silence these 'moderate' reformers.' Other true warriors have asked for us to be 'burned without mercy.'

Add to these the Russians who warned me off after my piece on their treatment of Chechens, the Hindu fundamentalists who want me never to set foot in India and the 'Friends of the USA' who want people like me or Robert Fisk or Mark Steel first tortured then dead, and you begin to understand the chaos of the twenty-first century.

The one issue I have found deeply problematic is that of Israel and anti-Semitism. It is absolutely my right, indeed it is an absolute obligation, that I should unequivocally condemn the policies of the Israeli government when necessary. I have to present the feelings of Muslims around the world who watch the grave injustices perpetrated on Palestinians. The debate is unbalanced. Although there are honourable journalists who do report this conflict dispassionately, there is, to date, no Palestinian British journalist (even though refugees have been here for forty five years) and yet there are always intelligent, fair minded people in our public life who can and do speak up for the rights of Israel and Jewish people.

It is always possible because anti-Semitism is always with us that some people are using the politics of Israel to vent an ancient hatred. But it is also possible that many of the individuals who cry anti-Semitism when Israel is censured are doing so calculatedly to disable the critics. Then there is the question of standards. Do we judge Israel more harshly than other countries which do worse? Or is Israel immune from the standards we apply to, say Iraq or Pakistan? We never, ever demand transparency on Israel's WMDs for example. Or is Israel, a democracy, rightly judged by its own declared standards?

Two of my own colleagues on the Independent have had serious misgivings about my position on Israel; one publicly presumed to doubt my empathy with the Jewish cause and support for the idea of a safe state for Jewish people. He notified me authoritatively- a combination of Moses and an Oxford Don- that Jews would not be 'slandered'. I answered him back forcefully in a follow up column. Eight hundred emails flooded in. At least a third were brutally anti-Semitic. One young man sent an email to praise me on behalf of Allah and confided he was planning to be a martyr but hadn't yet fixed on a cause so if I thought he could help... (it sounded genuine) and thirteen chieftains from Afghanistan wrote in to say I was their sister forever. The moral merry-go-round of modern life.

In the months that have followed the war against Iraq. Americans in particular are triumphant, insulting, incredibly arrogant, insensitive and convinced that the 21st century is theirs. They are wrong. The war without end in Iraq shows how wrong. The next century will not be dominated in this way; people will find other ways to fight back and no tanks or WOMD will be able to stop them. That is the lesson the US and its allies have not learned, will not learn.

British Multiculturalism, immigration policies and race relations inevitably form a key part of what I write. These issues matter, and increasingly so to the whole nation as we enter a new phase in our collective histories, as we struggle to make sense of what it means to be British now. In 1999 I wrote the book True Colours on the duty of government to lead positively on race and immigration. Tony Blair endorsed the book at the launch. But that was before the fall of New Labour into the pits where asylum-baiting is the new national sport. Then came the controversial Runnymede report on multi-ethnic Britain which demanded a new definition of Britishness. I was on the panel of respected people responsible for this important book, although I believed then and even more so now that too much credibility was given in the text to 'communities'. We were denounced as rogues and traitors by most of the media and criticism came from the right as well as the left. Jack Straw, then Home Secretary, was contemptuous. Hugo Young was scathing. The deputy editor of the *New Statesman*, Cristina Odone, hired a hackette to demolish my reputation. Some on the panel got threats from the public.

We were forced to re-examine the landscape and our assumptions. I went on to write two further books – *After Multiculturalism* and *Who Do We Think We Are? Re-Imagining the British Nation*. Both these suggested, over-boldly perhaps, that old multiculturalism was now utterly unsuitable as an ideological basis for enlightened policies. In truth it had kept black and Asians playing marbles in the ghetto, away from the real centres of power and influence. Devolution, globalisation, renewed tribalisations, the end of communism had created a different country with new dilemmas and a more profound engagement was needed with all its citizens if the centre was not to fall apart.

Multicultural policies did make some difference when immigrants were settling in and through into the Thatcherite years. The first four black and Asian MPs came into Parliament, broadcasters, publishers, educators began to address a heterogeneous nation, citizens of colour gained confidence and made real demands. But as time went on, just as affirmative action outlived its moral authority so it is with our brand of multiculturalism. It does not connect. It is not modern. It is not useful any longer. In fact, it is worse than useless.

I only understood the extent to which Britons of colour are still thought of as guests in this country when I returned my MBE after witnessing the admirable position taken by the poet Benjamin

Zephaniah who refused an OBE because he loathes the implications embedded in the honours business. I realised I should never have accepted mine, especially as I am a republican. The war on Iraq and the new empire made it impossible for me to hold on to the bauble. There was flack, much of it deserved, because unlike Zephaniah I had shown no courage or conviction initially. But I was not prepared for *Guardian* writers to slag me off many times over and nor was I ready to be reminded that I had to behave better because I was an unwanted visitor to this land of tolerance.

Imagine this scene. In the next election, a black woman gets selected to fight for a seat in Middle England. She goes to the constituency and asks to meet the leader of the ethnic English community. Who would she be taken to? The editor of the local newspaper? The vicar? The mayor? The chairwoman of the WI? And would any of them or even all of them 'represent' the English people in that area? Of course not. Yet 'Take me to your leader' is what white politicians and others demand whenever they alight upon an area where there are substantial numbers of black and Asian people. If ever we needed proof that we are still regarded as aliens, it is this fact.

Not surprisingly, this demand for 'community leaders' produces a rash of individuals who are only too ready to stick out their chests and claim that they speak for Muslims, black Britons, Hindus, Asians, whatever. They run their own little mafia groups to keep people in order; they produce poisonous 'community' newspapers and, when talking to ministers and others with power, they constantly raise the spectre of 'extremists' and civil disturbance, the implication being that without them all hell could break loose and who wants that on this quiet little island? Powerful white institutions and individuals have actively helped to foster these invidious zealots.

I despise these so-called leading lights. They corrupt the meaning of democracy and crush individualism and independent thought. They stamp mercilessly on people – especially women. We may feel bonds with the various communities, which I clearly do, but we will not be bound by the tyranny and insanity of community politics.

I am a writer and a broadcaster, not a mouthpiece, not an envoy, not an agent, not an archetype, not an ambassador, never ever a spokesperson except for the think tanks for which I do some work.

What I do is no different from say, Polly Toynbee or David Aaronovitch. We all write and speak on issues in ways which are obviously conditioned by our different backgrounds. But they are white and I am not and this is what makes the difference.

One of the most pernicious effects of living in a racially unequal and divided society is that both sides conspire to rob you of your individuality and liberty to be who you are. It is only in the last four years – fourteen years after I started in the business – that I have been permitted by some imaginative white editors to express views, however controversial, about all those issues which I am interested in, including national politics, sex, food, children as well as race, class religion and ethnicity. This is obviously too shocking for some to take. People like me are not allowed to have to distinct, innovative ideas. Everything we are has to fit into simple labelled categories; all that we say is believed to be representative and all that is expected are platitudes from a brain washed of the capacity to dissent.

Many of Toni Morrison's early novels explore this quest for a self which needs to live and breathe even as it locates itself within ethnic, racial, religious and political territories. In *Tar Baby*, for example, one of the characters, Jadine, says that she feels guilty for liking Ave Maria better than gospel music and Picasso better than an African mask. Sometimes, she says, '[I long] to get out of my skin and be only the person inside – not American, not black – just me.' I know exactly how she feels. It is not that we wish we were white. Just that we cannot just be cows in a branded herd throughout our all too brief lives.

The deeper question here is about identity. Few of us have a single, all-defining identity which you can use for all seasons. When the Lawrence case was so much in the news, I felt black. This was our battle – whether Asian, Muslim, Hindu, African – against racism. On forced marriages, I react as an angry Asian woman. Watching ripe young Palestinian boys dying, my emotional response comes out of feeling with them as a Muslim but more out of a burning belief in basic human rights and self-determination. But when Palestinian men carry out honour killings or torture their own, I condemn them absolutely. And since devolution I have felt profoundly British. All of us – black and white Britons – feel this multitude of allegiances, some connected to an ethnic past, some not. In his stirring new book, *On Identity*, the French Lebanese writer, Amin Maalouf deconstructs this very modern phenomenon:

I'm challenging the notion that reduces identity to one single affiliation and encourages people to adopt an attitude that is partial, sectarian, intolerant, domineering . . . Their view of the world is biased and distorted. Those who belong to our communities are 'ours' . . . but if they are thought to be 'lukewarm' we denounce them, intimidate them, punish them.

Or worst of all deny them the right to be free human beings with choices about when they support a cause and when they can't; when they operate as individuals and when they place themselves within a group.

*

The writings in this book have been divided into four areas: The Enemy Within contains pieces on immigration, geopolitics, British politics and Britishness. In Culture Clashes I have gathered writings on multiculturalism, race and identities. Reform Islam is a self-explanatory category. Finally, in Feminism, Family, Football and Fornication are columns on feminism, relationships, sex and popular culture. These are broad categories which can overlap. All of the pieces are from the *Independent* except where noted, my thanks to all of the publications who have so generously given permission to use the articles in this book.

The Enemy Within

T he veteran writer and journalist Edward Pearce sent me an e-mail in the spring of 2004 saying: 'You are the most gifted nuisance I know.' It was a compliment I shall treasure. In this section are some of the most annoying, infuriating pieces I have written over the years. They were not written to whip up needless irritation. Some columnists are exceptionally good at this game and enjoy the outrage they deliberately generate. They are celebs, cocky, playful, rich provocateurs, but insiders all the same. I am not one of them. I loiter and observe from the periphery. Occasionally, I am allowed close to power, and it is never easy for either side. The rules of engagement, so evident to them, are incomprehensible to me. Why, for example have, or trust, a clique of parliamentary lobby journalists? They cannot, ever, whatever their good intentions, say what they truly think because that would lose them the privilege of intimacy with politicians.

I write what I believe as honestly as possible. I change my mind. Once I relished humiliating the English – revenge for the Empire. Now I feel that was wrong and that the English identity has been denied respect for too long. I have been at times spectacularly wrong and/or naïve, and my views are unpredictable except on a few issues where I have remained steadfast – immigration most of all. Today the centre left and right have gathered forces to poison the waters even more for asylum seekers and migrants. For the descendants of immigrants, the battle for rights has taken on a new, bloody urgency.

Loyalty is much in demand in the world today. It is an insistent, tyrannical stipulation calling on people to give an absolute, unquestioned approval to this group or that. I feel no such unconditional *loyalty to all members of my family, my 'community', faith, nation, political party, culture or continent. Yet there is a menacing mood growing where one is denounced (sometimes condemned to death) for so-called transgressions and betrayals. New Labour, multicultchi Tories, the monarchy, Zionists, Muslim apologists, British nationalists, black and Asian appeasers, have all described me as the 'enemy within'. In this first section, you can see why.*

The Siege of Britain

Guardian, 25 October 1995

Recently I asked shoppers in a suburban shopping mall in Ealing, west London, what they felt about refugees seeking asylum in this country. The antagonism expressed by the majority of them was shocking. They were convinced that most applications were 'bogus', and that thousands of grasping people were flooding into Britain using implausible sob stories in order to enter and get at our council houses and benefits. Only four people out of sixty were outraged that many asylum-seekers are incarcerated without a hearing, for an average of 154 days, and that there have been a number of recorded cases of self-mutilation and suicides among those denied refugee status.

And yet the people I was talking to would see themselves as caring, compassionate folk, who believe in justice and fairness and who even express pride that this country has always been a sanctuary for those in need. But these days so contaminated are public attitudes towards refugees that there is an outcry when a tiny proportion of lottery money is given to an Eritrean refugee centre. These attitudes are appearing elsewhere too: the European Commission recently advocated that governments should engineer 'an evolution of public and political perceptions of immigration and asylum issues'.

The hostility and intolerance towards refugees, particularly from the non-white world, has been deliberately fostered by an increasingly desperate government in search of cheap political gain. And over the next few months we are likely to see an acceleration of this. Michael Howard, Peter Lilley and colleagues barely let a week go by these days without some punitive action against those in search of asylum. This summer, income support and housing benefits were axed for those whose applications are being processed. Salima, a Somali student of mine whose husband was killed in the war and who has four children, sobbed over the phone: 'These people can feel sorry for the cows and the goats but not for people like us.'

Hawa, another Somali widow seeking asylum, told me that she was at the immigration office in Croydon when a Kurdish man burnt himself to death. She recalled how one of the officers joked about the smell of kebabs. And, she said, she had thought she was coming to a civilised country.

Now the Home Secretary intends that countries such as Algeria and Nigeria – where there is currently appalling political repression – are 'safe', where refugees are supposed not to be at risk. This endless and vindictive assault on refugees means that even those who have a right to be here are treated as feckless dependants on a country which is already under pressure.

This siege mentality may be politically useful in the short term but the damage it is inflicting on the ideals of this country and on those who have had to make their lives here is unforgivable. I was a 'refugee' from Uganda. I came here with other Ugandan Asians, because I had to. It is never easy to lose your country and your home, to live in exile, forever insecure and having to be grateful. But what you do when you find yourself without a country is to reclaim your self-respect. You do not scrounge. Quite the opposite. You want to regain control of your life. You want to succeed in order to feel safe again. Look at the Ugandan Asians: when we came here, people stood with posters at airports telling us to go home. The city of Leicester placed advertisements in newspapers telling us we were not welcome there. Today the same city has been regenerated by those very immigrants. My people have created 30,000 jobs in the Midlands. In medicine, science, the City, Ugandan Asians are making their mark.

In 1972, I remember being spat at by a weedy taxi driver who threw my money back into my face and cursed me when I told him I was from Uganda. Visiting some of the refugee camps near Oxford where I was studying, you could see groups of distraught people huddled together, talking about how they were going to get started again, and how they were going to exploit any tenuous connections they had with people who were already settled here.

So it is with most refugees. History has taught us how much they can and do contribute to the life of a country – from books to business, our culture has been enriched by the Jewish refugees who arrived in the 1940s. But these days, instead of using the talents of the people who have come here, we let them rot or misuse their skills.

Such attitudes are not just economically wasteful for the country and destructive for the individual refugees. In the end they destroy the soul of a country. Rabbi Dr Jonathan Magonet of the Leo Baeck College put it like this: 'Allowing the gere [stranger] to contribute to society is to offer them the chance to express their own self-worth and dignity ... We are defined as a human society precisely by the way we treat the ones who don't belong to us.'

It is not as if the government didn't have the evidence close to hand. A Home Office report published this spring showed that the majority of refugees in this country have substantial work and educational experience. (Unsurprisingly, it is a report the government was reluctant to publicise.) Most asylum-seekers, the research study noted, face 'a high rate of physical and psychological suffering, largely consequent upon the past experiences that led individuals to seek asylum, and because of separation from their families'.

Its conclusion: 'The celebration of distinctive cultures makes a positive contribution to the richness of modern British life. Intolerance and bigotry are best combated through personal relationships across ethnic and cultural boundaries: through, that is, the sharing of cultural difference.'

Come the Queen's Speech, perhaps someone will mention this to Her Majesty.

The Commonwealth's cannon fodder

12 November 1998

It would have been crass to write this column yesterday. It is essential to write it today. The morning after the weeks before when the country drank in war memories is a good time to ask: 'Why do we wear the poppy and keep a two-minute silence when the real significance of both these gestures has now become so degraded?'

Yes, we do remember, but only the bits that suit the purposes of certain groups involved in the conflicts. Too much else has been edited out and so the remembrance services themselves become endorsements of myths rather than memories of the truth. These rituals will mean less and less unless we begin to do better on the narratives of the past.

This is even more crucial now because so many who were there have since died, and because the young barely care about what moral choices mean in the modern world. I talked to a gang of pre-teen smokers outside the local sweet shop today. They think that the Russians helped Hitler, and that the Allies consisted of the British and the Americans. One thought the French 'did some fighting', too. They did not know – and most white Britons have never remembered – that 1,700,000 men and women from the Commonwealth died in the two wars. The First World War, which is a potent force in the national psyche, was our story too.

And such a story makes me want to whip my own moderation and make it rise to fury. Here were men, thousands of them, caught up in a war that arose out of European powers bickering over empires that had made my ancestors subject people. The colonies were not consulted and yet India, being the richest, was obliged to supply £250m of material help. A further £200m was raised there in war loans in 1917. The economy was drained, and nothing could be done for 16 million victims of a flu epidemic immediately after the war.

But the most astonishing contribution was that of the soldiers whose pictures, staring out of trenches, are unbearable. They were ill-equipped for the weather, unused to the terrain, and still they fought with such bravery that a German soldier wrote of them: 'Today we had to fight against the Indians and the devil knows those brown rascals are not to be underrated.'

The Indian soldiers wrote long laments home. Some used coded language describing how the 'black pepper from India' was all being used up and that much less 'red pepper' was being used.

The historian Rosina Visram believes that these letters show how Indian soldiers were used as cannon fodder on the Western front. This is the subject of an excellent play, *Across the Black Water*, by the novelist Mulk Raj Anand, currently playing at the Hackney Empire in London.

At the unveiling of a memorial on the South Downs in 1921 to honour these soldiers, the Prince of Wales said: 'It is befitting that future generations should not forget that our Indian comrades came when our need was highest – free men, volunteer soldiers – who gave their lives in a quarrel of which it was enough for them to know that the enemies were the foes of their sahibs, their Empire and their King.'

But the nation did forget, as it did the role of Africans, Caribbeans and others too in the Second World War. Yet we all faithfully wear that red flower on our lapels hoping that one year, black and Asian Britons will not have to make these abject pleas for recognition and that every programme and newspaper and every opportunistic politician, too, will say how we, too, helped to make Europe great and potentially safe.

This matters, because only by learning this will we be accepted as the true Europeans we are. Europe and the West will then be forced to reconsider its obligations and its recent actions.

'Never again,' they said and say still. It has become a fetishistic phrase which, besides making people feel better than they should, allows them to ignore the sufferings of Bosnian and Kosovan Muslims. For the only way that Nato and the US can live with xenophobic massacres on European soil right now is by pretending that twentieth-century Europe owes its existence only to Judaeo-Christian soldiers and that the rest cannot be covered by their honourable post-war intentions.

Never has there been such a massive capacity to stop such slaughter, and yet the great powers do nothing except make loud noises, play bugles and turn memorials red with solemnity and wreaths.

Our forebears were there with yours, and together, surely, we should be asking that that story be properly told, and that our leaders should not betray the ideals which they all died for.

The Jewels in Your Crown
are Ours, Ma'am

2 March 2000

I think I was about ten and a half when I became a republican. It was in Kampala, Uganda, during the glory days of the Empire. Like every other child I knew, I saw the British as awesome people, hand-made by God to rule over the world. Their administrators walked tall, talked little and behaved with immaculate arrogance. I grew to believe that no other people on earth were as clever, orderly, morally dependable as our rulers.

Then my Marxist teacher, Mr Shah, father of six boys who shared four pairs of shoes between them, told me about the Koh-i-noor, one of the world's biggest and most beautiful diamonds, once owned by Maharajah Duleep Singh of the Punjab before it was annexed by the British in March 1849. The bloody British had stolen it (said Mr Shah) and stuck it in the middle of Queen Victoria's crown: 'Do you call that honesty? We can never hold our heads high until these English thieves return the treasures they have taken.'

Duleep Singh was haunted by the diamond and carried on demanding its return until he died, impoverished and broken, in Paris in 1893. Lord Dalhousie, the viceroy responsible for the ignoble acquisition, said that the diamond had 'found its proper resting place'.

The story touched a raw nerve. I threw away my scrapbook containing all my pictures of Queen Elizabeth and Princess Margaret and I gave up on the British royal family.

I remembered that militant moment last Tuesday when, once again, we were reminded of how much Jewish-owned art was stolen by the Nazis during the Holocaust. Hundreds of priceless paintings – including some by Picasso, Renoir and Delacroix – in the British Museum, the V&A, the Tate and the National are (allegedly) part of this Nazi loot. Anne Webber, head of the Commission for Looted Art in Europe, and other luminaries want them returned or paid for. I hope they succeed.

But is it right that certain historical injustices are endlessly championed while others remain shrouded politely in the past? We discuss this issue only when Greeks bring up the Elgin Marbles (again and again) or when the well-connected Jewish lobby, quite properly, demands redress. Why have Indians not campaigned for the return of, or (more realistically) fair payment for, all those treasures shamelessly purloined first by the East India Company then by imperial representatives? Are we (ex-colonials) still so locked in mental subjugation that we dare not even ask?

Well, I am asking. Let us at least demand an audit of how many objects of value – paintings, fabrics, statues, jewels, sculptures, precious Korans and other books and anthropological artefacts – belonging to great civilisations in the former colonies are to be found in our museums, stately homes, government institutions (have you seen the grand rooms in the Foreign and Commonwealth Office?) and Oxford and Cambridge libraries.

And once we have such an audit, I suggest we can begin a process of creative negotiation. Some countries could choose to have parts of their foreign debts written off in exchange for a legal settlement. Other countries – Egypt and Iran, for example – could be offered free places in good British universities (plus grants) for their students to the value of the objects appropriated. India, Pakistan and Bangladesh might choose to settle for more generous immigration allowances.

The British government should fund the publication of books showing these treasures, and the books should be provided free to the countries concerned so that their children can learn what their ancestors achieved. Our sly mother country has indulged herself long enough on our diamonds, treasures and (these days) spices. It is pay-back time.

The truth is the Tories have always resented people like me

19 April 2000

I think it was a dream. Or maybe it was my head conjuring up images to fit my despair at the way British politicians (who like to be known abroad as fair, tolerant and decent) are using asylum-seekers as cheap bait to hook voters for the forthcoming local and London elections.

I saw a flaming gold chariot carrying a mad-eyed Ann Widdecombe, her intimidating chest covered with armour with a crown blazoned on it, and a huge whip in her hand. (If this seems grossly insulting to an 'honourable' Member of Parliament, I do not apologise. A well-seasoned football hooligan would have been shaken by her verbal violence in the Commons last week. I have never, ever seen such a depraved performance.) Jack Straw and his junior, Barbara Roche, were her exhausted horses who tried their best to outrun her whip but couldn't. They were tied to her, you see. Then I woke up to the sound of James Naughtie on the *Today* programme talking about William Hague and his brilliant new wheeze to have internment camps for asylum-seekers, including children. Manacles to the walls near the bed too, surely. They worked a treat with pregnant prisoners. Widdecombe must have other ideas too, seeing as she has discussed prison reform with Charles Murray, the American academic who believes in genetic inferiority.

Huge numbers of us are appalled at the way New Labour ministers have allowed themselves to be driven by the Tories on this issue. The Tory Party has a damp and dingy soul where real, overt racial prejudice dwells and festers. That's one thing we could not say about Labour or the Lib Dems. Indeed no Tory would ever write what Mike O'Brien, another Home Office minister, did in the *Parliamentary Monitor* this month when he accepted, like a man, that the Home Office is 'institutionally racist'. For all the many quarrels I have with him on asylum, this was a brave admission.

Tories have given the nation Enoch Powell, Norman Tebbit, Winston Churchill junior, Margaret Thatcher, Terry Dicks, Charles Wardle, Michael Howard, and now Ann Widdecombe – all have used their positions to poison the minds of British people.

The history of the Tory Party on race and immigration is almost wholly ignominious (with some exceptions like Edward Heath who refused to attend the funeral of Enoch Powell) and I cannot understand how so many Asian and black people can bear to vote for a party which has always resented our presence. In my forthcoming book, *Who Do we Think We Are?* I examine this history. In the Cabinet papers of 1955, the Commonwealth Secretary, Alec Douglas-Home, said: 'We do not wish to keep out immigrants of the good type from the old dominions... [but] immigration officers could, without giving rise to trouble or publicity, exercise such a measure of discrimination as we think desirable.'

This ingested discrimination of immigration officers operates to this day and we are already hearing mutterings of how white Zimbabweans are 'kith and kin' who should all be brought home immediately. In the 1964 election, the slogan 'If you want a nigger neighbour, vote Labour' was used to assist in the defeat of Patrick Gordon Walker, the then shadow Foreign Secretary, by the Tory Peter Griffiths. Today the Tories are pushing pamphlets with false costings showing the 'burden' on local taxpayers.

Enoch foamed in 1968 with his Rivers of Blood speech. In the seventies, Thatcher made her remark about white Britons feeling 'swamped' by aliens and was one of forty-four Tories who were actively opposed to the Race Relations Act. Then we had Tebbitt's cricket test, and the calculated assaults on asylum-seekers orchestrated by Michael Howard and Widdecombe herself. The smarmy Tory Andrew Lansley has openly admitted that immigration was 'successfully raised' in the 1992 election and 'has more potential to hurt'.

So how has Labour responded to this long Tory onslaught on diversity? Since 1964, Labour has vacillated between enlightened policies and the politics of cowardice. During the second reading of the Asylum and Immigration Bill in 1995, I discovered that the word 'bogus' was used forty-seven times. Even with their massive majority, New Labour has not the courage or wit to transform the debate on race. They cling to the belief that they must soften the blow of a new race relations act by creating ever more inhumane immigration laws. As Sarah Spencer of the Institute of Public Policy Research points out: 'Once a government decides to appease rather than to assuage public concern, new measures have to be proposed to show that something is being done. Loopholes are identified, rule changes proposed, appeal rights abolished.'

Until the next time the Tories start up again. Far from improving race relations, as Bill Morris said, people become more anxious and unsettled and race relations get worse.

So what can Labour do to save us from these raging Tories? They can unbuckle themselves from the chariot. They can explain that the reason we are getting so many more asylum-seekers is that there are wars again in Europe and huge inequalities too since the end of communism. Instead of people suffering in faraway places – Rwanda, Congo – we are now dealing with sad and needy white Europeans who are near enough to come over. They can start using the word 'ineligible' not because it is a more accurate word than bogus.

Ten per cent of those seeking asylum are crooks. A large percentage have no status under the narrow definition of the 1951 Geneva Convention. Women in Kosovo today with rape babies are being rejected by their own, but they have no legal case to get refuge in this country. When are journalists going to ask the Tories and Jack Straw who are the 'genuine' refugees? Do they include the women above or those starving to death in Ethiopia?

We cannot take all the refugees the world is unleashing because we are a densely populated country. But the British public needs to be told that these are genuinely dispossessed people and that an ageing British population will need immigrants again. But Labour politicians can't do this because they are so scared, still so scared of the Tory Party. If Labour cannot oppose the racism of Tories now, when they are so unpopular, then Labour does not deserve to win a second term.

Why we must remember the dead in a Dover truck

12 July 2000

It all began on 19 June, the hottest day we have had so far this summer. I was asked to compere a TUC event launching an initiative to fight racism in the workplace. It was a jolly evening with celebs, steel bands, wine and five-star canapés. But many of us were distracted because this was also the day that the bodies of fifty-eight young Chinese men and women were found in the back of an airless container.

Imagine then how these poor people must have suffered as they suffocated locked up in a box in that heat. Like others who are profoundly affected by this tragedy, I am haunted by images. I see vomit and clawed flesh and hear wild screams and fists banging on the walls.

I am sorry to upset readers, but I think it is essential not to avoid the awful reality of what must have happened before merciful oblivion put them to sleep.

They died three weeks ago, and yet as a country we have not properly mourned them or remembered them. The nameless fifty-eight have vanished into the ether. Just compare this to the reaction, both in Australia and here, to the terrible deaths of the young travellers who died in that hostel fire. Well, a group of us who were present at the TUC have decided to redress this shameful neglect. We are holding a vigil today (at 4.30pm at the West London Synagogue, 1 Seymour Place, Marble Arch, London W1), putting down a white lily for each person who died, as well as a wreath for all those we will never know about who have perished trying to make it to a good life.

Some British Chinese mourners will be present, and we will observe a minute's silence to show both respect and shame. Following this remembrance, we will hold a public meeting to discuss the causes of such tragedies and the way we might prevent them. An incredible number of well-known and ordinary people have come forward to offer support for this initiative, which we have called Action 58. I am very very grateful that they have signed up. They, we, have done so because we wish to tell a different story about immigrants and asylum-seekers, because most of us believe that our laws, are, in part, responsible for these deaths.

Try not to think of these people as 'illegals' or 'bogus refugees' or, that most evil of categories, 'economic migrants', and think of them instead as individual human beings, sons and daughters who were young and keen and/or desperate to make a future. The wreath we are putting down will bear cards with words such as 'lover', 'gardener', 'mother', 'cook', 'dreams', 'hunger' and 'computer scientist'. Many of our children here in Britain have just graduated from university. Full of fear and longings, they are trying to cope with the gush of uncertainty that rushes in after graduation. These victims were also twentysomethings with their lives ahead of them, living through, I imagine, a similar range of emotions. The one-child policy in China means that each was probably an only child. We don't really know yet what the families are going through or what is going to happen to the bodies – or even when they will be properly identified.

These, then, are the human reasons why we should be responding with empathy to their anguish. But our Action 58 aims to do more than that. Many of us have argued on these pages that our asylum policies are dehumanising those already here and failing those who need to get here. I also believe that we need to take more responsibility for the promiscuous way we are exporting our economic system across the globe. How many British people know that much of the maligned economic migration is the detritus produced by this new global capitalism? The world that we now live in demands a more expansive and imaginative approach to immigration, international obligations and human rights.

No British politician at the moment seems to have the nerve or the wit to take up these challenges. Instead, we have the paranoid Jack Straw and the demented Ann Widdecombe who daily feed us reasons to be hateful to those who are simply doing what people have done for centuries.

As Adrian Mitchell says in a poem that he has written especially for the vigil: 'From the child-murderer Poverty/Or the claws of

Nightmare Police/Painfully over land and sea/They come seeking some kind of peace.'

Government and opposition falsely believe that this is what the well-fed middle classes want them to do. The list of those backing Action 58 shows both how wrong they are. Will they listen? Probably not. They will most likely dismiss us all as luvvie friends of Ken Follett. But we can make them listen by using this day to start building up a viable coalition of people who feel strongly that no more people should die because they dared to hope for better.

A matter of arithmetic – or racist scaremongering?

6 September 2000

Never trust a journalist, especially one who comes across as a soulmate within minutes. There I was last Saturday, emerging from a delicious afternoon nap, when the phone rang. It was a reporter from a newspaper, wanting to talk about the foolish panic generated in the United States recently by the US Census Bureau issuing figures revealing that 'white' people were now in a minority in some states (including Hawaii, which I never knew had whites in a majority in the first place), and that California was going the same way, mainly because the immigrant Hispanic population had grown markedly.

For committed Wasps (White Anglo-Saxon Protestants), even those of Spanish heritage don't count as white. Some of this panic was then wafted over here, and we had a few silly comments about how it could well happen in Britain, too. The journalist and I agreed that a) that was utterly improbable, and b) in any case, it was racist to talk in such terms; after all, the Nazis, militant Serbs and the Hutus used exactly the same scare tactics to create an emotional groundswell of fear and prejudice as they went about their barbaric business.

Imagine my shock, then, when I opened the newspaper to find not only a crass headline – 'The last days of a white world' – but a deliberately alarmist piece that will have served only to comfort those who have always abhorred our presence here. I felt the heat of this hatred this Monday when I argued on the *Today* programme with Norman Tebbitt, who could not accept that someone with my name could possibly claim to belong to his island. I was born elsewhere, he coldly reminded me.

There are others who do truly believe that, in the dead of the night, we people of colour are busy fulfilling the objectives of a major, planned breeding programme. Some un-named demographer claims that 'it is a matter of pure arithmetic' that non-Europeans (who are just over 5.5 per cent of the population) will become the majority.

So be warned: we intend to out-birth white Britons, who will end up as rare as red squirrels. I can just see it. The editor of every paper will be a Patel, and 10 Downing Street will house the outlandish and curly-haired family of Prime Minister Delroy Raggamuffin. Buckingham Palace will be a mosque, and William's grandchildren will be forced to rote-learn the Koran. All utter rubbish, of course. As more black and Asian Britons join the middle classes, their birth rates fall.

But let us assume that said faint-hearted demographer is right, and that Britain will have vastly more people of Asian, Chinese, Balkan, African, Caribbean and other backgrounds. So what? This is already true of London. In areas such as Newham and Southall, Wasps are indeed the 'ethnic minority', a fact that some find troubling. But on the whole, I do not observe white Londoners creeping about laden with deep sorrow. Most have never had it so good in terms of choice, whether one is talking about food or lovers. And in the past few years, this diversity has started to define London and to make the capital one of the most amazing cities in the world. A survey carried out in March this year by the London Chamber of Commerce and Industry found that business leaders put cultural diversity at the top of their list of what made London better than other European cities.

The poison of racism remains, and imperial attitudes are not hard to find, yet the English, particularly in large cities (and I do mean the English – just compare what we have here to the nearly all-white Edinburgh and Dublin), have embraced this diversity with uncharacteristic passion. I think it would be churlish to deny this good life to those who inhabit the white heartlands, but they will be able to share its benefits only if there are many more of us.

There is a more serious point to be made here. If there are going to be proportionately more young black and Asian Britons in the population in the next two decades (and that is a real forecast, not a fantasy one), it is equally true that their economic activity will be essential to support an ageing population, the majority of which will be white.

Are we grumbling about this demographic time bomb and the burden to come? Do we sit around panicking about the pressures this will create for us? No, because most of us feel British, part of a nation, citizens with basic obligations to one another, regardless of colour. That is why so many of us are angry with the hacks and researchers responsible for this manufactured discontent and apprehension about fecund 'ethnic minorities' and the rightful white inhabitants of this land. Perhaps in a hundred years' time, such people and ideas will have become extinct. Now there's a prediction worth taking seriously.

Why does questioning the nature of Britishness raise so much fury?

18 October 2000

What a week. Had to sell my hammer and sickle in a car boot sale after the right-wing papers denounced me as a 'semi-Marxist'. Got repeatedly accosted by strangers demanding to know why I hated Britain so much. Had more awful racist letters than ever. Felt like putting on a burka, that all-covering cloak with only a small opening for the eyes, and disappearing for a long, long time.

Various pictures of me and other commissioners responsible for the report, 'The Future of Multi-Ethnic Britain', were displayed for all to pelt with spit, stones and scorn. And on it goes as Kate Gavron, a commissioner, is derided this week for suggesting that Prince Charles should have married a black woman. (Trust me: that is not in our report. Would any self-respecting black woman want ghastly in-laws and a man with peculiar fantasies about tampons?) Without reading the report, people have condemned who we were, what we did and what they had heard we had written.

We have been accused of saying that the idea of Britishness was racist. Completely false. The report is about continuing racial disadvantage and exclusion (hands up any institution that feels it reflects the diversity of Great Britain) and makes recommendations on what to do about these injustices. The report also suggests that as the concept of Britishness is problematic for many inhabitants of these islands, black and white, we need a national debate about how we might imagine a modern British identity that would mean something to many more of us.

Anyone who is familiar with this column or has read my *Who Do We Think We Are?* and *After Multiculturalism* knows how passionately I feel about my British identity and this nation, which is in danger of fragmentation. Read Tom Nairn's *After Britain*, or Andrew Marr's *The Day Britain Died*, and you realise this is a burning issue for all citizens. Last Monday the BBC produced the results of a survey of 1,500 people that showed one in three English people want their own anthem instead of the national anthem, and in some regions the majority feel themselves to be English rather than British. Local radio is running a full week on this emerging English identity, and a good idea it is, too. Similar results have shown up in Scotland and Wales. Unlike us, though, these anti-Britons are not denounced as traitors to crown and country.

The commentator Bruce Anderson, the nation's verbal mugger, accused us of being stupid and of wasting lottery money, a charge that was repeated in *The Times* and the *Observer*. Lies. Unlike the Dome so promoted by Simon Jenkins of *The Times*, we received no lottery money. None of the commissioners was paid anything, either. The right knew this, but yet deliberately exploded a false story creating a mushroom cloud of fumes and provoking the kind of hysteria I have not seen since the Rushdie crisis.

On *Question Time*, the actor Nigel Havers said we were 'bonkers' and the usually perceptive Allison Pearson suggested that the commissioners should go to France to see how well they neglect their non-white people. The next time women complain about inequality in this country, I look forward to Ms Pearson suggesting that they should take an Afghan airline to Kabul and see what real pain is.

The rogue's gallery of the 'stupid' and the 'dangerous' consisted of six internationally respected professors, two peers and two knights of the realm, the master of a Cambridge college, a QC who advised the South African government on labour law, a senior fellow of an Oxford college and expert on criminology, a chief constable and a chief inspector of police, three prominent human rights experts, two senior social policy researchers, one popular broadcaster who is also the chair of the Greater London Assembly and, until April, Andrew Marr, an ex-editor of this paper and now the political editor of the BBC.

Between us, we have written more than a hundred serious books. More importantly, the report is the result of a vast number of consultations with key people and organisations, qualitative research, seminars and specially commissioned research. None of this matters to the critics. Or maybe it does, which is why they worked so hard to kill the book off quickly. The cowardice of Jack

Straw when faced with any right-wing onslaught is becoming a defining quality in the Home Secretary. He distanced himself from the report and made some extraordinary remarks about how the left does not like being patriotic. Tell that to the working-class heroes who died in both world wars.

In some ways we are a remarkable society, increasingly at ease with diversity – in London especially. But racism, inter-ethnic tensions and new nationalisms are equally strong features of what we have become. The future is uncertain, but I think a small place like this without any meaningful ties that bind the future looks bleak. And those ties cannot be the same as the ones that prevailed during an era when people who looked like me were subjects and white Britons felt they were born to rule. The British Isles are now irretrievably mixed, but the British identity does not naturally include black and Asian people. Not yet. Many of us claim it, but others don't always accept this claim.

Just a few months ago on the *Today* programme, Lord Tebbit could not accept that I was British in that sense which matters. 'I'm sure that she carries a British passport,' he said in that sneering voice. 'But I don't know whether she was born here or not.' Does Prince Philip have to go through such abject interrogations? Remember that until the seventies, many of us had British passports marked with the letter 'D'. It meant second class, people who needed visas to enter their own country. These are the attitudes the report was trying to highlight. We are still not seen as people of this place, and some of us still believe home is somewhere else.

I think the hostility the commissioners have faced – and I often meet – is like the fury that Snow White's stepmother felt when she looked into the mirror. She only wanted to hear: 'You are the fairest of them all.' Well, this mirror says: 'You are indeed fair, but not as fair as you think.' Stamping upon the mirror till it breaks will not change that fact.

For how much longer will we treat asylum-seekers worse than our dogs?

1 January 2001

A pretty man with golden hair tried to pick me up on the Piccadilly line the other day, and very nice the experience was too. My dear husband thought I ought to have been furious, but sisters who have reached my age will understand my excitement. What drew him to me (he claimed) was the bold, yellow badge on my coat collar.

It is shaped like a hand and says: 'Hands Off My Friend' on the palm and 'Defend Asylum-Seekers' on the thumb. Issued by the National Assembly Against Racism, the badge will officially be launched on 23 January at the House of Commons by a wide coalition of people who disagree about many things, but who loathe and fear the way this society and its political élite treats asylum-seekers and economic migrants.

And that is the point which needs to be banged into the dumb and xenophobic heads of the politicians who think that, in order to placate the majority of British citizens, they must be seen to be ever more brutish towards people who have dared to come to our shores to seek a better life. When will they realise that it is not only unkempt anarchists, revolutionary lefties and never-satisfied race warriors who oppose these policies?

I think that the year 2000 will be remembered for the most iniquitous asylum laws ever passed in this country by a Labour government (this was one reason why I left the Labour Party last March), and for disgraceful, deliberately incendiary press reports which were written to ignite fury against asylum-seekers, refugees and illegal immigrants. Coverage got so foul at one point that even Ann Leslie of the *Daily Mail* came out and said that she was mortified at the language that was being used by local papers in areas such as Dover.

Like jackals and buzzards, anti-refugee politicians and papers fight over and tear into the same dying gazelle, reinforcing the sense of power they thrive on. At a recent meeting organised by the One World Broadcasting Trust, we were shown a collection of such nauseating cuttings from the *Mail, Telegraph, Sun* and, worst of all, the *Evening Standard,* the paper for London, a city made and constantly renewed by immigrants and refugees.

And it will only get worse over the next few months with the election looming, the dispersal policies in chaos and new evidence that asylum-seekers are moving back into the capital, where they will suffer without any incomes but where they have support networks. As I write this, I can hear Michael Heseltine on Radio 4 growling like an ageing lion about 'bogus' asylum-seekers and why it is right to keep them out. Having shown little moral courage in the past, and being more vulnerable to criticism than ever before, what will Jack Straw et al do except match the howls of these Tory beasts who are roaming wild at present?

They would be very misguided indeed to do so, firstly because they cannot go on encouraging people to be vile to asylum-seekers. Racial attacks against them are getting worse; the latest victim, 42-year-old Cumali Sinangili, a Turkish asylum-seeker, lies fighting for his life this week. He was set upon, apparently, by three white men, in an attack which even the police describe as 'gut-wrenching'. We know that the European Union is concerned about human rights abuses in Turkey, and that this is the reason for keeping Turkey out of the EU. But the victims of those abuses are 'bogus' once they are here. Explain to me the logic of that.

In school playgrounds now, 'Paki' is a less insulting word than 'refugee'. An article in the *Reader's Digest* last November showed how anti-asylum-seeker hatred is the result of bizarre 'facts' that many people now believe. In one survey quoted, the majority of respondents thought that asylum-seekers get £113 per week, when all they receive is £36.00 in vouchers, that paper confirmation of their sub-human status.

And yet, in spite – or maybe because – of these relentless attacks, last year should also be remembered for the fact that many safely middle-class people, as well as the rich, famous and powerful, decided that they were no longer prepared to sit by and watch politicians and the right-wing press ostracise weak and vulnerable 'outsiders'. Bill Morris was one of the most vocal, and it was in this paper that he first made his demands that the voucher system should be abolished. He was promised a review, but expectations are low that he will get what he wanted.

Last July some of us, mainly journalists and actors – luvvies so hated by robust politicians – got together to organise a vigil to remember the young, ambitious and hopeful Chinese men and women who were found suffocated to death in the back of a lorry. We also wanted the powerful to rethink their policies. In just over a week, we had hundreds of letters and many cheques. Interflora gave us beautiful lilies and a wreath. Those who responded were hospital consultants, company directors, head teachers, theatre directors, city slickers, local authority workers, ballet dancers, photographers, pensioners, and Jewish, Muslim and Christian organisations.

Supporters included Harriet Walter, Colin Firth, Maureen Lipman, Arlene Phillips, Adrian Mitchell, Ian McShane, the Redgraves, David Suchet, Phyllida Law, Ahdaf Soueif, Tim Piggot-Smith, Jo Brand, Jeremy Hardy, Sophie Thompson, Maria Aitken, Sam Mendes, Laurie Taylor, Richard Briers, the Goodness Gracious Me team, Will Self, Andrew O'Hagan, Linda Grant, Francis Wheen, Annette Crosbie, David Yip, Steve Bell, Frances de la Tour, Linda Smith, Lisa Jardine, Sheila Hancock, Maggie Steed, Juliet Stevenson, Kevin Whateley, Billy Bragg, Malcolm Tierney, Tom Paulin, Alan Rickman, Barry Morse, Jack Rosenthal, Saskia Reeves, Ian Wright – no sleight is intended at all, but there are many, many more such names. Ordinary people from Kent, Sussex, Norfolk – Middle England, if you will – joined in to reject the methods and messages of politicians on an issue that touches deep historical memories for many in this country.

And now Anita Roddick has launched a pilot campaign through her Body Shop network to give dignity back to asylum-seekers. Posters and postcards (to send to Tony Blair) have been placed in key shops and the idea is to go nationwide and to pull in all those people who know that it is contemptible to treat any human beings – even lying asylum-seekers – worse than we treat our dogs.

Don't be fooled: the best immigrants are not always the most 'skilled'

6 February 2001

One of the most memorable moments for me on Holocaust Memorial Day was the appearance of Kemal Pervanic, the once-emaciated Bosnian Muslim who appeared in the media, standing behind barbed wire in the Serb-built Omarska concentration camp. He spoke evocatively in English about what he had been made to suffer, but this was not the same man who had been broken by starvation and humiliation. His smart suit, beautifully groomed long hair and supreme confidence symbolised the vital reclamation of a lost life. He came here in 1993, and is now a science graduate with an assured future. We, as a nation, gave him that future, by letting him come here as a refugee. It is what we used to do.

Thousands of South Africans fleeing apartheid were similarly sheltered and given opportunities. Today, many are in top jobs in South Africa and they are finding productive ways of paying this country back for the gracious and generous way they were treated. The mean-minded among us so often forget the importance of this reciprocity and the reputation that Britain – in many ways, justifiably – built up after the war. The reason so many more asylum-seekers and economic migrants are coming here is not because the country is a 'soft touch' but because people can see what immigrants have accomplished here in spite of racism. Just compare the lives of migrants in Britain with those in Germany and France.

Staggering numbers of non-indigenous Britons are home-owners and well settled into middle-class lives. What's more, we have massively influenced the national character of this country. No other European country can match this achievement; as a pro-European, I say this without any jingoism or arrogance. This is what the anti-immigration Tories do not have the wit to understand. It is not the palatial council flat and fat giro cheque, but Blighty's good name as a land of opportunity that draws those with fiery ambitions and hopeless lives. And in time, many give the country much more than they ever take from it.

But, I hear you say, I am only saying this because of self-interest. Yes, can't deny that. But hark, a new Home Office report, 'Migration, an economic and social analysis', confirms these assertions.

Levels of entrepreneurship and self-employment are 'higher among migrants in the UK than elsewhere in Europe... [migrants] appear to perform well in the UK labour market compared to other EU countries.' Unemployment rates for migrants in the UK is about 6 per cent. In France, it is 31 per cent. The report also exposes the fallacy that there is a fixed number of jobs, some of which would be snatched away by migrants. As more migrants are of working age, the fiscal impact of recent migration 'is likely to be positive'. There are all those unquantifiable benefits, too, in sports, the arts, pop music, food – all of which would have withered on the vine without the new energy brought in by migrants and developed by their offspring on this soil. Zadie Smith and Sir Magdi Yacoub could not have been transplanted from elsewhere. They are a product of the searing and creative interactions and exchanges that migration forces both on those who move and the inhabitants of the places they move to.

Can you imagine special work permits to bring in good novelists and artists, or even pioneer scientists, because politicians and officials decide that the country 'needs' them? Yet this is the thrust of new government thinking on immigration.

Ministers realise that an ageing population and economic changes will soon force them to go shopping for immigrants once more. They also know that they are going to have huge problems getting the British public to accept this because, for half a century, immigration has been described as a problem that can never have enough controls and regulations.

Politicians are throttled by their own propaganda. So they try to sell the idea of targeting IT specialists, nurses and teachers, and importing them from countries such as India. This could begin a shift in attitudes towards immigration and is great for those individuals who want to emigrate. But is it moral to use our money and might to encourage a brain drain from countries that are still so unequal and impoverished? These people trained in countries that have few resources. Are we going to pay the national governments for this before we steal their experts?

And can we really pretend that we are developing a more positive immigration policy when we are so unforgiving of those who are seeking to do with their lives what we are choosing to do as a nation, namely improving their quality of life?

If, in a globalised world, we plunder the world for markets and highly desirable talent, by what right do we then deny those in impoverished and troubled countries to plunder our world for jobs and a decent future? And even worse, how does this then sit with merciless actions against asylum-seekers, thousands of whom are being deported and sent back into very dangerous situations?

The senseless and heartless message is that IT experts that we pick are brilliantly good for us, but self-motivated immigrants and refugees, who might become brilliant IT experts, are a disaster. For proof, read what Tony Blair wrote this weekend. He is co-operating with his Italian counterpart, Giuliano Amato, to stop those trafficking in illegal immigrants by building a stronger barrier around the western Balkans. He wants a debate '[which] should focus, not only on the repression of criminal activity connected with immigration, but also on supporting appropriate opportunities where in the national interest, for legal immigration into a diverse and tolerant society'.

By attacking those vile people who deal in human cargo, Blair is being disingenuous. The merchants are wicked. But why do they get business? Because there is no legitimate way in for people who simply want a chance to make good. Our government is not imaginative, brave or ethical in the way it is dealing with immigration. The US takes greater risks, is more open and benefits much more from its immigration policies. We could take a lead from the US by, for example, assigning quotas to different countries, and using a lottery to fill them.

I believe in controlled immigration that takes into account both what our country needs and the needs of those who have nothing but their dreams. This is a small country, I accept that. But people like Kemal Pervanic should be proof that the most crushed migrant can grow roots, blossom and enrich the whole landscape, particularly in this green and pleasant land.

Stop bombing, end the sanctions and open up the gates of Britain

20 February 2001

I am so pleased we bombed Iraq last week. Yes, truly, I am. At least it has broken the torpor, the dull indifference towards policies that have been pursued in our name for a decade. If the letters to newspapers are an indication, the British public has been shocked into reassessing what it is that we think we are doing to Iraqi people. You don't have to be a boring old bleeding heart like me to see that our actions are ignominious.

For twenty-two years, these citizens, once among the most cultivated and sophisticated in the world, have had to live under a ruthless dictator and face wars they never asked for. They are victims of daily bombing raids by the US and the UK (7,000 sorties to date), and the ever more despised sanctions, which have resulted in massive food and medical shortages, a collapse of the infrastructure, and thousands of children dying, many from 'new' cancers, attributed by some to the weapons used during the Gulf War.

A few months back I had an e-mail from the tireless campaigner Felicity Arbuthnot, who had just returned from Iraq. She found out that all of the many sick children she had photographed ten years previously had died. She wrote: 'These children, wistful, listless, smiling, utterly joyous and wracked by unimaginable pain scream at me from the shadows; Jassim, my little poet and so many others.'

According to the Cambridge-based Campaign Against Sanctions in Iraq, the UN's own Sub-Commission on the Promotion and Protection of Human Rights issued a statement saying that any embargo 'that condemned an innocent people to hunger, disease, ignorance and even death' was a flagrant violation of basic human rights. I don't care if Saddam is hiding essentials in order to incite anti-Western feelings. He could not do this if there were no sanctions.

Thank god Peter Hain isn't listening in to this opening paragraph. He has been taken out of the Foreign Office, and not before time. For Mr Anti-Apartheid Hain, critics of these policies are 'apologists for Saddam', not people who are just a little more aware than he wants us to be that we are actively adding to the misery of an already oppressed population and making Saddam's hold over them stronger and not weaker.

Iraqis were already suffering immeasurably when the Kuwaiti crisis burst upon international stage. From 1980 to 1988, the Iran–Iraq war martyred hundreds of thousands of young Iranian as well as Iraqi men. The Gulf War added further fatalities and casualties ; we will never know just how many conscripts were killed, many of them sitting ducks, powerless before the superior air weapons of the allies. Kuwait was rescued, but the war was a vicious and unequal one, with those on the winning side not unduly distracted by old-fashioned ideas about the rules of conflict. Then came further repression by Saddam, and the bombings-plus-sanctions policy in which there has been little public interest in this country.

Have you noticed how quiet the churches have been on this issue? Our media only rarely report on the cumulative effect of our policies. Exceptionally, the journalist Sean Langan does that in his compelling new BBC2 series, *Langan Behind the Lines*, which starts next Monday. Again it is the bewildered suffering of the children that gets to him. Politicians too have more or less forgotten to ask the tough questions that Tam Dalyell used to ask Margaret Thatcher about the Falklands War.

I want to know, for example, the total cost of the bombing raids to date. Will the relevant minister please produce a figure for the readers of this newspaper? It would be good, too, to see some footage on television of where these bombs land, and what they do to the terrain. What a jolly idea it would be for the pilots to have some excited male journos on board to film their actions and let the rest of us share the buzz. Maybe someone could also explain why so many sheep and young shepherds are bombed. Are they part of some new terrorist network?

Then there is that little matter of support. Blair, Bush, Hoon and General Colin Powell (a black hero whose right-wing foreign policy views are truly scary) partly justify their approach by invoking the plight of the Iraqi Kurds and Marsh Arabs who have been targeted by Saddam for years. The Kurdish journalist, Hazhir Teimourian, whose views I find alarming, argues that we should increase the bombings, but his is a minority view. Not even the Kuwaitis and the Iranians believe that this long punishment is achieving anything.

Since the PM is so irritated by cynicism, let us believe. Perhaps for some deep reasons that only these clever men understand, Kurds in Iraq (but not in Turkey) and Marsh Arabs have been selected as victims to be protected out of all the millions of others in the world. Well then, send out a luxury liner (loaded with Baby Gap clothes, chocolate and bouquets) to France immediately and bring back the 908 Iraqi Kurds who have ended up in France after a hellish journey. These hopeless dreamers obviously believed the earnest propaganda of the UK government.

Ah, but Jack Straw wouldn't like that, would he? His 'modern' asylum policy seeks to keep victims as near to home as possible, not to come bothering us over here with their sad children and sorry bogus tales about torture and fear.

'Only connect,' wrote EM Forster. More people would trust Tony Blair if he put his compassion where his propaganda is and stopped assuming that The People are so dull-witted that they don't understand that there is a direct link between our foreign and domestic policies.

It kills me to say so, but the only political leader in recent years who understood this was Margaret Thatcher. She hated communism with such pure and real passion that it pushed her into accepting thousands of Vietnamese refugees. With typical gusto and conviction, she then 'sold' this immigration to the British people, so that the refugees were warmly welcomed into the 'free' world and she won a minor PR victory.

To gain any respect back after last Friday, the British government must stop the bombings and sanctions, or open up the gates and accept any asylum-seeker from Iraq. Preferably both.

Our schools should be places of integration, not faith-based separation

27 February 2001

Back in 1920, H. G. Wells wrote: 'Human history becomes more and more a race between education and catastrophe.' Eighty-one years on, this race has only intensified.

The recent government Green Paper with several key proposals to deal with failing 'bog-standard' comprehensives has aroused much debate and anger across the nation. The plan is to increase the number of state-funded single-faith schools in England and Wales. Fundamentalist liberal secularists, such as Richard Dawkins, have gone on the offensive. These are erudite and influential people (whom I respect enormously most of the time) who are on a jihad, an uncompromising mission to secularise and rationalise this country, to liberate it from backward superstitions and the power of religious faith.

They despise blind faith, but do not ever see how their own passions have blinded them too, rendering them incapable of appreciating how important and beneficial religion can be for individuals and society. Theirs is only another kind of self-righteous evangelism which is contemptuous of those unlike themselves. As one of them, a prominent scientist, said to me: 'The next thing will be state-funded mullahs and mass baptisms in the Thames. Just get them praying young and they will never think for themselves or learn that the world is in their hands, not with fake fakirs or conning clerics who live off the great brainwashed.'

Their opponents – church-goers – have come out fighting too. They say there is an increasing demand for their schools, which is why they are forced to refuse places to so many children. Church schools can legally discriminate against children from other faiths, or even other churches. A single black mother was told that her daughter – who was already at a C of E primary school – would not

42

be accepted at the secondary school because the mother had not shown her commitment by contributing to the video camera which was purchased by the congregation.

So precious are the places at some schools that parents use some very unholy means indeed to get their kids in. They suddenly start going to church and become conspicuously generous with donations to good churchy causes. Church leaders say – and this is indisputable – the academic standards are impressive and there is less reticence when it comes to teaching children basic morality. In the past ten years, there has been a fruitful and powerful coalition of the various major faiths and this means that it is not only Christians who are delighted by the new proposals. Once the church schools have their money, Muslims, Sikhs, Hindus and Jews will demand and get parity.

I think both these camps must rethink their positions. There may be fewer people going to church but the need for faith and spirituality is manifestly not disappearing. Last week on GMTV's Sunday programme, I interviewed Derek Draper, who told me he had become a committed Christian. I didn't burst out laughing. It may be another fad, but I believed him when he said that he was tired of living a shallow, meaningless life. A 'God list' which is due to be published by Channel 4 on 11 March shows that, although traditional religious leaders are less respected than they themselves believe, people do attach great importance to individuals who they feel touch their inner lives. Cherie Blair, Rabbi Lionel Blue and Anita Roddick are among those at the top of the list and this wine-drinking, flawed Muslim female columnist appears at No 20.

Many of us support schools with faith-based values because they can counterbalance the devouring consumerism which is sweeping across the globe. The homogenised and technologically overpowering world is another reason why people are seeking the quiet and permanence of religious faith. The relationship between the state and religion is changing everywhere from the US to India, even though both countries do still have a commitment to secular state education. In this country, religious discrimination will be outlawed within the next five years and two documents published this week by the Home Office explore the options and nature of the forthcoming legislation. Religion is here to stay and grow, which is no doubt why the government is going for the faith-school idea so vigorously.

But the policies they are proposing are misguided and ill thought out and here I completely agree with the objectors, Richard Dawkins and others. What we need in the future are global citizens capable of understanding those who are different. How can separate education provide these skills? If your beliefs as a child are never interrogated by others and vice versa, you end up like many of those arrogant American Christians or Pakistani mullahs or Israeli orthodox rabbis who think that they are the only chosen ones with a god-given mandate to deride or destroy outsiders. Too many of our young are already too tribal. Schools should be places of integration not separation. The Green Paper is muddled about whether this is what the government believes or whether it is now opting for state-sponsored religious apartheid.

I sent both my children to the local Church of England school so that they could learn about Christianity. Eighteen years ago, my son was welcomed as a child from another faith and he did get a brilliant education. Three years ago, with my younger child, several unfair obstacles were put up by the same school. She had to be baptised and (I say this with some shame) her father started going to church again after many years of indifference. But although she was well taught, the atmosphere was much less inclusive than previously and we took her elsewhere.

The solution may lie with having two types of schools. Let the state get rid of all separate religious schools and create instead faith-based schools where all the major religions are taught. The second choice would be schools which are enthusiastically secular with no religious teaching. There would still be a common national curriculum and citizenship education. Both should be obliged to deliver diversity, international awareness and mutual respect. Parents can then choose schools on the basis of both academic results and values and we can move on from this overcharged stalemate.

Where is the voice of Asian women?

17 July 2001

The Muslim Council of Great Britain wants a Scarman-style inquiry to look into the racial riots that have flared up this summer in northern England. This idea (first suggested by *Independent* leader writers, by the way) does make sense although I wonder how much now that we have a hard-hitting Ouseley report. This tells us what a number of us have long argued, that many multiracial areas around the country are rotting, oppressive, hopelessly segregated and mistrustful, and lacking in any sense of optimism or civic culture.

Racism is rife and now has a place to go with the re-emerging influence of the far right. For several years, Margaret Thatcher and her coterie neutralised extremist nationalists and we had a credible organisation in the Anti-Nazi League (this is why I want Iain Duncan Smith as Tory leader. The others are too wet-New Labour, which means right-wing voters will have no respectable option and will be drawn to the increasingly urbane BNP leadership). It is horribly different today. We must never underestimate the power of racism and xenophobia to influence resentful whites left behind in this bright, new, zappy, digital age.

Those clamouring for an inquiry will be very satisfied if the focus is on the threat of the BNP in the disputed territories, or if we have a race audit to show that local councils have operated with criminal indifference, and at times active racism, against brown Brits. Gurbux Singh, who chairs the Commission for Racial Equality, is horrified at the levels of discrimination in Oldham and Burnley. The Muslim Parliament is demanding a 'statutory commission', based on the Northern Ireland model, to combat religious discrimination. Complaints are rising about inadequate resources. Call me a cynic, but watch now as voluntary and help organisations use the riots as a lever to get more funding. Always happens. Happened in Brixton, Tottenham, Liverpool. Some of these organisations can make a difference. Many of them are worthless and actually part of the problem.

But if this investigation begins and ends with such a limited analysis it will be a useless document and may even make the volatile situation worse. Other aspects of the problem need to be addressed urgently before effective interventions can be planned. No, I don't think that all the young Asian men rioted solely out of frustration that they are not given opportunities or because they have had enough. Being abused and rejected as 'Pakis' all their lives must have had an impact but, like some of the white thugs involved, these British Asians are now nihilistic and unmoved by the pain they cause to others, even their parents.

Their upbringing has been distorted by families who want them to belong to some mythical land in a magical time where all good and Allah prevails. *The Burning Mirror*, a sharp new book by Suhayl Saadi, a young Scots Muslim, reveals how this plays out inside the heads of young men. The imagined faraway held on to by the elders was important once as a way of surviving the hardships so many of them faced here. But to force these escapist fantasies on to their sons is resulting in an anarchic mindset. None of this is inevitable. Many young Asian men with just such a background have made a great success of their lives and they need to be part of the story told by the inquiry.

Too many furious Asian men expect respect, control and a life of ease. A son born into an Asian family is treated like a deity, especially by his mother. Only now, this automatic status is fast slipping away from them. The culture shock must be devastating. This leads on to the next issue, almost invisible so far. Where have all the women and girls gone in these conflagrations? At the launch of the Ouseley report there was a shocking lack of Asian women who could give their version of what life is like. One bright young woman did ask why the female perspective was being ignored. Her teacher was so frightened for her, she took off her name-tag.

When I was with northern politicians during the election, I saw no other woman at any election meetings. They are excluded from this discourse because they deviate from the anti-racist agenda by describing their hellishly circumscribed lives policed by the same young men we saw on the streets. These women are desperate to go to college – one reason why so many of them run away from home.

I have just received the annual report of the Muslim Women's Helpline. Racism is indeed one of the problems people seek help for. But the majority of the problems are to do with forced marriages, child abduction, polygamy. (A new interim report, 'Forced Marriage: An Abuse of Human Rights', by the Southall Black Sisters, claims that the state is still not taking real responsibility for these violations.) When there is this much anguish within families and communities, is it any wonder we are getting so many dysfunctional young people?

Other thorny issues must be tackled if we want these places to thrive: the conscientious Labour MP Anne Cryer has not joined the conspiracy of silence one sees in Roy Hattersley, Gerald Kaufman, Jack Straw, Marsha Singh and others who know about the internal crises among many (not all, obviously) Asian families in their areas of influence.

This week Ms Cryer was once more attacked for saying something that needs consideration at least. If Asian families could start to arrange the marriages of their children with other British Asians, the marriages would be more fulfilling and the economic potential of the couple would be better than if they marry people from their home countries who take years to learn the language and the system.

The uproar that followed said people had the right to choose who to marry. The point is that, in most cases, the young people have no choice. Any real inquiry would have to confront this and immigration regulations which are leading to forced marriages abroad.

Separate schools so encouraged by New Labour (but now worrying Estelle Morris, the new Secretary of State for Education and Skills) are another major fiasco. Muslim parents did not move to their enclaves only because of racism. They do not want their children to become too British. I have interviewed Asian parents who never let their children stay overnight with white friends. White parents are just as nervous. Segregated housing was partly a result of poverty, harassment and housing policy. But both groups will resist any attempts to create mixed communities because, in spite of sharing space for decades, they don't know each other at all. Confidence-building projects are needed urgently.

Finally, what about the white people who feel so disenchanted?

Are we going to dismiss them as 'powhitetrash' or damn them as racists? How does increasing anti-discrimination activity help these people feel more at peace? And what if some are victims of Asian abuse? Do we do nothing? If so, the fires next time will be bigger still and we may just get BNP MPs and local councillors. Democracy can be an effective form of revenge.

So yes, let's have a worthy to ponder the past and the future. But let him or her have broad vision and courage. Otherwise don't bother. It will only waste expectations on all sides.

Where can we blacks holiday then?

23 July 2001

You have no idea how much I fret at this time of every year. It is the same frustration when the skiing season is upon us and at Christmas time. Nobody from the media ever asks me about my holidays, what I like drinking and eating when I am abroad, or if I might go on a nice little freebie with the lover and/or the children to the Maldives and then write it up. Perhaps they think my tan is good enough already.

I long to be asked what books I will be taking with me. It is such a mark of being a somebody and of establishing your credentials as a very cultured person. Since you ask, I am taking George Orwell's *Essays on England*, Abdulrazak Gurnah's *By the Sea*, a novel about exiles in this country, two books by Anne Tyler, *My Kind of America* by Jeremy Poole, new novels by Asian women writers, *Smell* by Radhika Jha, *Salt and Saffron* by Kamila Shamsie and *Felix Holt* by George Eliot. You see, I am one of the élite really; erudite, adventurous and not a reader of trash, even on holiday. So why do I feel so wretched?

Because holidays planned at home or abroad, if you are a black or Asian Briton, often feel like acts of resistance, brave forced entries into places which have chosen to exclude us. We, you see, are not expected to go on holiday by the media and the leisure trade.

Internal tourism in this country is just as problematic, possibly more so. I am sitting here with major weekend newspapers all replete with travel articles, holiday destinations and honey-sweet adverts to entice punters. There are happy campers, beach bums, adventurer holiday-makers, about 222 images, across 89 pages from two tabloids and three broadsheets, including the *Independent*.

Except for the musicians, Lionel Richie, Ladysmith Black Mambazo, and one ordinary black man with swimming trunks digging into a conch shell with a laughing blonde woman, all the other images are white.

We looked through thirty brochures before making our choice this year and there were several pictures of non-white people, most wide-grinning waiters serving multicoloured cocktails in the Caribbean and a few Arabs guiding camels. I know Thomsons has made a black consumer central to this year's adverts and brochures, but this is so rare that you notice and remember. Other advertising has moved on and you get all sorts of Britons, white and black, used by companies, including in the financial sector.

Then there is the problem of sorting out which countries in Europe to go to if you are black or Asian. Rural France will never again attract me because I will not go to places where they treat like scum anyone they think is Arab. The last time I went, residents of a town in Brittany were unforgivably nasty to my teenage son and when my six-month-old daughter smiled and touched the head-scarf of a woman in a shop queue, her hand was brushed off and the woman stormed off muttering in disapproval.

Parts of Germany are very difficult for black, Asian and mixed race families. Some areas of Northern Italy are showing signs of blatant racism. In urban Britain, where most of us non-whites live, these hostile attitudes are still confined to some areas and small groups (important to remember this in the wake of the recent riots) so why should we spend good money to experience meanness and intolerance? No wine, food or landscape is worth that kind of humil-iation.

Southern Spain is good, so are some of the Mediterranean Arab countries such as Tunisia and Morocco, particularly for European Muslims who are hungry to see the old Islamic civilisations and to experience Islam which is easy with itself. The fear is that these places will harden and force changes of the sort we see in parts of Egypt, another country I cannot visit because they would expect me to cover my head as a Muslim woman, which I will not do.

In Britain, similar obstacles stop too many of us wandering around the countryside. How many black and Asian Britons would you get joining the Ramblers Association? The Black Environment Network does some valuable work trying to change the white heartland image of the countryside and the environmental movements. The director, Judy Ling Wong, who lives in a village at the foot of Snowdon asserts:

'The wonderful countryside, with its treasures of heritage is also ours. Beyond the physical and legal ownership of land, we have a need to feel that we have a spiritual ownership of the landscape.'

Wong has done much to get rural areas to embrace diversity so that black and Asian people are not seen as a threat when they enter the ancient hills and cliffs, the walks and villages. It is an uphill battle and who wants that on holiday?

So go to the Third World, I hear you say, full of black and Asian people, your people who will make you welcome.

More difficult than you think actually. Long-distance tourism – one of the fastest growing industries in the world – is still attached to the imperial idea that it is white rulers of the world who travel. They can behave there as badly as they wish (can you imagine how this country would react if wealthy tourists from Bombay set up their version of Benidorm in Bournemouth?) because, although the Empire is long gone, the world still belongs to these people, white Britons, Germans, French and others. In the late twentieth and early twenty-first centuries, Japanese and North American tourists and sometimes very rich Arabs have been allowed to join in.

Many of us black and Asian Britons are getting richer as the years go by and with these disposable incomes come desires for expensive holidays abroad. The first generation of immigrants never took a day off and any money saved for travel had to be used to make rare and important journeys 'back home' – usually carrying many suitcases of presents to show the folk (or pretend) that your long journey of hope had indeed delivered. Other trips would include pilgrimages to Mecca or Amritsar and journeys made for weddings and funerals. Now we want the luxury trips too, but how should the children of ex-subject people behave when they go on these trips?

Tourism Concern, an organisation which usefully highlights the effects and morality of modern tourism, is seriously critical of the arrogance and carelessness of first-world travellers who exploit places, cultures and people with no regard for equality or respect. Worse, most of the income generated by tourism – 60 per cent – goes to companies based in the West.

Imagine how it feels, then, if you are an anti-racist warrior and you go to India, Kenya, the Caribbean, Hong Kong as a Western tourist carrying the money and kudos. You feel guilty, implicated and sad too that you have lost your place in the old place. This is why I have not been to India since 1972 and why I only go to East Africa if I can use local people and local agencies to arrange the trip.

After all this navel-gazing, the holiday when it comes is all the sweeter. Until the next time, that is, when the soul-searching begins all over again.

It's time we were all proud to be British

Good Housekeeping, August 2001

I remember the exact moment when I began to feel this country was both physically and emotionally my home; when I suddenly felt profoundly British and longed to be in London. It was in 1994 while staying near Limoges in one of those dull French villages that never really light up, not even in the summer.

Like many others we'd fallen for the myth of idyllic rural France, but our holiday was thirteen days of misery. The villagers (who narrowed their eyes with suspicion and shuffled just like those in the brilliant film *Chocolat* when the gloriously free and foreign Juliette Binoche appears in their village) had clearly decided I was an Algerian because of the way I look.

My daughter Leila has a Middle Eastern name and my teenage son Ari could pass for an Arab. My English husband was treated fine, but they ignored me in the patisseries and the children clearly gave them the creeps. Ari was thrown out of a bar where he went to play pool. When Leila reached to touch a woman's scarf in a shop, her hand was brusquely brushed away. We left and I burst into tears. Again, I was that unwanted stranger I'd been in 1972 when I arrived in the UK from Uganda and white Britons screamed abuse at us, telling us to go back where we'd come from. We weren't refugees, remember. We had British passports. But the 1968 Immigration Act (which even Auberon Waugh, not known for his liberal-mindedness, described as among 'the most immoral pieces of legislation ever') had redefined British nationality to include only those with a British-born parent or grandparent. Our passports meant nothing unless we could secure visas too.

In Uganda we dreamt of Horlicks, Trafalgar Square and the Queen, and the greatness of Britain. But arriving here, we found the visas and passports had been reluctantly given and we were second-class citizens. It still hurts when politicians start unsettling debates about how this is an 'Anglo-Saxon' country. But the interim years have been extraordinary. London, and Britishness itself, have been transformed by the children of the Empire who came to stay, and by those indigenous Britons who were prepared to open up.

For centuries, the idea of Britishness has been based on myths about colonialism, racial hierarchies and cultural purity. The Queen's husband and children aren't pure Anglo-Saxon and everything, from the English language to Handel, proves this is a hybrid nation. But that's not how it has chosen to see itself.

Panic about contamination was present as long ago as the sixteenth century, when writers began to complain about mixed-race sex, and Elizabeth I issued an order asking for 'Blackamoors' to be banished from her kingdom because there 'are allready to manie consyderying howe god hath blessed this land with great people of our nation'.

But after 1948, with post-war reconstruction and large-scale immigration, the face of Britain had to change. Those who came were no longer colonised subjects. Most loved the Motherland and were immersed in British traditions and literature. In my school in Uganda we used to perform Shakespeare and George Bernard Shaw plays three times a year; my children here have never had that privilege.

Racism tore at this love but out of acute disappointment and terrible rage came a new creativity and determination to remake the British identity. Hundreds of thousands of indigenous Britons welcomed these ambitions. Their lives were spiced up; they fell in love (Britain has among the highest numbers of mixed-race families in the developed world); predictable, dreary, post-war Britain changed utterly. I fell in love with my husband after he spent a whole train journey enthusing about immigrants. 'Couldn't get a decent aubergine before you lot got here.'

I have heard white women describe how charming, elegant Caribbean men – fab dancers too – turned up at dance halls in the fifties and stole their hearts. Today, when Robin Cook says this is the land of chicken tikka masala, he's describing an indisputable reality. Trevor McDonald is the nation's favourite newsreader; the next king wants to be a defender of all faiths; a black actor plays Henry VI with the Royal Shakespeare Company and the Hindu temple in Neasden, London, sits proudly, lighting up a bleak landscape.

Welcome to the new Britain, which is finally starting to define itself as a nation of diversity. TV comedy *Goodness Gracious Me,* the architect Zaha Hadid, Ali G, Naomi Campbell, the high-profile mixed marriage of Dawn French and Lenny Henry are all part of this Britishness that came out of that searing interaction between those who have moved here and old Britons, the descendants of those who never could remain confined in this small place.

Italy, for example, is what Italy has always been. Britain is a modern, global place alive with all the important historical episodes of the past fifty years. You want to know what happened in Rwanda? Go and have a drink at the Africa Centre in Covent Garden – some soulful Rwandan will tell you stories. In the Persian areas of Kensington they can't forget life under the Shah. But these people won't be going back anywhere. Their identity is now new British. They take democracy and their liberty for granted.

Britain is today unsteady, fragmented and unsure. Integration into Europe, devolution, multiculturalism and immigration have shaken old Blighty. A Mori poll for *The Economist* in 2000 found only 18 per cent of Scots, 27 per cent of the Welsh and 43 per cent of the English describe themselves as British. But go to Brixton or Leicester and the overwhelming majority of black and Asian people will claim they're proudly British. How ironic. The people who are still often seen as foreigners are now the most fervent defenders of the British nation. I'm one of them. It's fine to have other ethnic or national loyalties, but without an overarching British identity and ties that bind we'll end up even more fragmented than we are now.

In 1972 in Uganda, when I saw a journalist attacking the government, I expected him to disappear. Today I treasure my right to speak out. Gender relations, too, have changed among the 'new' as well as the 'old' groups in Britain. When my ex-husband – an Asian himself – and I parted, my elderly mother said: 'Some men can't bear women who are cleverer than them. We sacrificed our lives. But you must not do the same.'

Britishness should now be our common cause; Britain is the place where we meet, exchange secrets, touch flesh, laugh and cry and find meaning beyond our own little ethnicities and nationalities. Without such an umbrella identity we'll get wretchedly tribal and paranoid. I'm very content with being an Indian-Pakistani-Ugandan-Muslim-Brit and the wife of an Englishman. To opt out of this and to inhabit a world of forced simplicities? No thank you. Complexity is what makes this nation great. And I thank Idi Amin for enabling me to become part of it.

Mrs Thatcher's lesson in compassion

07 August 2001

M C – the name appears Kurdish – sends this e-mail: 'I have no chance of warding off the emotional tauntings and assaults of some peer groups of white guys. How should I act in this situation and continue preserving my self-esteem and not start behaving like them?'

Every week I get a number of such desperate e-mails from asylum-seekers who obviously use their meagre allowances in internet cafés in order to express their grief and rage at the way they are forced to live. (Home Office officials will scurry off to advise ministers that this is a wasteful use of taxpayers' money. The voucher system was, after all, meant to dehumanise these people so that all they can do is eat and drink – just enough – urinate and defecate, sleep and wish they had never dared to come here, seeking generosity from a nominally Christian country.)

Many of those contacting me are men, young men who feel emasculated by the fear and loathing that they endure on the streets and in the allocated places they are forced to inhabit as a result of punitive dispersal policies. One such young man, 22-year-old Firstat Yildez, was murdered last week in what is thought to have been an unprovoked racist attack in Sighthill, Glasgow, a city that has received 4,000 asylum-seekers since March this year.

This murder adds one more case to an ever-increasing number of violent attacks in some localities. Mr Yildez was not Stephen Lawrence, a young, ambitious son from a settled, middle-class black family. Politicians will not rush across and have their pictures taken with grieving relatives or friends. They will not attend the funeral (even in Germany, the EU country with the most nefarious asylum regulations, when there are racist murders of asylum-seekers many Members of Parliament attend the funeral. Not here. Never here) and Ann Widdecombe, David Blunkett et al will not be rushing around the studios standing up for the basic right to life of asylum-seekers.

He was not one of us. He was just another one of those who are invading our shores as we sleep, bringing with them nothing but rabid lies and pestilent needs which plague us and destroy this fruitful land. So, sad as it is that a mother will break and want to die to hear the news of her son, and although none of us decent folk of Great Britain would ever condone murder, we must remember that most of these people are 'bogus' scroungers.

On Radio 4's *World at One*, a bullish Jeff Rooker, a minister in the Home Office, was keen to let us know that most asylum-seekers fail to make their case and that those awaiting decisions get less money than British nationals. This was his response to a question about whether politicians should be doing more to change the hostile attitude of the public towards refugees. He is probably proud too that, as the *Independent on Sunday* revealed, more than 1,000 asylum seekers are currently in prison without having been charged or convicted of any crime and that many of them are picked on for special treatment by inmates and officers.

If these were nice dogs or sheep or lambs or even foxes, public sympathy could easily make a difference. If they knew that these animals were being brought across in appalling conditions, then forced to survive on as little as possible and kicked around and killed by drunken thugs on our streets, the uproar would be heard in Calais. And if there were cute little babies among them, the good people of this island would never let it happen.

Asylum children however – there are, for example, more than 1,200 orphans currently in Kent – are more likely to arouse fear than sympathy among millions of British citizens. Politicians and their policies and some sections of the media have ensured this. Richard Littlejohn and Gary Bushell have even written sick 'novels' about bastard asylum-seekers and then had them serialised in the tabloids to incite and excite people who never read books.

It is that coupling between the press and politics which makes public opinion and if you want to see how it can work to create a positive outcome, even in the fraught area of immigration and asylum, astonishingly, the best examples are found not in Labour governments (which are always dishonourable and cowardly when it comes to this issue) but in two Tory prime ministers, Ted Heath and

Margaret Thatcher. I choke as I write this. Ted Heath, no great egalitarian and very Tory, nevertheless took on Enoch Powell when he let
in Ugandan Asians who had been expelled by Idi Amin. He got his
ministers to talk up the skills and contributions of the exiles. He said
Uganda was losing a great asset and Britain was gaining enormous
entrepreneurial capital. Many newspapers took their cue from him
and promoted this line. This meant that when 20,000 British pass-
port-holders arrived here, large numbers of Britons felt moved by
our plight enough to offer us genuine sympathy and material help. I
went into the camps carrying dozens of winter coats and baby
clothes which daily arrived or were brought over by people of all
classes. There was brutal racism around too and life was hard, but
the goodwill helped immeasurably. Although there are still many
Britons who support asylum-seekers today, their numbers are much
diminished.

An even better example of a committed positive policy was
evident when Margaret Thatcher decided to take in Vietnamese
refugees in the early 1980s. Her hatred for communism was much
greater obviously than her concern that Britain was being 'swamped'
by alien cultures (this is what she said in 1978 in a television interview) and typically, when she decided on this gesture, she went for it
with all the conviction which made her such a formidable politician.
She presented the refugees to this country as people who loved
freedom and enterprise. Resettlement was organised and funded.
Thatcher's favourite newspaper editors were co-opted to churn out
sentimental stories of escape and suffering.

This week on Channel 4, *Secret History* shows how the *Daily Mail*
under David English had already embarked on this propaganda
mission by orchestrating an airlift of ninety-nine Vietnamese
orphan babies in 1975. This meant that on the whole, Vietnamese
refugees – although they too faced hostility and official hypocrisy –
managed to enter the country without that hail of hatred we now see
everywhere.

Learn from this, Mr Blair. You know better than any previous
prime minister how to manipulate the media, but you choose not to
do so on this issue. This death of a young man seeking a better life
should force you to look again at your policies. Let asylum-seekers

work until you deport them if you must. Let them take back their dignity and some money with them. Inform your public that world unrest and inequality forces people out, to lie and cheat and try to get a living for themselves and their children. Tell them that as an overcrowded island we cannot take all the people who need help but that we will be as fair as possible. Develop a proper integration policy – teaching language, citizenship and work skills – and track the people who settle. Publicise the way the most wretched of the earth can flourish given humane surroundings. Why, for example, have you not made public just what this country has gained since giving refuge to South African exiles for many decades?

If you don't do this, more asylum-seekers will die under your leadership; asylum children will be beaten up in playgrounds and that moral authority you radiate will lose all credibility.

The English have feelings, too

17 August 2001

Some say it is the deep love of an Englishman (and mine for him) over a good thirteen years that has made me go soft on the English. Maybe. I have a young child who is half English too, with long ancestral roots in the South Downs, that most English of landscapes. I'm no longer comfortable in stereotyping and deriding Anglo-Saxons.

Once, as a rabid anti-imperialist (which I still am), I would have applauded anybody who publicly humiliated the English. If it was done cleverly and with panache it was even more satisfying. Like other nationals who had been subjugated for so long, these small affronts were liberating, a way of confronting that arrogance of Englanders.

But these days I feel more disquiet than wicked delight when the English are gratuitously slagged off. The outrageously offensive remarks that referred to English immigrants as 'foot-and-mouth disease' and as 'oddballs, social misfits and society dropouts' have left me, well, outraged.

I understand why the Welsh feel protective of their language and are furious with the English who expect the world to speak only English. Wales has long been exploited, abused and denied. The media's racist treatment of Neil Kinnock in 1992, and 'clever' columnists expressing their prejudices about the Welsh, were and still are contemptible.

Remember the smooth critic AA Gill describing the Welsh as 'loquacious, immoral liars, stunted, bigoted, dark, ugly, pugnacious little trolls'? Responding to the furore, the BBC broadcaster Huw Edwards and the writer Hywel Williams, both Welsh, movingly described the anger of dependence and having to please England. But the offending remarks were still very wrong. England is fragile, uncertain, feeling very unloved. This is not the time to start a campaign of historical revenge against it. The clamour for an English parliament is a search for a home by a lost tribe, which once

61

knew its identity and power, and is wandering, as Jeremy Paxman describes it, in a 'land of lost content'.

The US poet Ogden Nash wrote in 1938: 'Every Englishman is convinced of one thing, viz: That to be an Englishman is to belong to the most exclusive club there is.' Some of that inherited superiority does undoubtedly survive. On holiday in Tunisia I met an ex-Foreign Office chap, who was loudly explaining to his sons (Harrow public-school boys) on a coach that black people had invented nothing, 'not even cement', and that all they were doing was 'occupying space in the world'. He was badly dressed and well spoken and described himself as an 'absolute racist' when I confronted him.

So yes, imperial attitudes do still infect some, but the breed that believes so completely in English superiority is dying. These days you are more likely to come across the thoughtless mockery of the English, often by the English themselves (as if they must do this before others do it to them), and by others too. Yesterday morning on Radio 4's *Woman's Hour*, for example, there was a discussion of how English women lacked the confidence of other European women. Apparently, they are tormented by fearful complexes while their Continental cousins can pad around in their bikinis without any self-consciousness. This is ludicrous. All women feel under pressure to conform to beauty myths. Why pick on the English in particular?

If any English people feel themselves to be part of an exclusive club, they know the building is collapsing, the paint is peeling, the servants are no longer deferential and, like those left in the last days of the Raj, fear for their future, rather than hubris, dominates their inner lives.

Why is this happening now? Because of devolution, Europe, globalisation and, most importantly of all, the reality that Britishness is now no longer synonymous with Englishness, which is what it once was. Englishness is just another ethnicity within that large canopy of Britishness. Not even Radio 4 feels like home any more with received pronunciation fast disappearing to be replaced by any number of different accents. If it was hard for the British to retreat back into this grey little island when the Empire finally ended, think how much harder it must be for the English to retreat into a smaller space on that island and to share a national culture now influenced by so many different tribes as well as English tribesmen and women.

Actually, if these bewildered Englanders could be persuaded to think differently, they might survive this trauma and emerge with a more healthy sense of pride befitting these new times. As the novelist and poet Maureen Duffy writes in her new book *England*: 'When our self-image seems to be at its weakest it also seems most important to examine the making of that image, its icons and imaginative components and to [seek] options to clothe the body of England in the twenty-first century.'

The images of England evoked by John Major's sound of leather on willow in the village green, or by Ann Widdecombe – 'tea on vicarage lawns, roses in a summer twilight, people keeping themselves to themselves, well-fed cats purring on hearth rugs' – are sad, wishful and pitiful. I too could claim that my true culture is somewhere back there in the great courts of the Mughal emperors or the courtyards of Persia where my ancestors hail from. You would think me foolish if I did so. Besides, such longings make a mockery of the great multifarious land that is England today.

The English have proved somewhat better than the Welsh, Scots, French, Germans, Italians and others at adapting and accepting difference. Their imagined superiority is not an adequate explanation of this. The French are equally culturally arrogant, but they are, even now, much less at ease with change. Post-devolution Wales and Scotland have yet to reflect diversity in their political institutions and the stories they tell themselves. I would say that no other ethnic group in Europe has been as culturally promiscuous and adventurous as the English. London is emblematic of that hunger and openness. Asylum-seekers like being in London and Leeds, another fast diversifying city.

Most of our top non-white British novelists, playwrights, actors and artists live and work and flowered in England. I am not English and do not wish to be so, but I do fear the rise of xenophobia and the British National Party in England because that would destroy so much of what post-war Englanders have created in spite of racism. And a shared understanding of this rich harvest is growing.

In the collection of short stories *England Calling*, (edited by Julia Bell and Jackie Gay), various writers from Julie Burchill to Alexei

Sayle and the new Englanders Pavan Deep Singh, Leone Ross and Courttia Newland reflect how this land is being revitalised again.

This New England will not tolerate claustrophobic ideas of community and nationalisms. Perhaps this is why conservative Welshmen fear English immigrants today and see them as misfits and oddballs, and why I find the Welsh prejudices so abhorrent.

Stuff your 'British test'

16 December 2001

A week has passed and, in spite of mollifying words from the Home Secretary, many black and brown Britons remain in a state of high upset about the humiliating debates over demands that they adhere to British 'norms'. The otherwise excellent report by Ted Cantle, written after the flare-ups in our northern cities this summer, recommends the establishment of an oath of allegiance for immigrants to create a cohesive society. In other words, we darkies must prove again that we are worthy of equal respect because, after all, as David Blunkett said to this paper, we are in someone else's 'home'. Presumably, it truly belongs to the poor natives who have so long had to suffer our presence.

This is how the message has been received and it does not matter a toss what Mr Blunkett's intention may have been.

I would rather be stateless than succumb to this kind of pressure. I love London and would go to battle for it and for the country too if there was a genuine threat. But I would do that willingly and not because otherwise I might lose my right to be treated as an equal citizen.

Such fitness tests will not, I imagine, be demanded of immigrants such as Germaine Greer, Clive James, Janet Suzman, Peter Hain, Barry Humphries, Loyd Grossman, Madonna, Antonio Carluccio, Barbara Amiel, Conrad Black, Elisabeth Murdoch, and all those other white South Africans, white Zimbabweans, Australians and Americans who have magically managed to enter every one of our institutions, often doing jobs that somehow still elude black and Asian Britons. Will the people of the 'four nations' be asked to sign their hearts over to the idea of Britain? If so, James Naughtie, Gordon Brown and Alun Michael had better sharpen their pencils. I can't see the good people of Glasgow being too happy about the prospect.

It's all very odd when you consider that more of our black and Asian islanders think of themselves as British than do the Scots, the Welsh or even the English. And then what about the dissenters? Will all those who are against globalisation have to sign up and agree to the exam? What will happen to republicans and those of us who loathe class deference – that defining British norm? Will our holiday hooligans have to re-take the test of what it means to be British or do they think they represent true Britishness in the way they behave? And will our government encourage Zimbabwe to ask their white citizens to live according to black 'norms'?

Just before he died in 1994, Dennis Potter confessed: 'I find the word "British" harder and harder to use as time passes.' The term had lost its old meanings and symbols. It is time to bury that version and plant a new vision which brings together all the tribes of Britain. That is going to be much harder to do after last week when so many of us have been made to feel like interlopers once again. The more I think about this, the more my head overheats with the absurdity of it all. Vast numbers of black and Asian Britons are more immersed in British traditions and culture than some home-grown natives.

My father, who looked like Jeremy Thorpe, loved his British passport so much he kept it in a safe in the bank and whenever he could – once between the time I was conceived and when I was fifteen months old – he would run away from the family in Kampala, Uganda, and come to England, where he lived like an English eccentric until the money ran out and he had to return.

I have read almost all the authors in the traditional literary canon. I can make the most wonderful Victoria sponge in the world. The vote, parliamentary democracy, the idea (if not the reality these days) of probity in public life , these are all profoundly important to me and always associated with Britishness. I am pleased, too, that I have learnt, since living here, to treat domestic pets with kindness and to give my children greater autonomy than I ever had as a child.

One of my neighbours, on the other hand, a rough chap from Yorkshire, has never read an English writer, has never voted, hates this 'bloody country', eats shop-bought curries and Chinese food, has convictions for violent behaviour and a basic vocabulary of about two hundred words plus 'fucking' and 'shit' which he uses a lot. Just who should take Mr Blunkett's test?

Even money can't buy acceptance

25 February 2002

As the media hangs on with its teeth to the many fine coats of Lakshmi Mittal, the Hindujas are beginning to surface again. Sir Richard Packer, a former permanent secretary, has come out blazingly in defence of the British Ambassador in Romania, Richard Ralph, who has been left holding the responsibility for the infamous letter sent from 10 Downing Street supporting the successful bid by Mr Mittal's not-quite-British company, LNM, for the nationalised Sidex steelworks.

Now evidence is emerging to show that the Prime Minister himself brokered the £1m donation by the Hindujas to the Dome, uncomfortably close to the time one of the brothers was trying to get British citizenship. Other stories were surfacing about cosy tax arrangements available to such businessmen who have special status as 'non-domiciled residents', which allows them to pay substantially lower tax than the rest of us.

Once more, tiresome though it is, British Asians are called upon to explain why we are such a dodgy lot, still carrying the venal ways of our hopeless homelands, now dragging down upright English and Scots gentlemen and women of influence, who, as we all know, can never ever be corrupt. Unless they are tricked, that is, by wily oriental gentlemen who dazzle and confuse, maybe hypnotise their gullible victims and get them to do dishonourable things. Then, one day, the politicians wake up, rub their eyes, blink and lo! find themselves in the middle of a glaring scandal which upsets them terribly.

Now I am no acolyte of the excessively rich, Asian or otherwise, as readers should know by now. But these lingering prejudices of the Raj are execrable and even worse are the assumptions behind such scandals.

For there is, in our country, an undoubted hierarchy of villainy. A Jewish no-good is much worse than an Anglo-Saxon crook and an Asian or black rogue is worse still. This applies as much to small-time muggers as it is does to clever millionaire fraudsters. And when misdemeanours are discovered to be a collaboration between Jewish and Asian plotters, just observe the froth, wrath and convulsions around the nation.

When these already suspect people indulge in the normal dirty business that keeps the Establishment going, they are judged by higher standards. You can almost taste the sneers and disapproval when reports emerge about Lord Levy's activities as a Labour Party fundraiser. He is Jewish, you see. As was that other one, Robert Maxwell. Can't trust them.

And watch them, especially when they do business with other Jews or Asians who think they can infiltrate Britain's sacred spaces. It was easy once, of course, to keep these enclaves clean of unpredictable outsiders, but now that all the political parties and other institutions need their cash, ways must be found of getting at this loot. But how to do this without terrible compromises?

These hapless custodians are likely to feel ever more vulnerable as the number of thrusting Asian millionaires continues to rise exponentially.

The latest list of Britain's richest contains fresh new names – Tahir Mohsen, Jasminder Singh, Vijay and Bhikhu Patel, Tom Singh, Gulu Lalvani. They will soon be on many unexpected party lists (of both sorts) now that they have been named among the supermen. Their troubles will then begin, as they try to understand the peculiar and slanted principles of their sparkling new white admirers, values which still confuse me.

Is it any more disgraceful to use money to get what you want than to use your name, friendships, university and school connections and all those many skilful and invisible ways that facilitate the flow of positions, status and wealth-making enterprises in Britain? At least money is a kind of equaliser and you can find the stuff if you really want something that badly.

But how do I acquire the surname, say, Freud, or the intimate contact with the powerful that is available to the children of Margaret Jay or Paddy Ashdown, or the lifelong friends of Ian Hislop or Alan Bennett, or Ken Clarke? Not that I am not trying. I was once congratulated by a commissioning editor of a liberal newspaper for the 'genius stroke' of adding 'Brown' to my otherwise alien-sounding name. I wouldn't have made it 'so big' without this comforting appendage, he said.

I was with an acquaintance at a conference in Sweden last autumn. He is proudly English and a powerful operator and we were joined by one of his friends. Within ten minutes, the latter had offered a job to a relative of the former. It was an exchange of favours. 'I owe you' were the last words I heard as they parted.

I was caught somewhere between admiration and envy, nothing more noble, as once more I was made to understand just how this fair and meritocratic society works. And so it is when names are thought of for non-executive directorships, consultancies, selections for political advisers and candidates, arts critics, chairmanships of big bodies and so on.

If you are not a born insider, you will never be given prestigious slots in the media (not even the BBC, which would still rather promote trusted white names than take risks with swarthy inter-lopers: check out the main line-up for its new channel, BBC 4) or the chairmanship of the Arts Council or get that call from Tony Blair asking if you would like to take over from Alastair Campbell, who truly needs a break.

There is something iniquitous and dishonest about minding so much when coarser forms of influence are revealed, while never questioning this hidden trade in nepotism. Mr Mittal, for example, gave £200,000 to the London School of Economics just before his daughter tried and failed to get into the prestigious college. This is seen as yet another stinking example of illicit influence which on this occasion didn't work. But hang on. The openly amoral and syco-phantic Woodrow Wyatt confessed a few years ago that he had to ring not one but two chummy vice-chancellors to get his daughter places at the universities they ran. He was successful both times so the girl had the luxury of moving from one to the other. I know which method I think is the more pernicious.

Remember, too, that in many societies around the world money changing hands for favours is not regarded with much disapproval – it is just what people do, just as instinctive clubbishness is what people expect here. And if you live in a country where money is the only thing people really like about you, can you be blamed for using this advantage in any way you can? On Friday, Doreen Lawrence, the mother of Stephen Lawrence said: 'We black people are still on the outside looking in. That has not changed.'

She is wrong. Some people with jangling pockets are now inside. But their terms of entry are tendentious and they are learning that flattery and gifts will only get them a temporary membership. However well they learn the smoozing tricks of their white patrons (I can't tell you how many of them have started sponsoring awards, fundraising bashes, expensive dinners in Park Lane hotels, graced by Cherie Blair), they are still really thought of as unreliable little wogs, best avoided if only such a thing were still possible.

Why I'm boycotting anything 'made in Israel'

15 April 2002

First let me say the following as clearly and loudly as I can: I have fought against anti-Semitism all my life, against friends, colleagues, lovers, anyone who expressed anti-Jewish sentiments. I remember one night in 1974 when I stood for four hours under a lamp-post in north Oxford recovering from a screaming row with my ex-husband after he accused me of being excessively emotional about the Holocaust. My nine-year-old daughter was taken to see *The Merchant of Venice* in the week when all her friends were flooding to Harry Potter because we feel she needs to understand anti-Semitism as it arises around the world once again. I refused to support the UN conference against racism in Durban because I feared it would give licence to people to abuse Jews and it did. And as I observe the unsheathed hatred of Jews among many Muslims here and around the world, I feel shame and rage.

I condemn the acts of suicide bombers whose own hopelessness makes them target Israelis in cafés, at weddings, in street markets, bursting open the bodies of the young and the old and themselves; and by each act blowing away peace and progress. Israel – as it was originally created – has an absolute right to exist and to flourish, without fear.

But Israel has absolutely no right to do what it wants, to use such overpowering weaponry against mostly unarmed people (we will never ever know how many are being killed in the current deluge) and justify that by referring to the horrendous history which led to the creation of the Jewish homeland. In fact, I would suggest that Ariel Sharon should be tried for crimes against humanity in Sabra and Shatila, and Jenin and other occupied areas and be damned too for so debasing the profoundly important legacy of the Holocaust, which was meant to stop for ever nations turning themselves into ethnic killing machines.

Remind yourself of this. Read the gripping new biography of Primo Levi by Carole Angier to understand the inimitable humanity of great Jewish thinkers, people who had every reason to surrender to the abomination of all-out vengeance but never did. Levi's painstaking testimonies about what happened in Auschwitz illuminate connections and avoid the traps of special pleading. He surely would not have been able to witness without protest the depravity of the current Israeli leadership.

Sharon can only carry on with his invasion of the West Bank because Colin Powell and his master in the White House crumble before his brutish ways and the US pro-Israeli lobby. He knows too he has the blind support of Americans and Britons whose anti-Arab racism has this year reached new lows. One columnist writing in a US journal captures the view held by many: 'Israeli tanks should mow down Arab youths as they throw stones. Kill them. Keep going until the Arabs decide whether they hate Jews more than they love their children. I don't think the Israelis would have to dispose of too many Arab children before the white flag would go up.'

So do we just blink back our tears and wait for these deaths? No. That would be like killing all imagination and optimism. I have just come back from Cape Town where I met inspirational people who fought those long, long years against apartheid. They gave me courage that all is not lost. We don't have to depend on craven British ministers who still insist on blaming Arafat (no saint he) more than they can bring themselves to accuse Sharon.

These South African liberationists have already persuaded many people not to buy anything from Israel. No, they admit, apartheid was not exactly the same as what is happening in Palestine. Yet, they recognise the familiarities. The racism against Arabs which fuels hard-line leaders; the systematic violence and humiliation to force a population to succumb to what is an unjust deal; the bulldozers, oh the bulldozers, which evoke such trembling memories in so many South Africans who remember how they too had their homes and lives turned to dust not that long ago.

They have not forgotten either that Israel for many years supported apartheid and that some Tories thought white South African rulers were just fine people. Nelson Mandela was also declared a terrorist for not denouncing the use of violence against the iniquitous system built on a permanent state of heightened paranoia, just like Israel today.

I think we – all those who want Israel to leave the occupied territories – should follow the example of the South African activists. I have already started looking at labels and putting back anything made in Israel. Many of my friends are doing the same. We are e-mailing organisations – not those based on religion because Palestinians are not only Muslims – but all those who want to see a world committed to universal human rights. Money will count more than words. The US will not be able to prop up the economy of Israel for ever and these hard wars are expensive.

We should call on unions, especially Equity, to advise artists and others to cut relations with the state of Israel. Exchange trips should be off; no holidays in sunny Eilat (perhaps this is happening already because of fear), even Christian pilgrims to the holy places need to think if this is when God may want them to delay the trip. Please note these actions are not directed at Jewish people but at the Israeli government. We will not, for example, stop buying from shops in Britain owned by Jewish people.

I was heartened to find out that others are doing their bit. Professor Stephen Rose and Professor Hilary Rose have started a boycott of institutional, cultural, academic and research links with Israel. They have collected three hundred names across Europe. Jewish academics have signed up too. The signatories must know that this means cutting off much that is of value. There are hundreds of joint research projects between Arab and Israeli academic institutions – scarce spaces where decent dialogue and co-operation have been able to carry on. But I think they are right to sign up because we are in the middle of an unprecedented inferno which politicians are doing nothing to quell.

We know some Israeli soldiers are rejecting Sharon's strategy and that small peace groups keep going, enduring rejection, accusations of treachery and worse every time another suicide bomber goes off. Several Jewish women who work for human rights are trying to find ways to make their objections heard. They know they must tread carefully so as not to give succour to Jew-haters but unless they take an ethical position, they will be violating all that they stand for. As one Jewish South African friend, an artist, who lives in London put it: 'I owe it to my father who fought against apartheid and my grandfather who died in Germany, not to let my people turn into fascists. Don't name me but I say that many of us are beginning to think that Israel is a burden on our backs instead of the imagined haven we grew up thinking it was, the place of safety and honour in an evil world. I will not stand by and let them do this in my name.'

She is not alone. These brave Jewish dissidents and others who refuse to retreat and cower will stop the tanks; or, if not, at least they will ensure the nameless hundreds who are being killed did not die undefended as the world looked on helplessly. So remember to read the label; put it back if it is made in Israel. You will know you did a little something.

Oh dear, I have flunked
the Tebbit test again

10 June 2002

Things are not good in this household at the moment. Apparently, I am out of order, unbelievable and plain stupid because I said it was a shame Argentina didn't win The Match seeing as the country is collapsing economically and they lost the Falklands War (and boy have we reminded them of it this year, in spite of not playing fair with the Belgrano) and because we are rich and secure and doing so fine under the bonnie Blairs. Anyway, it is not Christian to hold such long grudges – Maradona's devilish hand was sixteen long years ago. I am not crass or brave enough to express these views in pubs with wide-screen TVs, but I thought I was safe in my own home, muttering quietly as old people do, at the kitchen table.

The reaction from my children – the 24-year-old son whose voice is hoarse after days of joyous shouting, and the nine-year-old daughter who imitates her brother's every whim and preference – was a mix of fury and stupefaction. England, oh England, my children are your children. I have only just understood how intuitively they stand up for you. Ari, my son, is dancing again because Lennox Lewis beat Mike Tyson and to irk me further he says he will jump even higher when England beats Nigeria, which is of corruption. So this is patriotism, this heady feeling, this intoxicating emotion which rises to catch your breath at certain key moments wiping out all caution, sorrow, reality and – especially – rationality.

I have never, ever known patriotism and never will because fate gave me a life where it was not possible to bond with any country to this extent. The most I can feel is a gentle love for London and Europe, a love which is neither blind, dumb nor deaf but real enough. There are haunting connections with India, Pakistan and Persia because my community – Ismaili Muslims – originated in these parts, and as I grew up in Africa, I find myself often having to defend that continent and its strong people. These days I feel an obligation too to stand with maligned Muslims and against the monstrous fanatics who have hijacked the faith.

None of these allegiances feel as strong and pure as the patriotism my children have just displayed. I am too aware of the weaknesses, the lies and dangers of these identifications and by nature I recoil from any cause which demands unthinking devotion. I am dismayed, not stirred, to see millions of good folk thronging the streets to throw their love to the ruthless royals or to witness rallies where people proclaim their countries right or wrong and poison the air with their rhetoric of hate. I guess I still believe what George Bernard Shaw said: 'You'll never have a quiet world till you knock the patriotism out of the human race'. And yet all over the globe, as the World Cup progresses, you see that primitive pleasure of nationalism glowing on faces as they cheer or jeer the teams.

Just as I can't ride a bike because I didn't learn as a child, I can never acquire the habit of this simple patriotism. There are many others like me and increasingly so in a globalised world where people are on the move, perhaps for ever, leaving places which are rapidly altering anyway and making lives in lands where they can live and make good but where they will never truly belong. I walk the walk and talk the talk and believe absolutely that I should be a good British citizen, but as some of the less forgiving readers of the *Independent* remind me, I cannot be one of you, not really.

The colour of my skin is one problem, but these days that is perhaps less important than all those Tebbit and Blunkett tests which make hideous demands of us only to keep us ever on the outside. These same leaders never mention Gibraltarians and white Britons in southern Spain who refuse to become more Spanish or declare allegiance to Spain. I don't suppose the villa owners in Umbria or Bordeaux feel the need to display undying fidelity to Italy or France either. Australians and Italians living here expect to remain attached to their own country and nobody minds. Yet the pressure is constantly on black Britons to prove that they are truly the sons and daughters of this nation. Meanwhile, Pakistan, India, Jamaica, and all those other 'homelands' still doggedly lay claims on migrants who left fifty years ago and on their children and grandchildren too.

Further complications: more and more indigenous Scots, Welsh and English people are turning their hearts away from Britishness and the British collective nationhood. In work which I have been doing for the Foreign Policy Centre, I have found that young people identify more easily with their localities, regions and with Europe than with Britain. As for our dementia over Europe and the euro, I am not clever enough to hazard where that will take us. In his fine and radical new book, *Patriots*, Richard Weight dares to take on the amnesia which has gone into the making of our national identity since 1940 and the confusion we are in today.

So who would we black Britons die for in this mélange? What if India and Pakistan went to war? What will we do if restless England – where most black and Asian Britons live – decides to secede from Great Britain? On whose side do we fight if the Western allies, along with the Russians – such good friends now – mount a major offensive against Muslims everywhere, good and bad?

Until 11 September, until the riots in the northern towns of England and until this year of monarchist madness, patriotism was worn lightly in this country and I still think that natural restraint will hold us back from embracing cloying US-style proclamations of patriotism with flags in every home and self-conscious self-dotage imbibed and regurgitated generation after generation. But there is a menacing mood about, which is unsettling for those who may just find themselves denounced for their lack of real patriotism or even of treachery, particularly in an England which fears globalisation, the devolved nations, Europe and just about everything else. I feel for the English as much as I dread where this may take us. It was not only my republicanism which made me recoil from the jubilee celebrations. This was old England smothered in whipped-up pride, and the victory over Argentina has just added the ghost of Thatcher, another fearful symbol of English hubris.

Weight, a young man of infectious idealism, believes we can and should recast English patriotism to release it from itself. He quotes Will Self, who wrote in 1999: 'The old idea of a mono-cultural landscape is impossible to sustain, England, the centre of that great rolling, post-colonial ocean of cultural ferment, is alive and kicking.' Amen to that I say, with enthusiasm. Englanders have many other qualities to admire – not, as Dennis Potter said, the imperial identity, or the flags, drums and trumpets, or 'billowing Union Jacks and busby soldiers and the monarchy and pomp', but the bravery and steadfastness, the creativity and industriousness, the endless line of rebels with a cause, the respect for individuality and eccentricity, the institutions of democracy and law, and most of all the insatiable cultural promiscuity. For all these reasons I feel proud to be living in England. But that pride will never trigger the kind of Argie-bashing I have witnessed in my own children.

And yes, I secretly hope that Nigeria wins, because Africans need some good news.

We need to ask why these Chechens use terror

28 October 2002

Well, at last, and for the worst of all reasons, we are buzzing about Chechnya like furious bees. In that sense, at least, those homicidal men and women who took over the theatre in Moscow achieved something.

They were callous. They imprisoned the innocent, killed three of them and terrified the rest, until the Russian authorities stormed in leaving more a hundred dead and many more injured. The media and the Russian authorities describe them as Muslim separatists, not as paramilitaries fighting for freedom from Russian occupation, which is how they see themselves. We may loathe their latest act of terror – and I do without reservation – but that is no excuse to misrepresent deliberately the excruciating struggles of the Chechen people, which, in the eyes of radicalised Muslims is just one more example of how unfair the world is to their people.

Depressingly, the only time Muslims get seen and heard by the world is when the pitiless among them turn to sickening violence or if they threaten Armageddon. Until this happens, their grievances and aspirations are ignored or crushed by the powerful. When it happens, moral authority is claimed by the latter to perpetuate accusations against all Muslims. Serb nationalists are not seen as Christian terrorists, nor did their activities ever blight all other Christians. But Muslims are different. We now know, guys, that damned Muslims are the indisputable barbarians in the new globalised world where all the rest of humanity has embraced the postmodern universe of pleasure and profit.

Even Russia, our old enemy, now smiles and shakes our hands. Old communists are so much more civilised than these clothheads who did the twin towers, Bali and now Moscow, not to mention all those sniper murders in and around Washington. All bloody al-Qa, obviously. I wouldn't be surprised if Ulrika was molested by a Muslim (you know how they are with blondes).

You could see this as the continuation of what Edward Said and other scholars have called 'Orientalism', the demonisation of and unjustifiable violence against Muslims through history. Did you know, for example, that Muslims were persecuted from 1820 to 1920 across Eastern Europe and the Caucasus, including in Bulgaria, Georgia and, yes, Russia? Tolstoy described this in the 1840s: 'Russian soldiers did not let the women and children escape the horrors that followed as they entered the houses under the cover of darkness, horrors no official narrators dared describe.'

For months now I have thought about an eight-year-old girl who was repeatedly raped by Russian soldiers in Chechnya after watching her mother go through the same. The child apparently did not cry at all and let the men push her on to the next, then the next rapist. She told her aunt she did not want to upset further her bleeding and screaming mother. Her father had been shot and her two brothers had disappeared, and like the African-American writer Maya Angelou, who was raped as a child, this girl is now wilfully dumb.

Chechnya is full of shallow mass graves with chunks of bodies, hacked or blown apart. Vanessa Redgrave last year hosted a meeting in London with Ahmed Zakeav, the Minister of Culture in Chechnya, a deeply civilised man who condemns terror and the vengeful brutality of extremist Chechens. I believed his account of the human rights violations by the Russian army ignored by the US and UK. As the Palestinian academic Daud Abdullah says in a recent essay: 'After 11 September, international criticism of Russia's human rights record in the Caucasus faded into silence. By playing the "war against terror" card, Russia managed to deflect attention [from] the extra-judicial killings, detentions, torture and sexual abuse.'

The rape story was e-mailed to me by a human rights activist. I have known her for many years, and she is no apologist for all things Muslim. Before this she was in the villages of Pakistan where tribal leaders were using rape as a weapon against families who transgressed. She, like me, is a Muslim by birth and one who struggles to keep her principles steady at this time when Muslims do so much wrong and are also much, much wronged.

If the raped child ends up with explosives strapped to her body to blow up theatre-goers or sports supporters or travellers, is it possible to understand her actions? Or is this understanding itself criminal because it is, in fact, showing tacit approval of horrific acts by suicide bombers who are increasingly targeting civilians? Yes to the first and a resounding no to the second. We need the courage to ask difficult questions just when anger and outrage are pushing us towards retribution where again the innocent will pay a greater price than the guilty.

In this new world order, how do the oppressed secure their rights or even have their voices heard? Passive resistance would have no impact. They cannot win straight battles because they are utterly out-armed whether by Israel, Russia, India and, ultimately, the US, whose expenditure on arms now exceeds that of every other country put together. The Gulf War and the war on Iraq to come are calculatedly unequal, with no deaths expected on our side and no need to count the bodies of the opposition.

To make things worse, this axis of good busily promotes the worst leadership in troubled areas, mostly people who can be bought off cheaply in return for ensuring that nothing like real democracy or civil society can emerge. For what will the powerful globe runners do if there are assertive democracies in Saudi Arabia, Pakistan, Iraq and Chechnya, or breakaway republics in China? Why would they say anything unpalatable to the Hindu fundamentalist Indian government that allowed 5,000 Muslims to be massacred in Gujarat after Muslim extremists killed hundreds of Hindus?

Am I here turning Stalinist Muslims into the real victims? No. I hate what they do. I hate their idea of Islam. I hate their hatred for all things Western. I reject the idea that the end justifies the means.

Suicide bombers, whatever the injustices they are fighting, do more harm than good. They make it easier for the enemies of Islam to make life even worse than it has been for Muslims in the last twenty years. The majority of Muslims worldwide would agree with me. But we will not be believed because we cannot provide the proof that is required of us; we will not parrot the lies of Bush, Blair, Putin or Sharon, or of the BJP in India. We can see too clearly that these leaders share the responsibility for the terrifyingly unstable world we are all now trying to cope with.

Unless they understand this, more and more angry young Muslims will turn up to join groups that offer their rage direction and weapons. And be very afraid because they, too, are globalised; they are fighting a guerrilla war in a world without boundaries. Unconfirmed reports say that the women who held the hostages in the theatre were from the Middle East. Like the Britons fighting with al-Qa'ida, these are the new transnationals. They are indestructible because they are happy to die. They will always find support and places to hide because, for millions of the disenfranchised, these obscene counterblasts may feel like the only way to get a better deal for themselves and their children.

Britain should welcome immigrants: it needs them

2 December 2002

Immigration today is as volatile an issue as it was in the bad old days of Powellism, only people in power then had mettle. They blocked any ambitions which Enoch may have had to determine the course of history.

Edward Heath was the unlikely braveheart who chose to sack the popular white nationalist. But Heath was no liberal anti-racist. When Asians were thrown out of Uganda in 1972, he dithered for weeks because he feared public opinion. However, in the end, he delivered us safely to our country (we had British passports) because he understood that most immigrants have hunger, zap, dash, manic ambitions, imagination, super-high expectations of their children, and a phenomenal capacity for hard work over long hours. We made good and gave Britain thousands of jobs.

Choose young asylum-seekers next time, Jamie Oliver, instead of those sullen young Brits who had to be dragged through their chance of a lifetime.

European politicians have never quite understood the dynamism that immigrants bring, as long as the state ensures they have freedom, equality and real opportunities. Blair, like them, is a retro, led by anti-immigration hysteria, ill-suited to facing the biggest challenge of our times – the unstoppable movement of peoples around the world.

Franklin Delano Roosevelt described such timid conservatives as people 'with two perfectly good legs who, however, have never learned to walk forward'. Such conservatives barely understand the implications of globalisation. Read Frances Cairncross's fiery essay on this in *The Economist* (2 November): 'However much governments clamp down, both immigrants and immigration are here to stay. Powerful forces are at work. It is impossible to separate the

globalisation of trade from the global movement of people...
Immigrants bring new customs, new foods, new ideas, new ways of
doing things.' But all European Union governments want to be seen
doing is condemning immigrants, treating them like battery
chickens.

It is the stupidity of this which grates, even more than the injustice of it. Findings by the American National Research Council show
that although first-generation migrants cost the US an average of
$3,000 (£1,900), the second generation produces an $80,000 fiscal
gain. A Home Office study last year found that immigrants paid 10
per cent more in taxes than they received in state expenditure. In
Essen in Germany, a cost-benefit assessment reached similar conclusions. We grudgingly pay out aid money (much of which goes into
the pockets of corrupt ministers and generals) instead of allowing
Third World workers to come here, work, and send or take back the
money they have earned with dignity.

Most migrants don't wish to die in foreign places even if they
manage to acquire that semi in Harrow or a car they could only have
dreamed of in Ethiopia or Malawi. I believe that, had we not had a
series of lock-out immigration policies since 1968, many settled
immigrants would have chosen to go back – as long as they had a
safety net: the chance to return here for economic reasons. After the
mammoth gains made by Britain through colonialism, they had that
right. Hence the paradox: the immigration laws themselves have
created a larger immigrant population. Ask the first generation of
Pakistanis, Caribbeans, Bangladeshis and they will confirm this.
Many immigrants would, of course, have settled for life, made new
lives and helped in the eternal renewal that this country goes
through. But we are forever treated as a problem.

Now we have to tolerate a new right-wing organisation,
Migrationwatch UK, which is suddenly being treated with undue
respect. This wants no more immigrants and warns that blacks and
Asian Britons are having too many babies. Yes, I have bred a litter of
future scroungers myself.

New Labour panders to such rubbish and carries on with the
tradition of botched immigration laws, failing to understand the
needs of modern Britain. The economist Nigel Harris believes that

migration controls disable economies in the developed world, where serious labour shortages hold back growth, and in the poorer economies, where high unemployment pulls down incentives to succeed. We should allow a flow through rather than build useless fortresses.

Business leaders across Europe understand this. Top British executives tell me they want all migrants and asylum-seekers to have a National Insurance number so they can be employed. They already are, but illicitly. Wander around London at dawn and you see them at all-night petrol stations and cleaning offices. The exploitation is awful but the workers tell me they cannot afford outrage. This gives them a way through an otherwise hopeless life.

'A' came to the door last year, bedraggled, a little scary. He was a farmer from Romania. Could he cut grass for £7 an hour? Fine. A year on, our garden is unbelievably beautiful. He is now legal, so has to charge £9 to pay taxes. Six other neighbours employ him: 'After three years, I will have a house in Romania,' A says optimistically. He will too.

None of this is easy for indigenous Britons and settled immigrants, who feel under threat every time a new wave comes in. Ugandan Asians hated the Hong Kong Chinese arriving because they were bringing competition. Immigration brings clashes, challenges. The poor feel ever more excluded, and now of course there are the dangers of global terrorism. A proportion of immigrants and asylum-seekers will turn to crime or end up being a burden on the state. But there is still more to gain than lose. Just watch the BBC's Mega Mela, a celebration of Asian arts. It is just one more event showing how much immigrants (including Jewish, Italian, Polish and Irish arrivals) and their descendants have given this country while rising themselves.

There is another even more important advantage. If the fight against Islamist Stalinism and other fanaticisms is to be won, immigrants are vital. Some may become the enemy within, but more will imbibe social-democratic values, the best of the West, and become the reformers of the future. For example, one of the most compelling writers on modernity and Islam is Leila Babes, a French Muslim sociologist. The Islam she promotes sits well with those of us who are passionate about individual autonomy and gender equality. Her ideas are already travelling to where such rights are yet to be won.

I organised a conference on immigration in Spain last month where paranoia is growing alarmingly in spite of the fact that Spain, like Italy and Germany, needs young immigrants to maintain the size of the working-age population. Compared to these EU countries, immigrants in Britain are more powerful, successful and vocal. Depressingly, however, Blair is more keen to be seen as the leading anti-immigrant leader than one who leads the most successful country of immigration in Europe.

I am sick of this betrayal. Let us have a 48-hour strike of immigrants and their offspring. See what happens to this ungrateful nation without cleaners, doctors, lawyers, waiters, nannies, actors, ushers, curry cooks, bouncers, drivers, teachers, newsagents, social workers, nurses, gardeners, newscasters, shop staff, dancers, pop singers, sex workers, dinner ladies, childminders, City brokers, accountants, pharmacists, off-licence staff...

Do Muslims not belong in this Christian Europe?

16 December 2002

Awfully dejected this week after Turkey was yet again rebuffed, discouraged from even thinking it could be considered as a member of a European Union described by Valéry Giscard d'Estaing as a Christian club. The sentiments were echoed by Germany's conservative leader, Edmund Stoiber, and others too. Ah, yes, now I understand these particular values which form the basis of this wonderful Union of theirs. They are to be based only on Christianity. So that's why Europe had to energetically burn those millions of Jews fifty-plus years ago. The continent's terrific human values could not be sustained when it contained such a large number of un-Christian souls. How interesting that it is the German and French leaders – with their shameful anti-Semitic history – who are keenest to keep Europe Christian.

And now other threats are being made by all manner of barbarians knocking at the doors: Hindus, Sikhs, Baha'is, Buddhists and – most of all – those infernal Muslims. We allowed them to enter our countries so we could exploit them, and now they think they can actually belong to this ancient civilisation. The cheek.

Their decision has knocked back reformist European Muslims who are fighting against Islamist ideologues who also see Europe as 'Western' and a place with alien and abhorrent ideas which must be rejected or terrorised by true 'jihadis'. The humiliation of Turkey gives the ideologues ammunition against all that Europe stands for, including many of the precious principles so many of us Muslims espouse, not because they are white and Christian but because they are universal and right.

Turkey so far has proved itself worthy by holding a fair election and sticking with the result – an overwhelming victory to the Islamic Party – even though the result alarmed the secularists who have held power for decades oppressing, among others, the opposition Islamic parties. (I think the West would have been better pleased if the victors had not behaved with such sophistication and as proper democrats. If only they had started chopping off hands and stoning adulterers, it wouldn't have been so hard to dismiss their latest application.) Yes, many human rights abuses still remain to be sorted out and Turkey's ruling party has to prove itself. But this should be another reason to encourage Turkey to join us and to start to live by the rules which the EU holds sacrosanct.

Millions of people live in Turkey today who, until this week, were undecided whether their destiny lay with the West or with the Islamic nations to the east. They supported Nato and they thought of themselves as a meeting place of cultures where hordes of Western tourists could drink themselves to a good time as long as they stopped to listen to the calls to prayer, always hauntingly beautiful. Many – too many – will, I fear, veer towards groups and nations which are uncompromisingly anti-West. Powerful people such as Abdullah Gul, an adviser to Recep Tayyip Erdogan, the leader of the ruling Justice and Development Party, already feel Turkey should stop begging to gain entry.

As an ardent European, I feel let down and embarrassed by the EU leadership this week. Tony Blair was the only one in Copenhagen who appeared to understand the consequences of the EU's stupid and discriminatory decision on Turkey, and its criminal lack of imagination and of basic knowledge on its own history.

The East bedazzled Europe for centuries and its goods, peoples, thoughts, ideas, books, fabrics, jewels, crafts, arts, music, sexual practices and foods were craved, hunted down, brought over, admired and absorbed by every corner of European life. From Seville to Sarajevo and beyond, no corner of Europe can claim to be free of Eastern influence. Espresso coffee, hand-painted tiles, fountains and squares, science, medicine and mathematics all contain the cultural DNA of the Ottoman empire (which was, like all empires, both good and rotten), of the Egyptian and Persian empires, and many other civilisations, including China and India. I was in that most English of places, Lewes in East Sussex, last weekend and loved it for its palpable presence of history, Tom Paine and all that.

Wandering around the house of Anne of Cleves, I saw huge old tapestries with pashas and Turkish princesses as well as Chinese and Indian characters.

In his book *Islam in Britain 1558–1685*, Nabil Matar shows how 'Muslims and their Arab-Islamic legacy were part of the religious, commercial and military self-definition of England'. Coffee was brought here and installed in coffee houses by Turks, who took slaves from undefended British coastal areas. Love and hate came and went between the two just as it did, and does, between France and England. The influences were more profound and long-lasting in Spain, Italy, the Balkans and some former Soviet satellite states. Philosophers such as al-Farabi (who died in 950) re-established Greek thought and wrote on statecraft in books which informed Thomas Aquinas. Ibn Sina (known in the West as Avicenna, who died in 1037) built on the teachings of Aristotle and wrote some of the most respected books on science and medicine.

Today the traffic is the other way around. The West bedazzles the East with its technological developments, arts, literature, goods, ideas and ideologies. These are craved, hunted down, found and absorbed by so-called Eastern civilisations. For centuries, neither the East nor the West has existed without the other.

The effects of the EU's decision on Turkey will be pessimism and more mutual antipathy. It gives strength to those with the meanest instincts, the determined xenophobes, and encourages a wilful ignorance and misrepresentation of Europe's identity. It is a betrayal of many of us who pay taxes to keep EU grandees in the lap of power. If the EU is only Christian where do we, the non-Christians, fit in? Do we bulldoze our temples, mosques and synagogues and walk with red holly wreathes whistling Beethoven's Ninth to show that we belong?

It is said that the EU is holding back Turkey to stop the increasingly popular, far right-wing parties from exploiting a mood which is at present susceptible to Islamophobia. I scream with frustration when I hear this dangerous garbage. Yes, as a BBC journalist, Angus Roxburgh, reveals in his new book *Preachers of Hate: The Rise of the Far Right*, since 11 September support for fascism has reached 17 per cent in Europe and is rising. But, by refusing to get going on Turkey's admission to the Union, such abominable ideas are only encouraged.

And how do reformist Muslims get out of this one? What do we say when we are asked, as I already am: 'So what about your Europe now? Where is their equality? Where are their just values?' While Europe plays these games, hundreds more bright young Muslim men and women, who see through the cant, will seek affirmation in the company of people we should truly fear.

The EU has arrived at a moment of destiny. It needs to become a credible and dynamic world player to counterbalance the hyperpower. Unlike the US, it has a long relationship with the Muslim worlds and it is more trusted when it comes to the Middle East. Yet today it has betrayed these possibilities and stands condemned by those of us who had such hopes. What else, but dark despair?

A little honesty might help the government's case against Iraq

17 February 2003

Yes, I was there on the stupendous anti-war march on Saturday, in my red beret, with my ten-year-old daughter and my husband, feeling both the futility of what we were doing – Blair is as obdurate as Margaret Thatcher – and the power of people when they voice their views clearly and as one.

Even the hostile papers concede that hundreds of thousands came out around the rest of the country, and a million and a half inhabitants demonstrated in London, although our public service broadcaster, the BBC, claimed the number was nearer 750,000. It was a dignified march of people of all backgrounds and political ideologies (I met my first viscount, courteous gent he was too). Unlike the last Stop the War demonstration, we didn't have Islamic Stalinist groups distracting us from the cause. And for every person who walked, count at least three armchair supporters.

We made history, but that is not the point. A more profound assessment is needed of this mass display of the will of the British people, particularly in light of the forceful, almost zealous speech made by the Prime Minister in Glasgow at his party's spring conference, delivered just as the marchers were getting under way. He warned that our 'weakness' will mean the people of Iraq will pay in blood as they are tortured and murdered by their dictator. Now, apparently, what unites Saddam and al-Qa'ida is that they both want to destroy the West, not that they are working together. New day, new claim, new Labour.

Weapons of mass destruction are sidelined now; Blair wants to make a moral case, as does his party chairman John Reid, who delivered an identical set of remarks, albeit in a less pious and more street-cred Scottish style. That working-class token John Prescott also jumped to attention to defend his leader's sermon, adding a touching confession that he was wrong to oppose the Falklands War. The millions out marching should remember, they all chorused, that the same number had died or would die in Iraq without military action.

Offensive as I find these last remarks, I am prepared to engage with the core arguments made by the PM. I am more circumspect than many about mass protests. Democracy is a precious thing, but elections and referendums can deliver abhorrent ideologues or inhumane policies, or actually institutionalise the exclusion of the powerless for generations. I have misgivings about a wholly elected House of Lords, because I think that will only replicate the profile of the Commons, ending up a place mainly of white, middle-class men. Blair is right when he says that leaders do sometimes have to risk unpopularity to do the right thing. How would I react if a mass protest was staged to bring back the death penalty for paedophiles and other killers, or to reintroduce corporal punishment, or to stop all immigration? So impassioned are views on these issues today that such demonstrations could easily be organised. A progressive prime minister would have to ignore the yells and banners.

But there are two problems with this latest New Leader posture. Blair has been a willow tree, bending to please Middle England since 1997. He shows no courageous captaincy when it comes to the populist hatred of refugees; he panders to it. He sacks ministers if the press hounds them, sometimes unfairly. He is still nervously sitting on fences on the euro.

So how can we believe this new commitment to bold leadership? And would he stick with his views if, say, Bush unexpectedly decided to do business with Saddam? After all the US has done this before without any conscience.

Then there is the matter of Iraq itself. Yes, I would believe his concern for the torture victims of Iraq if in the same stirring demagoguery he told us that we are partly responsible for the state Iraq is in. Say it, Mr Blair: 'I want to apologise to the people of Iraq that we supported the tyrant. I am sorry I am sending back so many Iraqi refugees every week from this safe haven, so serious is my moral commitment to them. I am ashamed that in 1989, soon after some horrific genocides in Iraq, our closest ally gave Saddam more credit to buy goods from the US. I know that in 1991, when the Kurds and Shia Muslims wanted to challenge Saddam, the US watched and tacitly approved as Saddam crushed this uprising. We have armed and encouraged this beast for too long. I have to accept too that our weapons in the Gulf War and sanctions have destroyed ordinary Iraqis.'

If such honesty were forthcoming, there would be some moral basis for what Blair wants. It isn't.

The policies of the UK and the US have long been dishonest. Read *Iraq Under Siege*, edited by Anthony Arnove (Pluto, 2000). My eyes water every time I open this book of essays by various truth-tellers with facts that most of us don't know. And the lies persist. Take two quotes from 1999. In the words of Peter Jennings, the ABC news anchor: 'The US did want Saddam to go, they just didn't want the people of Iraq to take over.' An economist, Edward Herman, who is a critic of recent US foreign policies, wrote: 'One of the tricks of imperialism is to pretend that a target enemy has been offered a negotiating option, quickly claim that option has been rejected and then ruthlessly attack or continue sanctions that may be taking a heavy human toll. The beauty of this system is that no matter how many are killed by bombs, and how numerous the children who die, it is not our fault.'

That is exactly what is going on. To wrap these intentions in morality is odious.

In his awesome performance on Saturday, Blair also read letters from Iraqi exiles who will not be blown to bits when we rain bombs on their land. Of course, these people want to see their country free. Being dispossessed is a dreadful thing. But thousands of Iraqis do not want these attacks, and we should treat the pleadings of those who want war with some caution. When the ANC was in exile fighting for freedom, it risked lives by participating in operations in South Africa and neighbouring countries. It didn't simply advocate actions on their behalf while living in relative safety.

John Prescott says Blair is a man nobody can fail to believe. Wrong. Blair is a man who thinks he must always be believed and trusted. *Democracy Under Blair*, a new book by David Beetham, Stuart Weir and others, gives much credit to New Labour for constitutional reform but is scathing about the centralising instincts of Tony Blair, his lack of respect for the public and Parliament and the dangers therein. The cover shows Mr Blair as Louis XIV – 'L'état, c'est moi'. Perhaps that is why he was so furious with the demonstration and why this was a victory for us. We won't stop the war, but the state is more than Mr Blair. And we made a more plausible moral case than he and his have managed.

The life of an exile can never be made whole

10 March 2003

Iraqi political exiles have been appropriated by both pro- and anti-war camps, as the moment of battle with Iraq moves closer. Tony Blair summons them up in his ever more trembling speeches; Jack Straw does the same with a painful stutter; and those of us on the other side also try to boost our arguments by holding up examples of tormented Iraqis who hate Saddam but do not want bombs and depleted uranium raining down on the innocent.

Both sides claim they have the more accurate version of what these exiles truly feel after long years of watching their country devastated by a murderous dictator and by policies implemented by the 'civilised' West, of which they are now inextricably a part. The truth is that these exiles are as divided as the rest of the country, with some feeling Saddam is so evil that civilians may need to be sacrificed for a greater good and others appalled that any true Iraqi living in safety should even contemplate supporting such 'collateral damage'.

The politics of exile life are always strained and this is only one example of groups around the world who find themselves displaced and living in foreign lands while their own countries and countrymen go through tragic upheavals and cruelties that they can only watch on television screens or learn of from an irreconcilable distance. Our cities are full of them, people who have been in waiting, sometimes till they die, looking wistfully to the places they were forced to vacate. Some of those countries that disgorge refugees have gone from bad to infinitely worse in the interim years; others have experienced changed fortunes which herald hope. In either case, the exile, away somewhere else, inevitably finds it harder than he or she ever imagined to find a meaningful relationship with the homeland.

I often go to places where exiles gather. While politicians and tabloids carry on hysterically demonising asylum-seekers, across our cities in sad cafés they sit and wait. They smoke, sip coffee, eat old-home food, talk in repetitive loops, complaining about disobedient children who have become too English and plot wild plots before wearily heading back to bed after another night when it didn't happen. In my early years here, a Scottish friend sent me a consoling ballad that described 'the deep unutterable woe, which none save exiles feel'.

They may be Yemenis, Kenyans, Iranians, Ugandans, Algerians, Serbs, Croats, Russians, Indonesians, Nigerians and every other sort, but they all suffer from incurable nostalgia, repressed anger which rises like bile, and powerlessness. You see small acts of valour, too, as futile as the tiny blows of a small child trying to bring down a strong adult. In an Iranian café I go to, for example, they insist they are 'Persian' and that the Shah was the greatest ruler ever. In a Polish centre old exiles (bloody good dancers they are) say they can never trust the formerly communist Poland and that they are still waiting for the real old Poland to emerge. Vietnamese refugees I meet are vehemently anti-Viet Cong and reject the result of that long war. Two say they would fight to win back the country if only America had the guts to go back in. (I hope Bush is not reading this.) At the Colombian cantina, they feel there is no going back because the country and exiles no longer know each other.

'In this world without quiet corners,' observed Salman Rushdie in his fine book, *Imaginary Homelands*, 'there can be no easy escapes from history, from hullabaloo, from terrible unquiet fuss.'

Nonetheless, these people and their unquiet stories are the yet unvalued treasures in our country. As long ago as 1854, Giuseppe Garibaldi, the revolutionary Italian soldier-politician, said England was 'a great and powerful nation, enemy to despotism, the only safe refuge for the exile'. Every major event of the twentieth and twenty-first centuries walks our city streets. We are unique in this – not even the US has quite the vast array we have accumulated. Still alive (just) are people who can tell us what it felt to be ruled by the British, about the chaos of the partition of India, about hearing Stalin speak. Others remember in warm-blood detail the coup in Chile, torture in

Argentina, the death squads of Cambodia, Somali tragedies and much more. If we used these people as a resource in our schools and universities, we might be able to create new generations of Britons who truly understand history, instead of wallowing in a feel-good and falsified version of how great this country always is.

But when it comes to political influence from a distance, both in terms of time and place, what useful role can political exiles play? Sometimes, maybe often, the fact that they cannot forget what was done to them becomes such an obstacle that their influence is destructive. I wonder what might have happened in Iran had the Ayatollah Khomeini not returned from exile. Would Iran have ended up in the grip of such a harsh doctrinal plutocracy? An internal revolt may have produced a state less paranoid. One thinks of some of the rabid Cubans in Miami or the small number of escapees from the killing sands of Algeria who live in the UK so maddened that all they can feel is a generic hatred which must be satisfied.

As an exile from Uganda thirty years ago, I know how many Ugandans, Asians and Africans are stuck in self-pity and fury for a lost home, understandable responses to the horrific history that followed independence. If you want to understand, go to the new exhibit Out of Blue, at Tate Britain, by Zarina Bhimji, who was forced to leave Uganda as a young child. She recreates the terror we felt then and the perpetual sense of grievance we carry.

Exiles can also become brilliant advocates for progress in their old countries – Edward Said and Wole Soyinka are two striking examples. They can exert influence on foreign policy and possibly a deeper understanding of nations that we often stereotype. The down side is – and that is certainly being experienced by Iraqi exiles – there is a double guilt, of not being there and of knowing that the powerful countries you live in cannot always be depended on to do the right thing.

Then there is the population that never left and suffered on. The mistrust of outsiders and their own exiles among these people remains even when a good outcome occurs. In South Africa activists still question the authority and authenticity of returnees, even though ANC exiles took great risks with their own lives, even going surreptitiously into southern Africa where several were arrested and faced terrible punishments. In Kampala, which I returned to once five years ago, they had excised Swahili from the culture. I was told by my old university friends that this was because the language was associated with the Tanzanians who helped to free Uganda from Idi Amin, and those soldiers had behaved with disrespect towards Ugandan civilians. Hamid Karzai in Afghanistan is obviously trying hard and even succeeding a little in uniting that volatile country but, so far, too much – including his stylish clothes – mark him out as an outsider with limited influence.

When Iraq has been done over, pro-war exiles will gain gratitude and a little more power. But let them not believe all will then be well for them or the people of Iraq. For exiles there is no going back, except in dreams.

The Middle East is destroying my friendships

24 February 2003

I am walking barefoot on broken glass and eggshells with this column. I know well enough how it will displease belligerent Zionists and those Muslims who hate Jews. Others too, probably, because these days, there is a preference for crude and simplistic postures à la George Bush. We all have to declare who we are for (absolutely), otherwise we are presumed to be the enemy. Just as the world becomes maddeningly complex, political and religious fundamentalists jostle for conscripts – people who will surrender their brains and their hearts to follow their leaders. Some of us have, thus far, resisted this call of the sirens. We have, in small ways, crossed boundaries, entered the minds of 'others', and found a deeper understanding of our common bonds and obligations to each other. The challenge of this century is surely how to care about people who lie beyond our fields of concern, people to whom we owe nothing or even people who have long been our foes.

Which reminds me. The papers should have blazoned this piece of news but didn't, so low is our esteem for such activities. This Thursday, a British woman, Dr Priscilla Elworthy of the Oxford Research Group, was awarded the Niwano Peace Prize – £100,000 – for her work on the resolution of conflicts through non-violent means. She brings together Chinese generals with Russian weapons designers, Pakistani and Indian warmakers, and today has radical plans on unseating Saddam to which Tony Blair should pay attention. There is nothing weak-livered about wanting to find non-violent, humane slip roads to tackle the most intractable problems. It is a damn sight harder than pure, simple loathing.

For some years now I have been a member of a small group that brings together Muslim, Jewish, Asian and black Britons. We meet every six weeks and talk openly, often painfully, about all the issues that divide us and which we know we can affect if we work better together. And we have. We have helped refugee doctors to get retraining, and helped to make sure that the Stephen Lawrence inquiry was not left to gather dust. Two Jewish members have personally funded and participated in projects to prove that Islamophobia is getting worse. (How many Muslims have openly campaigned against the anti-Semitism that we all know is freely traded in mosques and other places?) This is not interfaith dialogue, because we have atheists too among us. Politicians, ministers too, have been invited for meetings, and sometimes even more controversial people – representatives of the Nation of Islam, for example.

This is the place where I feel best understood and safe. I know that if I ever need help or support outside my own family, these are the people who will stand by me. The majority of them, at present, are Jewish, because some non-Jewish people have gone on to jobs that do not allow such informal attachments. But for the first time ever, I am worried that this remarkable group will fragment. The political is pounding the personal so mercilessly these days, I wonder if we can survive.

Our alliances, painstakingly stitched together, are now stretched to breaking point. Trust, which survived the blasts of the many wars in the Middle East, the rise of fanatics – from George Bush and Sharon to the Taliban – and, until now, the pending war against Iraq, is fragile and frail today.

I see a direct connection between what we are threatening to do to Iraq and what we tolerate in Israel. I am becoming aware that this connection worries the Jewish group members. To them, there are other evil regimes (if I am honest, the vast number are in Islamic countries), and these human rights abusers get off without a mention. They may have a point. But as one of those Muslims who does not deny the right of Israel to exist (to its pre-1967 borders) and who has always been openly critical of our own societies, it is telling that today the iniquitous actions of Israel are consuming me. They illustrate too blatantly the arrogance of leaders who expect immunity because of the horrors of the Holocaust, the memories of which they betray.

I am not at all sure that my Jewish friends can understand the depths of these feelings. I don't bring them up because our relationships feel too vulnerable suddenly.

As my colleague Justin Huggler wrote in this paper last week, as the world obsesses about Iraq, Sharon is acting ever more like a licensed psychopath. Some six hundred or so Israelis have been murdered by Palestinians. That is unequivocally condemned by me. But two thousand or more Palestinians have been massacred by the overwhelming force of the Israeli army. Palestinians, old and young, are subjected to humiliation, beatings and torture, as was described in unbearable detail by Edward Said in a London lecture this January. We know what we call anti-Jewish prejudices, but what label do we give to the attitudes of some Jews towards Arabs, all of whom are seen as vermin fit only for extermination? Arabs too are Semites, so what do we call this Jewish hatred for other Semites?

Gaza is under siege and a dozen Palestinians have been killed because they were suspected, yes suspected, of being Hamas activists. Now the US is naming Palestinian academics in the UK and the US, pronouncing them terrorists without any proof. One of the victims of this summary injustice is the academic Bashir Nafi, who lectures at the University of London. His life is suddenly engulfed in suspicion. He may or may not be involved in unsavoury activities. But this is a violation of his rights. Aid agencies have called for our government to send food to the starving people of Gaza, deliberately denied sustenance by a government we do not condemn.

But I do continually question myself in feeling the way I do. Am I becoming more detached (for the first time in my life) from the genuine alarm at what many decent Jewish people see as a creeping anti-Semitism around the world? Is this evil once again uncorked and is it now tolerated because of the dreadful policies of the Israeli government? I think Linda Grant may be right when she points out in an essay in *Prospect* that 'Anti-Zionism, while not itself anti-Semitic, if pursued vigorously by enough people, lays the foundations on which it becomes possible to construct a political agenda in which Jews are principally responsible for the world's problems.'

Many Jewish people feel uneasy about going on the anti-war marches for this reason, and I understand this reluctance. Who would want to be out there among millions fighting for justice for Iraqi people when all the while placards accuse you of being a force of evil? I think anti-war march organisers should have focused only on Iraq, because that is the absolute priority. But when it comes to public discourse, you cannot have a credible debate about Iraq without direct and intellectually honest comparisons with Israel and other factors too, such as our complicity in keeping double standards for the two countries and the terrifying ambitions of Bush and Richard Perle and Paul Wolfowitz, the enthusiastic pro-war American Jew.

If we, progressive Muslims, Jews, Caribbeans and other antiracists, can't stand the heat of this, if we fall apart over the way the world seems to us today, then hope must itself have died.

A tidal wave of hatred is sweeping the world

19 May 2003

Let me try, as best I can, to describe the knots of fear, the coils of fury, the jumbled wires that mess up my head every time another act of violation explodes on the global landscape, splashing blood and horror and making inevitable acts of even more vicious retaliation. My responses are complicated and shared by millions who never have seen, and never will see, the world as the power merchants of the UK, US and Israel say we must.

So this week when the strange quiescence of al-Qa'ida (if indeed it was that rather amorphous, ill-defined organisation) broke to cause mayhem in Saudi Arabia, Morocco and Chechnya, and fear of mayhem in Pakistan and the east African states, while home-grown suicide bombers caused further turmoil in Israel and Palestine, I am sorry to report that I didn't react the way I might have if I was the kind of chap who expects to be invited to the *Spectator* summer party.

I cannot simply produce, on tap, platitudinous condemnations that seem to be required every time there is an attack by Islamic Stalinists. Yet more than two-hundred people died, and it is intolerable to imagine the pain that this has caused.

There is today a huge divide between people who see the universe through the eyes of neo-con America and its right-wing European devotees and satellites, and the rest of the world that feels disempowered and caught between all these New World barbarians who are seeking to dominate and destroy, to bully, threaten, humiliate and crush the will and spirit of populations the world over. Individuals or groups causing planned havoc are not more evil than states, even democratic states, that do the same, particularly as the death tolls they can inflict would be beyond bin Laden's most outrageous dreams. What is truly scary is that the powerful in the wild west coalition do not begin to understand (nor do they want to) just how much dormant suspicion and hatred are now spreading to all countries, many of which, during the Cold War, were on side and happy to be so.

The result, says Arundhati Roy, is a grotesque and permitted racism: 'There is a tidal wave of hatred for the US and its allies rising from the ancient heart of the world. In Africa, Latin America, Asia, Europe, Australia, I encounter it every day from bankers, businessmen, yuppie students. America is a nation of morons, a nation of murderers, they say (with the same carelessness that they say 'All Muslims are terrorists'). In the grotesque universe of racist insults, the British [are called] arse-lickers.'

This distrust is found across Europe, too, among many of us who feel powerfully European but have an internationalist sensibility that refuses to comply with the senseless US/UK geopolitical plans for the next decade. And it is because we care about these countries. The American historian Paul Kennedy was recently shocked when a Dutch journalist told him he was scared of the US. But many of us are as scared for the US and its allies. That is why I am contemptuous of American groupies who will not accept that criticism is exactly what that country needs today.

For we watch as the generous, idealistic, self-critical, enquiring and aspirational American nation is reduced to such paranoia that it cares no more about its own basic freedoms, principles of justice or capacity for productive coexistence with other nations. Guantanamo Bay will haunt them for ever. America is so greedy that it is making itself ill with ideological overfeeding and this habitual rush to unnecessary wars, with Britain as habitual ally.

Sensible British Tories can see this – read the pamphlet by the MP Andrew Tyrie (*Axis of Anarchy*, published by the Foreign Policy Centre). According to Tyrie, 'Bush and Blair are making the world a less safe place. The US is in danger of overreaching itself. Out of a curious mixture of a new vulnerability and a complacent and misguided sense of supremacy, a dangerous American foreign policy is being forged and a more reliable and orderly foreign policy discarded.'

We international 'objectors' (if you wish to call us that) want to understand why on 11 September those men in those planes wanted to wreck the sanity and security of America – which is not the same as excusing the crimes they committed. We believe the globalised world system can bring much benefit; but not if it is just another way of privileging those with ambitions for absolute cultural, political and economic hegemony. We are alarmed that our people are fed so many lies. As *Panorama* showed last night, the Bush project for increased US control was hatched long before 11 September. We know that only a real and transparently fair settlement between Israel and Palestine will reduce the power of the extremists on both sides.

We also know that, even if this were to happen tomorrow, bin Laden wouldn't deliver his troops to the International Court in The Hague. We 'objectors' never believed either the Taliban or al-Qa'ida were finished. Nor did some of us believe in the illegal war against Iraq which was never about the poor victims of Saddam whose corpses are now being used as shameful covers by duplicitous politicians. We want to know how many people were killed by our war. Yet we realise that, as with the hundreds of thousands of conscripts, these names and numbers will have been vaporised by our superior power. We watch with alarm as the reconstruction of Iraq degenerates into an occupation.

If our leaders don't understand these things, they will not be able to stop the rise and rise of violent extremists. They are already active in ninety-five countries, and reformists of all sorts are being swept away or silenced. Imams in Saudi Arabia are already calling for the murders of intellectuals and Westernised Muslims. In his book on al-Qa'ida to be published next month, Jason Burke is convinced that the network will grow and become more ruthless. All our lives are now endangered.

Most of the victims of this latest spate of terrorism are Arab or Muslim, the terrorists' own brothers, sisters and children – that is, if they really believe in the *umma*, the bond that unites diverse Muslims. For a good long while these Muslim terrorists will have ruined tourism in Morocco, Kenya, Tanzania and Uganda, and those countries will fall perilously now into economic chaos just when things were looking better politically. Talk to East Africans and Moroccans and they will tell you that they are traumatised by the bombs and threats thrown into their fragile countries by the suicide bombers. But they will add that they can understand why al-Qa'ida is attracting recruits and why this evil will not be beaten by Bush and Blair with all their weapons and hubris.

Blameless American citizens are today unsafe if they venture much beyond Europe; Britain has become the second most reviled country in the world; all white people, all Jews are now vulnerable wherever murderous Islamicist cells operate. The inhabitants of beautiful places that are terrorist targets are the collateral damage in this war and their deaths hardly ever count in this clash of the pitiless. And all we have to console us is George Bush with a silly smile on his face saying: 'These guys are on the run, we are going to get them.'

My patience is exhausted. I don't trust Mr Blair or the Hutton Inquiry

11 August 2003

The Hutton Inquiry into the death of the scientist David Kelly begins today. The judge is an independent, honourable man and for the family and friends of Dr Kelly this is obviously an essential process that will hopefully nail the people, who they say hounded Dr Kelly to commit suicide. But for me and almost everyone I know – black, Asian, Muslim and white Britons – this is not the story nor the inquiry that will give us the answers to the questions we seek. Quite the opposite in fact. The investigation that may result in high-profile resignations will be used only to keep Tony Blair in the life he and his wife have grown to love rather too well.

And as a strategy it will probably work. If Geoff Hoon, the Secretary of State for Defence, falls on his sword and Alastair Campbell, Blair's director of communications, goes off to earn a fortune, the nation will be placated and we will have a good many more years of Tony Blair, the man who always believes that all that he does is right and his right to do, the man who has got us into the mess we are in today – the UK is the third most despised country in the world after the US and Israel – and who announced recently that his appetite for power remains undiminished.

Something is rotten again in the state of Britain, and this time it is a Labour prime minister, the willing inheritor of so much of the mantle of Margaret Thatcher who is responsible.

This is why I have only limited interest in this inquiry and why I am exploding with frustration at the current discourse on the war, at the BBC, at the spin doctors smiling wryly in photographs instead of hiding their heads under thick grey blankets in shame, at the pleasing and appeasing language that allows New Labour to believe it can still get away with anything simply because it got rid of the Tories in 1997.

On Saturday morning when I appeared on the Adrian Childs programme on Radio Five, my exasperation burst through the humbug, dissembling, pietism, expediency, jockeying, sheer Machiavellianism that allows this rot to grow. I think the presenters were a bit shocked. I said that the Prime Minister had deliberately told the nation half-truths and untruths when it came to the war in Iraq and that he had, without our consent, yielded our sovereignty to the will of a warmongering Republican government in Washington.

I could blame the heat, but that's not it. Even now, when I have lived here for more than thirty years, I find it impossible to understand, let alone play, the obfuscating game of British politics: that gentlemanly pursuit of lobby journalists and think-tank wonks and insider gurus who know just how far they should go, in their own interests, in criticising the government. Otherwise, presumably, they would be flung into some bog to sink far away from the centre, never again to share a pricey meal in those discreet places where the off-the-record conversations happen.

Why do these cosy briefings take place? Is it because governments in good democracies really believe in the need for a well-informed fourth estate? Of course not. It is because the chosen ones – the majority of them white men, with now a handful of trusted women – can be depended on not to rock the boat in case they all sink. The most recent press conference held by the Prime Minister for various domestic and foreign correspondents, with all that mirth and flirty chatter, was a perfect example of that intimate little world. With so much going on, how dare any of the journalists succumb to summertime bonhomie? There are exceptions, of course, and on this occasion one or two journalists did seem to want to question Blair much more sharply, but they were lost amid the noise of merriment.

One senses, too, that Blair is still regarded with a degree of awe. 'Are you suggesting that Blair, a man of such integrity and obvious religious belief, could actually have lied?' I am frequently asked, by many who don't agree with the war but still prefer to believe that the Prime Minister genuinely believed and still believes the bilge he comes out with. And boy Blair does sincerity like no other, which is why the Americans like him to be forever on side. It plays particularly well in that sentimental country. But just because a politician says he is on the level and ardently uses the words 'absolutely sure' many, many times, it is no reason necessarily to believe him.

How much more evidence does this nation need that Blair backed the war because America wanted it and the occupation? We have had two former Cabinet ministers – Clare Short and Robin Cook – saying that there was no justification for the actions we took, particularly as that meant sidelining the United Nations. OK, perhaps these two have tainted reputations – I think they do. Cook presided over the disastrous sanctions on Iraq that killed many more than the war, and Short was not principled enough when she should have been. But they were insiders and would not easily rebuke their invincible leader without substantial knowledge of the facts.

Blair is guilty of political deception as serious as any the world has known. He never intended to take any notice of Hans Blix. Read the newly published 'war diary'(actually a very nice hagiography of the Prime Minister) by Sir Peter Stothard, fomer editor of *The Times*. There it is clear that months before the many charades that were played and the dodgy dossiers were prepared, Blair was quite committed to following George Bush, who was going to war whatever happened.

'The people of Iraq are free,' declare the warniks, and so what is the point of this relentless debate over the reasons that were given for the action? Because I believe that unless we hold the Prime Minister to account over this, it will happen again, and Blair will become even more contemptuous of our institutions and of international law.

The sad truth is that he is getting away with it because people don't want the Tories back and because Charles Kennedy is so addicted to his own affability that he is doing little or nothing – and that is a real shame for the Liberal Democrats and, more importantly, the country.

Come the autumn conferences, the New Labour tribe will reaffirm its leader – because it says there is nobody else to take his place, so great is his cult appeal now. As Roy Hattersley wrote recently: 'The victory of personality over policy is almost complete. We are fast moving into a situation where the party – as a democratic institution

– no longer exists. Its purpose is increasingly limited to the task of assisting in Blair's election.' People forget that polls have shown that it was not Blair wot won the election in 1997 but the Tories who lost it.

And it could happen again. New Labour has so betrayed all of us who voted them in, and the meaning of democracy itself, that many will proactively refuse to vote at all next time round. And who knows what that will mean? And all because Tony Blair deceived the nation and never understood the implications of that for the future.

The lessons we failed to learn from September 11

8 September 2003

This column is not an easy one for me. I write to reflect on September 11, because I feel I must, to balance the excesses and exaggerations, the merchandising of sorrow, the exhortations that will appear in our media at this time, and will doubtless be replicated in many other countries.

This is the week when the world feels pressured to reassure America that it was more cruelly and unforgivably violated than any other nation, before or since. This is a travesty, a dreadful negation of all that anguish suffered by all those nations through recent history. By writing about the event close to the anniversary, I unavoidably place myself among the many who will be rushing to place their offerings on the table of American grief, which will not give way.

Nor will the poisonous hate of those Muslims (a small but chilling minority) who rejoiced when they heard of the attacks. On September 11 this week, some of them will remember the 'Magnificent Nineteen' – the suicide bombers responsible for the mayhem. They are not alone in wanting to desecrate the memories of the people who died. An article by someone called Michael Santomauro (does anyone know who he is?) has been put on the internet. He feels no sympathy for the people who died because they were Americans who never cared about the lies and destructive policies of US governments. 'So what? Who cares? Bomb them all. In God's eyes this generation of Americans will never be missed.'

Two years on from those savage attacks which killed so many and assaulted the optimism that was the US's, have any really useful lessons been learnt by that country or its sworn enemies? Are we now more secure than we were? A resounding 'No' to both questions.

Only fools and the Republican neo-cons today believe the world is a safer place than it was two years ago, or that its colossal arms and arrogance will protect the hyper-power from further attacks. Only fools and Islamic fascists still believe they can bring down the US to create a Muslim global haven .

The rest of us know only deep unease. Where is the self-criticism, the honesty, the overhaul of politics and religion which should have followed September 11?

There was a moment when the waves of anguish, anger and unexpected vulnerability did make the US (all too briefly) think about the backdrop to this violence that came on a bright day, killing women, men, mothers, fathers, sons, daughters, lovers, friends, of all backgrounds.

A few months ago, Al Gore reminded the US of that moment of self-interrogation which he rightly said was squandered. Incurable self-pity, vengefulness and aggression washed away the trembling sorrow and questions Americans were finally asking themselves and their vainglorious government. The legally dubious victory of George Bush Jnr et al ensured that such soul-searching was swept off the stage of public discourse.

Today, apart from the usual chorus of honourable dissent – Noam Chomsky, Gore Vidal, Susan Sontag, Edward Said – and others such as Tim Robbins and Susan Sarandon, the US is grimly reinforcing the worst aspects of its politics and culture, and stamping out all that made and makes that country admired by billions.

And right-wing groupies of the US still cannot see the truth. Just read Geoffrey Wheatcroft's absurd twitterings in this month's *Prospect*. The left failed to support the official line; they didn't fall down on their knees to Ground Zero; they defended Islam and were guilty of 'Western self-hatred'. Even more worthless is the analysis of the sort propagated by the Princeton professor, Bernard Lewis, who still claims that September 11 was the most vile, the most wicked thing ever to have happened to a country which is only ever benign.

The land of so-called freedoms has spies in libraries, offices and neighbourhoods. Foreign nationals are held without charge, (numbers unknown, and we are doing this here, too) and deported to places they do not know. They can be Muslims, Hindus, Sikhs, anyone swarthy. Nuns and parents of soldiers trying to reach anti-war demos are stopped from getting there.

Blatant cowardice has infected the most liberal of journalists, and partial stories are thrown out for the public to guzzle. For a nation which prides itself on always being suspicious of too much government, how do they let Mr Bush and Co get away with so much? Some critics of Washington policy now claim that eleven countries warned Mr Bush about probable attacks on the US. Nothing was done about these. Where is the fury of the American people?

In his searingly courageous new book, *What Next?* the black American writer Walter Moseley asks the questions the US has stopped asking. Written for African-Americans (who have to deal with the confusion of having two of their own leading these policies of self-destruction) he writes: 'We know our nation's foreign policy is dedicated to imperialist gain, not the spread of democracy. If many everyday people in America know these things why can't they change the tide of world events? I want to argue against the powerful urge for us to dominate our enemies. I want to go beyond our fears and prejudices.'

In order to do that the US will have to learn to value lives which are not American. It seems pathologically incapable of that kind of human empathy. It is awful that Americans are dying in Iraq for a foul war; but what about the 38,000 Iraqi civilians who have died, several more dying each day? These people have no names; they now don't even have numbers. Even the Red Cross is not given these figures.

Astonishingly, still, across the world people are torn between admiration for the US and resentment against its unchallenged power. A British Council survey in Muslim countries revealed both views were alive among the young. But time will kill the goodwill unless the US wises up.

No better news on the other front either. Yes, Muslims around the world did wake up to the fact that their faith was being corrupted by intolerance and fascism, and that they had to reclaim their religion. But we are finding ourselves more powerless than ever as these ideas ensnare our young.

Too many intelligent, educated Muslims living in the West (like most of the hijackers) are withdrawing from the best that the West has given us. Some of us talk quietly about the need for a reformation, the transformations we need to thrive in modern times, our complicated allegiances which can never only be to Islam. But our vices are drowned out by the shrieks of the militants. Muslims, so long disconsolate, lacking in pride and strength, are now in the grip of a sickness ravaging minds and souls, says Abdelwahab Meddeb, the French Tunisian poet, in his new book, *Islam and its Discontents*. September 11 has only made them more sick.

In that sense Osama bin Laden has won. He has created global chaos and much loathing; he has distorted the minds of Muslims and destabilised them; he has enabled the US to behave ever more monstrously.

Remember that as you watch the sentimental bunting which will be hung out on Thursday.

Once a reactionary, always
a reactionary

3 November 2003

Horror of horrors. Can Tory MPs really be this chuffed with the choice they have just made? Are they suffering from collective Alzheimer's disease? Michael Howard was a revolting, reactionary Home Secretary from 1993 to 1997, and he will be the same as Conservative leader, mark my words.

Way back then, I gave a speech in a prison to inmates. It was a stark, awful place. On some of the window sills, I noticed wilted plants grown in tin cans. Orders from Howard, according to two prison officers. He had visited some days previously and was furious that the prisoners had grown flowers to cheer themselves up. So he put a stop to this little human and humanising activity.

I also watched him publicly humiliate Sir Herman Ouseley, then the chairman of the Commission for Racial Equality, which had called for a stronger Race Relations Act – now, thanks to New Labour, in place. At a conference, Howard was asked for his response. He was arrogant, contemptuous of Ouseley, uninterested in the document and didn't even try to pretend that the Tories took race equality seriously.

Oliver Letwin, Michael Portillo, Theresa May and Kenneth Clarke, who have given years of unrewarding service trying to drag the Tory Party towards modernity, must surely know that the person about to be crowned their king is an unrepentant, voter-repellent right winger. So what are they playing at?

They must think voters are halfwits. Howard wears slightly more fashionable spectacles and Widdecombe puts on a girly Alice band; they cheerfully say the past is over and we are expected to rush to them with hope. (Portillo is at least astute enough to understand that his incredible makeover may have got him lucrative offers from the BBC, but that most Britons still haven't forgotten he was once an unfeeling Thatcherite zealot.) The party faithful, last week so enraged at the behaviour of their MPs, are today as compliant as much of the media.

At various functions I attended last week, nobody was mentioning Derek Lewis, the prison chief unfairly sacked by Howard, who described the Home Secretary as a man 'with the menace of Uriah Heep and the sincerity of Bob Monkhouse'. This is why we all rose to applaud Jeremy Paxman when he asked Howard the same question fourteen times to get him to tell the truth about the Derek Lewis scandal.

Mr Howard will play the demagogue, but with precision and finesse. Watch him as he pushes New Labour into more and more punitive postures on law and order, as he savages good policies that advance equality and fight discrimination, as he trips up the progress slowly being achieved on legalising some forms of immigration, as he cruelly and knowingly further demonises asylum-seekers, the most voiceless people in our country. Like many of my black, Asian, Muslim and Jewish friends, I think that it is unforgivable when the children of refugees reduce the human rights of other refugees. Howard did this before and will again, given a chance. But then I feel the same about treacherous Ugandan Asians who have joined the clamour to keep out asylum-seekers.

Under Blunkett, although he can be illiberal and populist himself, we are getting some genuinely good developments – a new culture of citizenship, talk of green cards for migrant workers and, brilliantly, a new Equalities and Human Rights Commission to protect the rights of all Britons, white and black, who are victims of discrimination. All these and more are under peril as the new opposition leader sweeps in.

What will make it worse is that any criticism of the new Tory leader will be condemned as anti-Semitic. Edward Heathcoat Amory has already been branded an anti-Semite by Vanessa Feltz for writing that Howard is seen as a 'proper English gentleman'. Paxman the same because he does not show Howard enough respect. I too will get some slaps from those who weekly sniff my columns to finds words and thoughts which 'prove' that I have Jew-hating DNA. There is now a whole industry engaged in this new McCarthyism.

No matter. Michael Howard is one of the worst leaders the Tories could have elected, and nothing is going to make me flinch from saying this.

The good news is that a recent poll showed that 26 per cent of voters are even less likely to vote for the Tories under Howard than under IDS. So far, the people aren't convinced that the man who emerged so smoothly out of the dark is the prime minister they want for the twenty-first century. Long live their cynicism.

Why I have decided to give back my gong

1 December 2003

Damn Benjamin Zephaniah. I blame and thank him for this epiphany. On Thursday the poet, sweet and modest, vegan, always gentle, caused a nationwide eruption by announcing that he was refusing an OBE and then explained in a blistering article why he despised the honours system, this government and the monarchy. Zephaniah beamed a mercilessly bright light on the whole secretive and dubious system and the delusions which went with it. There was no escape; no patter that could diminish the force of his choice even though some of his arguments were questionable and were indeed questioned by decent black and Asian people who felt good and right about accepting their OBEs and MBEs and CBEs.

As a recipient of an MBE, I was thrown into chaos. Mingled with self-contempt, I began to feel that to hang on to the honour would be so dishonourable I could never again respect myself. After much too much internal turmoil, testing introspection, tortuous arguments, I have today made the decision to return the medal which will make me sink very low, I know, in the estimation of many, even friends, because there is little kudos in giving back something they feel I should never have accepted in the first place. This is rank hypocrisy, the worst of all positions, and I will have to weather the attacks private and public, in part because I deserve them. No getting away from that.

I also expect unfair attacks. I will be charged with being discourteous and manipulative, publicity seeking, for having no consistency, much worse I am sure. The wolves are already howling outside Zephaniah's door. They accuse him of being 'graceless and pompous' (that was Cristina Odone – the Catholic Queen whose tedious lectures on morality have not always been followed in her own life), being an ex-burglar and of criminal ingratitude (various colum-

118

nists). Even Trevor Phillips has asked the poet to live in the 'real' world.

When the formal letter about an MBE first arrived in 2001, I threw it into the bin. (I later did the same with the invitations to various palace events during the Jubilee.) Those I love most thought I should accept the honour because of what it would mean to my mother and because this was my country showing me recognition after a long, hard journey, still always infinitely longer and harder if you are black or Asian. Both reasons were sound and still stand.

Phillips has poignantly described the importance of such symbols for older generation immigrants who had to struggle against so many odds and barriers. Until this MBE, Jena, my mother, was constantly fearful that we would be deported from this country because I am so strident a dissenter. What happened in Uganda still affects Asians. Her panicky heart settled after she saw and touched the rather beautiful piece in its satin folds.

In Australia and New Zealand, citizens are honoured without inappropriate echoes of a disputed past. In France the state recognises the good and the great. We are still tied up with the emblems of Empire and monarchy but the meaning is the same as in these countries. And you don't enter the Establishment if you accept a medal – an accusation made against me by individuals I have been close to. In truth, some people who have refused the offer are more within the inner circles than I will ever be. Unlike me, they are seen at Chequers, or attending cosy soirées plotting the third term. Finally, it is important to remember that the little people are often in the lists which come out – nurses, community activists, dinner ladies – for whom such recognition is priceless and they can hardly be said to be members of the Establishment.

These were the original, credible reasons why I said yes. But Zephaniah's words still came as a wake-up slap. My current position is not morally sustainable. It is unethical and (a confusing one this) it isn't fair to the monarchy or government. As the sordid details of royal life creep out, after the Burrell revelations and the millions of pounds of tax revenue spent by Charles on refurbishing Clarence House, I am growing so opposed to this institution and the second-rate members of the family that they have the right to expect me to do the decent thing and give back their award.

Then there are the complicated questions about Empire. Unlike Zephaniah, I don't think colonialism, slavery, imperialism were evils entirely propagated by the English. All these projects depended on cooperation from the 'natives'. They led to us being here and claiming this country as our own, to the point of a stirring and volatile love.

Our collective history needs to be debated and told more honestly. It is indisputable that we have not even begun the painful process of addressing the generational damage suffered by subject countries and the economic base which was built by Britain through its domination and exploitation of these nations.

We Commonwealth immigrants are always asked to be grateful that we were 'allowed' to be here. Yes, sure, I'll be humbly grateful if the nation also expresses its undying thanks to the ruled children of the Empire whose blood and land helped to enrich and empower Britain. It is troubling to observe just how deep and enduring are the impulses which were borne out of that history, how so many indigenous Britons still believe they are always the best. And we encourage this sickness by promoting the old delusions of grandeur and greatness of Empire in our national awards system.

But there is a far more compelling reason why I must reject my own MBE. New Labour brutalises asylum-seekers, has no respect for the precious legal traditions so long rooted in this country and tramples on best principles. It colludes with the illegal and cruel treatment of hundreds of Guantanamo Bay detainees. Do I want to be associated in any way with this lot?

This Prime Minister loves his empires. In his victory speech at the Labour Party conference in 1997, he proclaimed proudly that this country once had the biggest empire in the world. Now he is committed to a new, even more loathsome empire, and is eager to join Bush and the neo-cons to reoccupy countries and steal their resources. How can I carry on being a member of the British Empire in the face of this new assault on the right of nations, however poor, to decide for themselves on their destinies?

So that's it then. The thing will be packed off today. Four things remain to do: 1) must tell Mother, slowly, and find ways to console her; 2) ditto my in-laws who were so proud of this; 3) reassure my daughter that her friends and their parents will not think her mother is mad, bad and dangerous; 4) solve the dispatch problem.

What is the right way to go about returning an MBE? A motorbike courier with a package addressed to The Queen, Buckingham Palace, or climb up the palace gates and hang up a banner before dropping the MBE over the other side. Or perhaps I should send it to 10 Downing Street via the Royal Mail with a savage letter to Blair, now that he says he is so interested in the views of his public?

The West must get humble and honest – fast

5 January 2004

For people in poor countries, life has always been fragile, unpredictable, risky, scary and murderous, which is perhaps why they believe so ardently in the next world, or try, even if it kills them, to reach places of wealth and safety. Although unfair trade agreements, grinding poverty, corrupt and pitiless leaders, illness, death, violence, degradation and natural disasters devastate generation after generation, they still laugh and sing and manage to dream a little.

These people are not today locked in any new and urgent sense of terror such as has gripped the Occident. That is our fate; the children of plenty who thought they could control and buy everything. In the past two years our certainties have been shredded, and although most of us carry on regardless, we have lost that innocent positivism which came out of historical privilege.

We too are now trembling before unforeseen forces. Suspicion is fraying the bonds of society – mistrust of fellow citizens, of politicians (who have manifestly been lying to populations that do not expect to be treated with such contempt), of intelligence sources, army spokespeople and media reports which are devoured, and at once believed and disbelieved.

Planes are grounded for days; alerts and warnings increase. Christmas and New Year celebrations were still jolly and expensive, but anxiety took a seat at most tables. When at midnight, on 31 December at a fab Scottish party in Somerset, we kissed each other, one of the inebriated guests said: 'Happy New Year – this may be our last the way things are going in the world.' I wonder how many millions shared that dread at that moment.

With one exception – the Aids crisis – the West has not known such internal turbulence for more than sixty years. Cosseted while the rest of humanity was buffeted, those 11 September planes heralded a hard reality for people softened by years of peace and prosperity. They demonstrated that the wretched of the earth were remarkably resistant and that some were capable of inflicting real and psychic wounds to the most powerful nations in the world, because they had nothing to lose.

Those leading these nations do not understand the power of this hopelessness. Please don't think I am idealising these killers as folk heroes. I am as frightened as everyone else of what they do, but I grew up in the so-called Third World, and I can see how such demon warriors can emerge from the flotsam and jetsam of a humanity that has been kept down for too long.

One of the most educative books I read last year was *When the Bulbul Stopped Singing: A Diary of Ramallah Under Siege*, by the humane and still sane Palestinian lawyer and writer, Raja Shehadeh. He describes the hardening of the hearts of good, caring Palestinians and the reasons for and consequences of this process.

This is why Bush, Blair, Putin and Co sound like fools when they say they are going to 'win the war against terror'. There is no way this is a 'war' which can be 'won'. And yet this invisible insurrection, with a limitless supply of kamikaze volunteers across the globe, can and does violate much of what is best in human civilisation through indiscriminate violence and destabilisation tactics. (It is important to remember that suicide bombers were not a 'Muslim' invention. Japanese pilots used themselves as weapons in the Second World War as did some of our own pilots of whom we think as brave. Tamil Tigers used young women suicide bombers, too.)

Look what the bombers have achieved so far, in spite of the successful defeat of their power base in Afghanistan. Count the money spent, the way the target countries have had to stretch their national defence and policing services, the cost to airlines, tour operators, the hidden expenses when leads are followed up to protect nationals.

World public opinion too is volatile and the bombers have more support than Westerners care to acknowledge. The homes, the streets and the playgrounds of the well-off are tense and paranoid places. It is possible that some of the frantic security measures today are instigated by set-ups. Al-Qa'ida and its satellites could well be doing what the IRA did for years – setting false trails and issuing threats that cause large-scale disturbance and economic damage – cleverly spacing these misleading clues between real explosions.

God knows what they know – the CIA, FBI, MI5, MI6, French, German, Italian, Turkish, Russian, Pakistani, Afghan, Saudi Arabian secret services and many others beyond. Some of the warnings are likely to be manufactured for cynical political reasons; some of the material, obviously, is unreliable. But I have no doubt that there are plots to stage another spectacular and another and another, whatever we do to protect ourselves.

In the long term, there will be a petering out. There always is. But our leaders must change direction now. They must fast acquire some humility, honesty and understanding. Laudable aims have been declared by Bush, and Blair, who went handshaking in Iraq this weekend.

Old tyrants held in place with our support (Saudi Arabia) or without (Libya) have been put on warning: democracy and human rights will be implanted in despotic countries. This weekend Afghanistan moved in that direction with its Loya Jirga agreeing on a constitution. The best news is contained in Article 35, which states: 'Formation or functioning of a party based on ethnicity, language, Islamic school of thought and region is not permissible.' This should be an example for Iraq. It is worth noting that India and South Africa, which in relative terms are good, working democracies, are civic and secular.

Joined-up thinking is urgently needed. The WTO, the World Bank, the UN and others cannot carry on disproportionately benefiting the rich or playing by different rules for different nations. As Noam Chomsky writes in his new book, *Hegemony or Survival*, we must get 'universality; we must apply to ourselves the same standards we apply to others, if not more stringent ones'.

We want human rights in Saudi Arabia? Yes. But we do not have the moral authority to demand these while hundreds are festering in Guantanamo Bay, US and UK prisons with no justice, or while allied soldiers in Iraq maltreat Iraqis and steal their resources, or when we promote pre-emptive actions and shoot to kill, or we prohibit weapons of mass destruction for some countries but not ourselves or Israel.

That universality applies to Muslims too. We too need more honesty, democracy, open debate, equality and freedoms. For the truth is that even if the West were miraculously to comply with all the above, the rot within Muslim countries would still wreck the lives and aspirations of citizens. This is why so many of the best and brightest Muslims in the world have flown to the West. In doing this they deprive their own countries and contribute further to global imbalances. And maybe therein lies a real solution, which is being missed at present.

Western Muslims could make a difference to the dangerous impasse we are in. They have imbibed democracy and human rights values; they know the world they fled. They could be employed by their new countries as envoys between diehard foes. Instead they are all seen as the enemy within, wearing explosive shoes to blow up planes.

The left's shameful betrayal
of immigrants

26 January 2004

Once upon a time, British liberals were keen to be seen to be on the side of freedom struggles, equal rights, internationalism, social democracy and immigration. They joyously endorsed the inexorable reshaping of class and other rigidities which, like a tight corset, had held together the country until the First World War. They appeared to love their rainbow nation and committed themselves to fighting the Little Englander mentality of Enoch Powell and later Margaret Thatcher and her gurus.

It was in 1978 that Thatcher said people of this country rightly felt 'swamped' by too many 'aliens' making demands on her country. It was the year my son was born and I never forgave her for those remarks and never shall. Left-of-centre liberals reacted with unequalled fury and we immigrants were given to understand that once they were in power, this nation would be ours too. At last.

They lied. They have turned out to be unreliable allies. And I don't just mean New Labour with its pernicious policies which destroy the hopes and lives of asylum-seekers. With few exceptions, influential British liberals today have shown their true colours. Using their box of sophistry week after week, they explain why immigrants and diversity are eroding the best of Britain.

They seek white schools for their precious tots; they move into areas without too many 'duskies'; they talk freely about how over-crowded the island has become. (Since they are barely reproducing, who else to blame but immigrants for this environmental and popu-lation disaster?) Sure, they still love fusion foods and Indian head massages and the feel of dark skin and forbidden sex, but oh God for the white Cliffs of Dover to be properly white again.

They have appropriated Thatcher's mean individualism and nationalism and have relaunched the products as brave new politics.

The most audacious among them has got to be the editor of the increasingly reactionary *Prospect* magazine, David Goodhart, who asks in the latest issue: 'Are we too diverse?' J'accuse Goodhart and other British neo-cons of threatening the new Britain that many of us are creating together. How confusing and upsetting that today I find myself more comfortable with Stephen Norris than with people like Goodhart and the journalist John Lloyd with their dodgy misgivings.

Goodhart claims there is a 'progressive dilemma' he shares with the Tory, David Willetts. The universal welfare state can only survive if the people who pay taxes believe recipients are people like them-selves. As Goodhart puts it, 'we are readier to share with, and sacrifice for, those with whom we have shared histories and similar values.' So I assume that if he were to see a small African child alone near his north London home, he would be less inclined to help than if she was as white as one of his daughters.

This, the latest of many reservations to emerge on immigration, is based of course on the idea that immigrants are only ever recipients and not producers of wealth, an outrageous assumption. Last year *The Economist* said: 'At a given moment migrants are generally net contributors to the public purse.' America's National Research Council found that while first generation migrants imposed an average fiscal cost of $3,000 (£1,640), the second generation yielded an $80,000 gain.

As a taxpayer for more than twenty-eight years, I have no burning need to see my money spent only on brown skinned women on the dole. I believe my society is bonded not through race and class and ethnicity but mutuality which cuts through all those categorisations. All those immigrant nurses, doctors, social workers, care workers who give their all believe that too. It may well be that human beings still retain close ties with their own people and may even want to live near them. That doesn't bother me at all. But in the past fifty years vastly more people than was ever expected have crossed imaginary and real boundaries, and today mixed-race Britons are the fastest growing minority group in the country.

European anti-immigration fellows also worry incessantly about 'assimilation'. The Dutch have now decided they want to remake a homogeneous country through social engineering because diversity is such a very bad thing. British neo-cons are excited by this new assertiveness in a partner country.

But what do we assimilate into when British society itself is so fragmented and volatile? And is it only immigrants of colour who must pass this test? What about English immigrants in Spain and Italy? Should they assimilate too? Or is it a question of when in Rome do as the English do? And who do we blame when immigrants change themselves and integrate only to find that they will never be properly accepted?

Nobody said it was going to be easy. We all have a long road to travel before we can create a strong sense of a new collective identity and each step is a challenge. As I have said many times before, no group can be exempted; we must all buy into a civic citizenship which can hold us together and enable our diversity to become a real asset for the future. If we can create this – as Canada has – and remain positive about managed immigration, we will be competitive in the globalised world. If we don't we are defeated, economically and culturally. And we certainly won't deserve the right to stage the Olympics.

Then there is the question of prerogative. These arguments about the welfare state and assimilation are based on a particular view of entitlement. The welfare state could not exist without the wealth that was accrued by centuries of exploitation of people around the world and without all the work that was put in by immigrants. I have no interest in keeping alive historical guilt in this nation. But to erase any historical sense of obligation to the children of Empire is surely a travesty.

At the World Economic Forum in Davos, Switzerland, this week, the demographic time bomb which awaits this country was once more discussed. A century back there were five people working for every retired person. Soon there will be one, and a large number of these will be the children of immigrants. Even President Bush, right-wing zealot that he is, understands the need for immigration and has granted amnesty to millions of illegal workers in his country. The Republican think tank, the Cato Institute, says immigrants are 'the lubricants' for the feisty US economy. In the UK, meanwhile, the

128

Home Affairs Select Committee, showing stunning immaturity, has gone in the opposite direction, asking David Blunkett (who was beginning to talk sense on immigration) to retract the amnesty he granted to 50,000 asylum seekers.

We are tired of having to justify ourselves. We have never been given the acknowledgement or appreciation we deserve. We are always asked to be more grateful to this country. When does our country show its gratitude to us for all that we have done and continue to do? And I am furious that these liberals have now given xenophobes licence to malign us further.

I am so disgusted with this latest bout of contempt for immigrants that I think it is time to arrange a national strike. Let us have a National Day for Immigrants. Don't go to work; don't buy anything either. Lose a day's wages or profits and for twenty-four hours show this nation just what we do. Neo-con liberals will not be welcome. We know who to trust now.

Must I vote Tory to champion immigration?

1 March 2004

What a week this was. We witnessed the first British citizenship ceremony – an excellent idea, though I could never swear loyalty to the Queen and Her family. But that is a quibble. At long last, in ritual at least, we are making recent immigrants feel this is their country and putting before them a clear social contract.

These new British citizens agree to live by the principles of social democracy. The state, in turn, I assume, will ensure their safety and promote equality of treatment and fair opportunities so they can grow healthy roots into the soil of this country and add to the ever-changing landscape. The recipients looked ecstatic. They appeared not to realise what an overwrought time and place they are coming into.

In truth I no longer know what kind of Britain I am living in either. It is all too bewildering. Traditional ideological maps are now obsolete. My old enemy Michael Howard sacked Ann Winterton, the Conservative MP for Congleton, for making an obscene, racist joke and now, it appears, Tories will be voting against New Labour's plans to remove the right of appeal from asylum-seekers.

Meanwhile, many key names on the left have been propagating views on immigration which are emphatically on the side of small Englanders such as the *Daily Mail*'s Peter Hitchins, who wants the old Empire back, please. Indeed the always-polite Mr Hitchins profusely thanked the new deliverer, *Prospect* magazine's editor, David Goodhart, for a searing essay arguing that too much diversity threatened the welfare state and tried his own patience. The *Observer* endorsed Goodhart and gave him a column to convert the unconvinced. The *Guardian* gave him another column, and then two full pages. Immigration has once more become a volatile subject, one of the three most contentious issues which are breaking up the nation.

(The other two are Iraq and 'the war on terror'.) The clashes go way beyond the numbers game into every aspect of state policy, including the economy, social cohesion, patriotism, civil rights, workers' rights, globalisation, diplomacy, war, the EU, gender equality, democracy, ethnicity and race, party politics, the media, national identity, demographics, history, education ... I could go on.

In the thirty-one years and eight months that I have been here, fighting for the right to be a true Brit, I have never known such chaos and confusion. This is as serious as it gets for immigrants, the descendants of immigrants and the indigenous Britons who have struggled with us against the mean streak that has always been present in this country and which is easily aroused by anti-immigration populists. Or populist intellectuals.

These intellectuals say they want a robust debate, but they haven't the stomach. As soon as we rebut them, and point out the flaws and prejudices which underpin their critiques, they burst into victimhood and claim they are being misrepresented or tarnished with accusations of racism. They are not racists, not in the way of a small and vanishing number of Britons. They don't want us to die in gas chambers or to be expatriated. They would not mind their sons and daughters marrying out and they love the writer Zadie Smith and actor Art Malik.

As Trevor Phillips, the chairman of the Commission for Racial Equality, notes, the genteel and learned can have exclusionary attitudes based on views of themselves, the country and its identity that are entirely in line with the old right's idea of kith and kin. Some of their best friends are not black, and never will be. Their use of 'we' does not include me, but does, I presume, include economic migrants from Australia. They have no objections to the army of US citizens in Britain. Their discomfort is aroused by Mr Patel in the corner shop but not Mr Starbuck. In the furore of the past fortnight, not one non-white Briton has defended the Goodhart thesis.

What about double standards, these nationalistic Britons believe that 'we' have the right to set up home and live where we wish – Spain, Italy or Bangalore (where they have very good services for old people). These brave new thinkers frequently whinge that they are being 'silenced' by the Politically Correct. Yet Goodhart, Anthony

Browne (an anti-immigration hawk who was awarded a prize by *Prospect* for his ideas), the academics Bob Rowthorn and Paul Ormerod (who reject the immigration solution to the demographic crisis) or Robert Putnam (who says diversity causes social fragmentation) can hardly complain they are not free to sell their ideas. They are everywhere – and I have debated vigorously against them at conferences.

It is vital that we, in the opposition, take on their theories. First, the welfare state. Professor Peter Taylor-Gooby of the University of Kent says: 'All survey evidence indicates that as societies become more diverse support for public spending grows.' Most human beings are not that misanthropic, thank God. Without doctors of South Asian background (making 27 per cent of the total) or black and Filipino nurses there would be no NHS today. Social work, teaching, transport are just as dependent on the people who are still debated about as though they are only receivers of welfare.

The energy in our nation comes not from the sleepy, homogenous villages of Suffolk (sweet though they are) but our messy, multifarious cities. Professor Richard Florida of Carnegie Mellon University has written persuasively on the creativity of diverse cities, the engines, as always, of dynamic societies. Remember too, under apartheid, society was very stable, and communities very close.

Finally, the 'national identity' which brainy retros are fetishising. Does our national behaviour now include due care in the telling of 'ethnic' jokes? Apparently so. Has it been changed by the 24-hour corner shop into a 24-hour culture? Obviously. With mixed-race relationships at record levels, is the very DNA of Blighty changing more than before? Yes.

When there is loose talk about British values, history and culture what exactly do we mean? I do hope we mean Shakespeare and democracy and not duplicitous prime ministers and horrendous levels of domestic violence and teenage promiscuity. May we include the artist Anish Kapoor and the vibrant talent of British Jewry? Had we not moved to this small island, we black and Asian Britons might never have known a Hanif Kureshi or Rageh Omaar or indeed *EastEnders*. What a joy it was to read a recent report by English Heritage and to see ourselves reflected as an intrinsic part of our nation. This never happened before; it is happening now because it must.

This is why this new leftie chauvinism is so outrageous. Theirs is a sinister invitation to liberals to abandon the nation we have jointly created. Some, not all, in New Labour find the ideas very attractive. The good news is that flying past their ears are yesterday's Conservatives, eager to catch up with modernity and its values. The clever, young deputy editor of the *Sunday Telegraph*, Matthew D'Ancona, wrote in a recent pamphlet, *Reclaiming Britishness*: 'Societies that close themselves from other cultures will wither. Those that don't won't. [Diversity] is not a threat to nationhood, but in modern times, the very essence of nationhood.'

Oh dear, oh dear. Does this mean I will have to vote Tory next time?

Is Christianity really better than Islam?

29 March 2004

Former Archbishop George Carey has just made, he claims, a thoughtful speech about the problem with Islam today. He believes the faith is associated with violence and political dictatorships; that a dark age has descended on Muslims in recent centuries which has led to creative stagnation.

He acknowledges the great Muslim civilisations of the past and their contribution to global progress (so he is not quite as ignorant as Robert Kilroy Silk), but now, he claims, we are a people without direction with hate in our hearts and bombs in our pockets.

He accuses Muslims of not condemning enough the suicide bombings in Israel. In his five thousand words he never asks more British Jews to denounce the murderous policies of Prime Minister Ariel Sharon. Ah well, we Muslims are getting used to doublespeak and double standards from our great and good.

All enlightened Muslims (yes, there are millions of them) feel a terrible pessimism and foreboding that authoritarianism, philistinism and barbarism are now the hallmarks of most Muslim states and too many Muslim immigrant communities – a barbarism which is killing hope, excellence, ambitions, life itself. We need reformation.

But we are also keenly aware of how leaders in the West – most of them the products of a Christian sensibility – have encouraged this backward state because it benefits their interests. How else do you explain the fact that the sanctimonious governments of the US and UK actively support the tyrannical despot in Uzbekistan, which has an appalling human rights record?

Not a week passes by without Islam being put in the dock. Carey says he meant to provoke a reaction. Well, I mean to provoke a reaction with this in return, my own sober reflections on the influence of Christianity today.

What with Easter round the corner and Mel Gibson's Christ dripping with blood and money, it is time to interrogate the faith and its

134

role in the world. Let us not go to the Atlantic slave trade or apartheid, both of which distorted parts of the Bible to justify the unjustifiable. Good Christians, after all, were central to the movements to overthrow both. But look elsewhere over the last seventy-five years and assess the impact Christians have had. Has it been wholly benign or often destructive?

I do believe Christianity, as originally envisaged, is a great faith, one I have learnt much from myself. Gandhi once wrote of Jesus: 'He was completely innocent, offered himself as a sacrifice for the good of others, including his enemies, and became a ransom of the world. It was a perfect act.' But faiths are more than their texts, their ideals, their stated principles or their heroic exemplars. Culture and politics invade, change, misuse belief to ignoble purposes, sometimes so much so that the faith becomes nothing more than useful spin. (A good question is whether it is faith which corrupts societies or societies which corrupt faith.)

Christianity seems to me the most redemptive and merciful of all the major religions. I remember as a child trying to comprehend this. Underneath the statue of Christ on the cross at the church near one of the four cinemas in Kampala were his words of sublime forgiveness: 'Father, Forgive them for they know not what they do.'

Many individuals do live by this testing doctrine. I listened to a British woman on Radio 4 this week who was married to a Tutsi killed in the genocide. She is going back to find the killers so she can forgive them. But where, oh where is that essence of forgiveness among the merchants of power today? Christians such as George Bush and Tony Blair are so consumed with the madness of vengeance that they feel they have the right to 'punish' the guilty and the innocent in their thousands because they can. The religion of peace has not prevailed. These faithful practitioners have become executioners and self-justifying bullies. Blair himself said in his speech in Sedgefield that he found a new uncompromising toughness in himself after the attacks on 11 September. The US will not budge on Guantanamo Bay, a purpose-built concentration camp.

Christ had humility and called for perseverance in the face of provocation – turn the other cheek and so on. Yet since the 1930s the body count produced by the so-called soldiers of Christ far, far outnumbers the deaths caused by other faiths on this good earth. I am including the two world wars and the Holocaust. Same story today. Hindus, Sikhs, Muslims, Zoroastrians, Pagans, Buddhists, Baha'is, or believers in Voodoo do not own most of today's weapons of mass destruction. Christians do.

Look at domestic policies and the view is just as ugly. Criminal justice systems in the US and UK are becoming so punitive they are almost totally un-Christian. Nothing, it seems, can expunge guilt any more. In Florida 600,000 exfelons, including those who have done time and repented, are denied the vote and civil rights for life. Death row bulges with the mad and young, whom the state will put to death without national shame.

The gift of love and hospitality to strangers is another tenet which has been crushed by the laws of Christian countries and their populations. It is OK to hate asylum-seekers and people desperately seeking a small living. Think of what we would do today if a swarthy, bearded, impoverished Joseph arrived with a pregnant wife looking for a place to stay for a few nights. In truth, although Muslim states have much that disgraces them, on this they have shown themselves more worthy than Christians. Even in Iraq, even as we were starving them first and then bombing them to bits, Iraqis gave surprised British journalists food, tea, warmth and care.

Then there is the issue of wealth. The rich in the West get ever richer (and the poorer ever more wretched) and human value is now measured in pounds and dollars. So what of Luke's account of what God wants: 'sell all that you have and distribute it unto the poor and thou shalt have treasure in Heaven'? This demonically self-obsessed and trashy modern culture of ours is a travesty of all that is good about Christianity. The Ten Commandments are ignored. Blair deceives the nation, Thatcher destroyed the will of working miners, and Christian children cannot go to school in Northern Ireland without a police escort to protect them from, well, other Christians.

By now, some readers may be splitting with indignation. You can't, they will say, blame the faith for the actions of politicians, princes, business people, and states. True. These people like Bush are not real Christians. True again. What about the great contribution

Christians are making to science, medicine, the arts and literature, to freedom, human rights and democracy?

Yes, I must accept these objections. We once were but now Muslims are not at the forefront of these developments. It is also unfair to focus solely on the bad that Christians do when they have also given the world so much.

But Islam and Muslims are constantly faced with such unfair generalities, disrespect and sweeping accusations. How does that make us feel?

Democracy is now a cloak for oppression

19 April 2004

As hostage-taking in Iraq becomes the next deadly tactic in this war without end, and increasing panic rises in the coalition countries, we are sure to get evermore self-righteous pronouncements from the leaders who planned this illegal occupation. We are daily instructed to express our outrage against the evil hostage-takers and other insurgents who, we are told, are motivated only by a hatred of liberty and democracy.

Oh democracy, how they debauch your reputation. Were you ever this callously used as a cloak for those who want to own the earth at any cost?

Democracy can never be perfect, but it is the best chance we humans have for decent governance and progressive politics. Until I was twenty-three I was only aware in abstract that in some parts of the world people could choose who they would be governed by. It seemed so far away from my own life.

I had absorbed keenly the history of the French and Russian revolutions, the American war of independence, other anti-colonial struggles and slogans such as 'No Taxation without Representation'. I was an avid reader of books on the suffragette movement, the plight of untouchables in India, later apartheid and the civil rights movement in the United States. But I had never seen a ballot paper until I came to Britain in 1972.

British rule over us was absolute and undemocratic and the first election when Uganda became independent was the last such event in that blighted country. I was too young to vote. It is still a tremulous moment when I go into the portakabin to declare my choice. And it drives me to distraction to hear that so many people in this country are uninterested in voting, except for *Pop Idol*. The next few months will bring on feverish voting excitement in many countries.

George Bush is already on his campaign for re-election, to add glory to his last dodgy victory. This month, the world's largest democracy, India, goes to the polls. I have just come back from that great country which today is buzzing with optimism and energetic political debates. The South African elections too are a reminder of the transformative powers of the democratic model.

And yet in all the above, and recently in Russia, we can see politicians brutalising the very thing they claim to represent. The ruling party in India attacks Sonia Gandhi, leader of the Congress Party, not for being an unproven politician, or for the many failures of her party, but for being 'foreign born'. They want to amend the constitution to prevent such 'outsiders' getting into positions of power. (By this logic, our Parliament should never have allowed MPs Keith Vaz, or Mohammad Sarwar, or Lord Parekh to take up their seats because they are all foreign born.)

The ruling BJP is also embarked on a mission to elevate Hinduism and relegate the practitioners of other faiths. An Indian friend of mine, who does street theatre with the poor of all backgrounds, has had his hand broken, his skull slashed by Hindu warriors who support these fundamentalist politicians. Corruption, intimidation, lies, deceit, the misuse of power and money distort the will of the people around the globe and will, in the end, destroy the democratic process itself, unless we wake up.

Many years ago, the American writer Norman Mailer wrote: 'A modern democracy is a tyranny whose borders are undefined; one discovers how far one can go only by travelling in a straight line until one is stopped.' How prescient those words, how even more frighteningly relevant today.

In volatile international politics, blatant injustices are now committed invoking the good name of democracy. Al-Qa'ida, Hamas, Hizbollah, Catholic and Protestant paramilitary fighters in Northern Ireland use religion to justify their terrible crimes against humanity. The US, Britain, Australia, Russia and others today use democracy to cover their tyrannical actions and policies. Israel terrorises and murders Palestinians in response to suicide bombers who terrorise and murder Jews. Vladimir Putin's troops crush Chechen communities but there is no condemnation from our leaders. Mugabe's crimes are nothing in comparison to what the Russian leader is getting away with. In all these cases, both sides ignore human rights, fair rules of engagement, various conventions and international law.

You may think it offensive that I suggest there is an equivalence between those we describe as 'terrorists' and the actions of civilised democrats. But to be scrupulously fair in this world, one does have an obligation to ask these uncomfortable questions. And we must expect better from those who say they are legitimate rulers who live in an ordered universe.

Passions understandably flare when blameless Italians, Japanese, Chinese, American and other hostages are snatched and held, sometimes cruelly slaughtered by the hidden enemies of the coalition in Iraq. We hear from ex-hostages from previous times how desperate they felt, how they went mad within days of being held. And we denounce these brutes resoundingly.

But these infringements of human rights and laws are simply a replication of what we have been doing in Afghanistan and Iraq, and the US in Guantanamo Bay. Men have been snatched and held without due process, sometimes tortured and killed, by our side. As Baroness Helena Kennedy QC points out in her new book, *Just Law*: 'For over two years hundreds of men have been detained in a legal limbo with no access to the writ of habeas corpus to determine whether their detention is legally justified. Links with al-Qa'ida have been made in very few cases. It is believed the majority were men in the wrong place at the wrong time.'

Some of these prisoners will undoubtedly have gone mad. Others are 'rendered' to countries where they can be tortured more rigorously and may have died. Useful outsourcing you may call this. Hundreds of people, including women and children have been blown up in Fallujah in the past few days. We still don't know how many innocent Iraqis have died or are dying as a result of sanctions and this war.

Do we really believe that such carnage and ruthlessness are OK, understandable, even admirable if perpetrated by democratic nations? Tony Blair and George Bush and Ariel Sharon and Vladimir Putin and others clearly do. They propagandise democracy to suit their own purposes.

Meanwhile, dictators, autocrats and various kinds of Stalinists carry on their campaign against the system which could empower their cowed and controlled people.

Thank God for real democrats who refuse to be fooled by the first lot or scared by the second. They will keep the flame alive even in these blasted times, people who remain truly and uncompromisingly committed to genuine political choice, to essential freedoms, to human rights and international laws and conventions, to common standards for all. Tony Blair was once among these spirits. In a book published by the Foreign Policy Centre in 2002, he wrote compellingly about internationalising democracy: 'We need to be clear what we mean by justice and community, the values of liberty, the rule of law, human rights and a pluralist society are universal and worthy of respect in every culture.' How hollow his words sound today.

Culture
Clashes

B ritain is evolving, constantly shifting. That is what happens to accessible islands. The tides of change keep hitting the shores. This is an inescapable reality. Trading with difference, domination, conquests, the ceaseless wash of migration, mongrelisation, cultural pollution and transformations are part of the contested identity of this complicated country. Unlike, say, Italy or Japan, though both countries are now having to deal with many of the same complexities as globalisation accelerates. Perhaps this helps explain the conservative heart of Britain – it cannot be easy being buffeted relentlessly.

The mélange inevitably leads to endless conflicts, tribal battles, quarrels over rights and entitlements, and value clashes. National and community narratives cannot agree on versions of the truth, past or present. Neo-imperialism is the new black, incredibly fashionable just as we enter the new imperial chaos in Iraq.

Politics and policies need continuous evaluations. The most innovative and effective interventions pass on as new times bring new challenges. White racism is still a blot on our landscape, and since The Satanic Verses, white liberals have revealed their deep, sometimes psychotic prejudices against 'the other'. But it would be dishonest to claim things have not got substantially better from the dark days of the sixties and seventies. Multicultural policies – which I once advocated with impressive ardour because they were needed at the time – are today responsible for dangerous fragmentations and may have held back progress towards a new, positive British identity promoting ties that bind us all. Alarmingly few English, Welsh and Scottish people call themselves British today. Black and Asian people can be as xenophobic as the worst of white Britons and a violent gangland lifestyle is emerging across the land. Young people are restless and emotionally homeless. Anti-racist polices, thoughtlessly applied, led to the tragedy of Victoria Climbie, the young African girl murdered by her adoptive 'aunt' and her boyfriend.

Our country is raucous, disorderly but yet rubs along; irreverent and reverent, questioning but too easily placated by the powerful. It can boast the highest rates of mixed race relationships in the Western world but the top 10 per cent of our institutions remain solidly white and the British National Party is gaining ground among many white citizens who feel disenfranchised. Culture clashes are unlikely to subside for a good while yet.

The long search for a homeland

Guardian, 22 November 1997

Kantaben, an elderly acquaintance I last met in Uganda, warns me in a voice trembling with disquiet: 'Don't say anything bad about England. Just keep silent. Because they also will throw us out and where do we have left to go?' A widow who arrived in Britain after Idi Amin expelled Asians from Uganda in 1972, she carries that unease of dispossessed people who have never had a spot on earth to call unequivocally their own. Having lost their ancestral place on the Indian subcontinent and been wrenched from their adopted country only to land on a cold and hostile terrain, they can never again take any chances and never forget. The wound of the expulsion is glistening fresh but their love is intact for that country they still call home. 'It was wonderful,' enthuses Kenti Nagda, a community worker. 'The valleys, rivers, the people, all carved in my brain. Without closing my eyes I can see it all.'

Intact, too, are the networks which served them so well in Africa. In minutes, the businessmen I am interviewing have determined my family background and found connections. Henceforth, any help I may need is guaranteed. Just as it was back home.

But there has been momentous change and not just in the form of the rags to riches stories that obsess the media; that myth of sorry little victims of the diabolical Idi Amin saved by Britain through her largesse and then converted into grateful millionaires.

In 1972 black Ugandans applauded Amin's policy believing they could at last feast at the economic table for free. Fuelled by Powell, Tebbit, Labour's Arthur Bottomley and the popular press, the British public erupted with unprecedented racist anti-refugee feelings. A week before the first refugees arrived here, Norman Tebbit wrote to Edward Heath saying the government was 'utterly and completely wrong' over accepting the Ugandan Asians. The Asians were not able or willing to recognise either the hostility awaiting them in the fair motherland or their own mistakes in Uganda. Time has transformed

145

all three players in that ghastly game, and a deeper understanding is now emerging of what really happened and why.

The story begins in the 1890s when the British imported Asians to East Africa to build the railway, to trade and, most importantly, to create a buffer between themselves and the Africans. Their early influence was beneficial, says Godfrey Lule, one time Attorney-General of Uganda: 'They were thrifty, hardworking, most welcome in the rural community as providers of services, credit and rudimentary banking facilities. There was mutual trust and respect.' But with increased wealth, Asians began to move into the towns which, says Lule, did not reproduce those relationships. 'These Asians were more arrogant, ostentatious and distanced from the African workers who had migrated to the city and so were only servants. They also controlled the visible economy. Some, only some, were involved in corruption and smuggling foreign exchange so resentment grew.'

This is half true, says Dayabhal Patel, poet and ex-politician. 'We may be blameable for indolence and indifference, but the British wanted to have those three layers in society, and there was bad black leadership.' There were also exceptions. Of two women elected to Parliament in 1963, one was an Asian, Sugra Visram, whose bravery against corrupt politicians is hailed to this day by Ugandans. She spoke local languages, wore African clothes, raised money for education and introduced family planning to Uganda, continuing the tradition started by her ancestor, Allidina Visram, a legendary pioneer and egalitarian who set up a network of shops and services for all East Africans. Visram often made her own community uneasy: 'Once I danced with an African family friend and there was such a hoo-ha about it. It hurt, but someone has to start things and then you get respect.'

Poor Asians were closer to Africans than their middle-class counterparts. Younger professionals also had different attitudes, says Kenti Nagda: 'Black friends came home to eat. It was hard for my parents but they didn't stop me, so the barriers were breaking down, though maybe not too fast.'

Nagda thinks seeing the Asian only as exploiter is wrong: 'People like the Madhvanis [major industrialists in Uganda] provided jobs for thousands, built schools, hospitals, libraries. The Aga Khan did the same and really built up the country. Somebody should write the history of our contribution.'

Manzoor Moghul, a financial consultant, feels that others should take some responsibility. Britain recognised Amin after his coup in 1969 with indecent haste and then humiliated its Asian citizens by denying them entry. 'That allowed that dictator to treat us like footballs for years.' It had become easy for Africans to pick on the Asian to explain away their own ineptitude and corruption. Asians thus felt insecure and the heightened state of antagonism helped politicians keep the heat off themselves. Politicians had the power to transform the country. Most chose instead to destroy it.

Even with all this poison in the air the expulsion order in 1972 came as a shock. 'It was terrible,' says Lule. 'I was losing good friends and as a lawyer I felt it was unjust. Then the mechanisms were so harsh, there was such mental torture But sadly there was support for it.' Kantaben cries when she describes how soldiers took her bangle off her, the only gold she had.

Their arrival here in September 1972 was the second big shock. Moghul remembers the racism, 'so thick in the air you could cut it with a knife'. Clusters of hostile British shouted at frightened Asians emerging from the airports. Leicester and Ealing councils put notices in papers telling people, as if they were contaminated, to keep out. A taxi driver threw my fare in my face when I told him I was from Uganda.

For these attitudes, Moghul blames 'the dithering government and the papers which created panic that 80,000 scroungers, primitives, were about to descend on them. In the end, 30,000 British subjects were accepted here – many stateless Ugandan Asians went to Canada and the US.

Dayabhai disagrees about the reception here. 'Some people were hostile, but the general attitude was very humane. Edward Heath was very very noble, and although they did not help us financially with loans, they received us with an open heart.'

This is the version Sir Edward Heath prefers. 'It was absolutely the right thing to take them,' he says loftily. 'Few other countries helped us so we had to. The British people are fair. We have a world reputation for looking after people.' He dismisses Tebbit and Powell as 'voices in the dark'. Sir Edward is even proud of his degrading dispersal policy. 'We were very careful to get them into a wide variety of places, so they would be spread out.'

There were generous people who provided enormous support but most saw the refugees as 'children and beggars', Kantaben says. The reception camps were grim. In one, they were moved suddenly because some whites expelled from Uganda were expected. One refugee recalls the scene: 'Our children were in schools, and when we complained they called us selfish. We had thirteen hours' notice. Even Amin gave its three months.' By December that year the International Voluntary Service reported that many Asians were in dire need. Wives begged for their husbands to be allowed to join them here, but some had to wait years. Refugees even faced death threats. Meanwhile, the media, especially the *Daily Express*, endlessly bemoaned the 'burden'. Few had the foresight of Antony Bambridge who wrote in the *Observer* 'General Amin, Your loss is our gain.' Even Sir Charles Cunningham, chairman of the Resettlement Board was afraid of becoming 'a permanent nursemaid'. But Manubl Madhvani knew his people better. 'The last thing they would do is become dependants. They are self-reliant people, who would make their own way.'

And they did. Recently the newspaper *Gujarat Samachar* celebrated the success of Ugandan Asians – the millionaires, doctors, lawyers, etc. – and with perhaps unnecessary enthusiasm, thanked the British government. One example – K.D. Patel, who lives in his mansion with swimming pool and peacocks – started work at a petrol station for £7 a week. Within months he became the manager and now owns a chain of stations. 'No television for five years,' says his wife Lata, who is now a Labour councillor in Brent. 'We ignored the hostility. We had no option, we just had to get financial security. It is our "broughtupness" that helps.'

Now these people are wined and dined by British princes and politicians; their money pours into trusts and funds. An estimated 30,000 jobs have been created by Ugandan Asian entrepreneurs in the Midlands. Maybe Lord Tebbit – who did not return my calls – has mellowed too. These people not only got on their bikes, they bought the factories. Ken and Joyce Brown once stood outside Ealing

Town Hall shouting they didn't want Asians moving in. Their son Steve later married Deepa, who was one of 'them'. 'She treats us like we are the most precious things in her life,' Joyce says. 'Her parents are so gentle, generous. We didn't know, you see.'

And now Uganda, too, wants the Asians, says Professor George Kirya, the high commissioner. 'We will all gain to have these brothers and sisters back. We need these entrepreneurs. We are giving their properties back with no ties.' Why now? 'We have diagnosed that it's human rights violations that brought it here and that only by addressing these issues squarely can we build a stable country.' He admits there are also economic reasons for the change of heart but denies they are following IMF instructions. 'President Museveni declared this policy while he was still fighting in the bush.'

Madhvani returned to Uganda in 1991. I talked to him when he was on a business trip back to London: 'I have a duty to my family to get back some of the millions we lost. And it is also my duty to help rebuild my country.' Its factories are now rolling again after twenty years of neglect. Lorna, a black teacher, is delighted. 'It is time to forget and forgive and to stop blaming the Asians for all our ills. We made a mess of the properties and the businesses.' The policy is not universally popular. Africans are being evacuated from premises without compensation. There have been death threats to Asians. But the overwhelming response is warmth. So the African has changed, but has the Asian? Or will the same conflicts flare up? No, says Kirya: 'Asians have realised their mistakes, segregating themselves and all that. Now they are talking of joint ventures. So there has been a deep shift of approach on both sides.' The returnees I met are indeed sensitive. 'We must treat them reasonably,' says Ruparelia. 'And if we go on about our property without thinking how these people have suffered, it is wrong.' And this is not merely a businessman's inherent expediency; many have learnt hard lessons in Britain.

This awareness is crucial, says Joel Kibazo, a Ugandan journalist with the *Financial Times*. He points out, 'Amin didn't just offend the Asians. Half a million of us were killed and you can count on one hand the Asians who died. So you cannot lord it over us or just take out what you can; my generation won't put up with that. Be

Ugandan and the future is great.' For the first time in twenty years my own heart starts burning to go home.

Most Ugandan Asians, however, are in Britain to stay, though they, too, are furiously searching souls. Many feel that more political involvement is needed. Without that, even millionaires can have no influence, 'just like in Uganda'. Others want the focus to move from millionaires to the problems of the majority, who work all hours to survive. Some argue that the community should be more assertive. Ingratiating yourself with the powerful becomes a habit and asking, as this country does of all its immigrants, a lifetime of gratitude is an unhealthy thing. Integration is another issue. Some Asians want to offer opportunities to Afro-Caribbeans to break the pattern where blacks resent and envy Asians who in turn fear and exclude them. The young provide new challenges. Raj, twenty-three, fumes: ''When. you face racism every day your folks see that treating anyone badly because of their colour, like they did, is wrong. I often wish we could go back. I don't know what they'll say about my sister's blackboy friend though.'

Asians in Uganda had three great fears. Violence, losing, their culture and their daughters marrying out – hardly anyone did. The irony is that racial attacks on Asians – rife in Britain – were virtually unheard of in Uganda. Intermarriage is growing and old values are disappearing. As Raj says: 'We fear the black man so much more than we fear the white man, who has damaged us much more. We should unite now, black and brown.'

Whose food is it anyway

Guardian, 25 August 1998

It is (too) often said that the most positive narrative about immigration to this country has been about food; the way the British opened their bellies to various culinary experiences and learnt to enjoy rather than fear the gift of difference, especially the 'other' from the Orient.

In this, at least, the nation has shown itself imaginative and confident enough to abandon what Philip Dodd has called 'fantasies of virginity [and] dreams of purity'. When I came here in 1972 you could not buy a green chilli in Oxford. Now, according to the *Daily Telegraph*, the national food of Britain is Indian. And meanwhile, the curry chef of the year award has gone to Simon Morris, a young, white Englishman. We (the Asians) came, we saw, we cooked and you surrendered, Or so it would seem. But talk to Asians and the story becomes more complex and less sanguine. Many young Asians feel like Bobby, previously known as Balwinder, a rich young entrepreneur who avoids Indian restaurants because 'even the air is thick with the past like those old-fashioned red curry pastes'.

There is anxiety about economic stagnation, an acute shortage of South Asian chefs (made worse by the ever-tightening immigration regulations) and as yet no reputable training establishment, although Thames Valley University (TVU) is starting up the Asian Academy of Culinary Skills next year.

Disaffection is everywhere, even among those stuffed full with profits. 'About time, too, that we said something,' says one South Asian owner of a superb restaurant. He begs, however, for such complete anonymity that I am unable to disclose the name. His reasons? Fear – the kind that comes from the deepest wells of historical memory of a people who were once colonial subjects and have never forgotten.

'No, please. These English, I don't want them to get angry or to think I am impolite. But I must speak out because this injustice is burning in so many of our hearts. We have struggled all these years to feed this nation and teach it about food. Today we are still slaves. They give us and our food no respect at all.'

This is a drama about history and about making demands and amends. It is the Raj again, carrying with it lust without love, contempt and appropriation. It is also a drama about class.

Indian food is still mostly regarded as the food of beer louts. History has something to do with this, as does the snobbery in British metropolitan culture. As a Radio 4 documentary next week reveals, unemployed Bangladeshis were among the first to start restaurants in this country. The areas they lived in were working class and the food was low cost. Indian food was not popularised by the porcini mushroom (£5 for three) set which needs things to be expensive to be able to savour them. Some of the finest South Asian food is shockingly inexpensive.

As Andrew Ward, head of corporate relations at TVU, says: 'Indian food was established as the cheap eating option and within the Asian community there is no link between the cost of food and quality, whereas the indigenous British have always equated low prices with poor quality.' Even malevolent French and Italian food is worshipped in this country while Indian food is treated with unforgivable contempt. I once read the haughty Drew Smith, an innocent when it comes to this food, proclaiming that much Indian restaurant food is 'filthy muck'. (He was most irritated by the cooked cauliflower because he was then into raw vegetables. Sorry, didn't know, Sahib.)

And new, Cool Britannia is reinforcing such rubbish. The Kinnocks loved Indian food like true voluptuaries. It is hard to imagine the new ruling classes or style gurus like Stephen Bayley tearing into a nan or breathing out words perfumed by spicy smells. This is determinedly the River Café set.

And we, the natives, are increasingly restless about this. Why has the people's food so little status in terms of Michelin stars, for example? Where are the top Indian chefs when it comes to television series and big-bang books? Television producers claim there is a language problem. Funny that does not impede Antonio Carlucci or Raymond Blanc. Madhur Jaffrey is the only exception. Last year, when I cooked her a meal, we chatted about this. She is a famous actress and an Indian-American. How many food critics can name our top chefs? People like Atul Kochar at the Tamarind in Mayfair or Cyrus Todiwallah who runs the Café Spice Namaste chain in London? Todiwallah agrees that the situation is ridiculous and that people need to get out of their shell and make a noise.

The powerful Restaurateurs' Association has one Asian member. There are no Asian food critics, restaurant critics either. Why not? 'It would be naive,' says Andrew Ward, 'not to recognise that there is racism at work here. Classic European is automatically high status and anything from the East is low status. And everyone who has power in this game is white.'

All this explains the extraordinary eruption this spring when Iqbal Wahab, erstwhile editor of the *Indian Food and Drink* magazine, made his disparaging remarks about Indian restaurants: the food was bad, waiters surly ('And why not?' one such waiter tells me. 'The bosses shit on us and the customers spit on us.'), ambience awful. Many restauranteurs banned him from their premises.

These people were furious because he was one of their own but more because it was one slight too many. One chef in west London told us in Hindi: 'Iqbal was wrong to betray us. But it is whites we should be attacking more. They don't know anything about our cooking and people like that [Pat] Chapman thinks he is the curry king.'

This brings us to the next big problem. Any little status which has begun to accrue finally to Indian food has been grabbed by white folk too. Take Pat Chapman, director of the Curry Club of Britain. He is guilty not of snobbery but of liking something so much that he took it. He is described as 'an authority' on Asian cooking and publishers love him as do many of his Asian acolytes because he helps them. At present he is supporting their fight to get more work permits for South Asian chefs. This is a symbiotic but imperial relationship. He has what they need, so they flatter him. It is what my uncles did with the colonial administrators. No one dares to ask him why he has entry into places where no Asian is allowed to tread.

Top cookery writers have incorporated South Asian food into their books and become big stars. Imagine how we feel when Delia

Smith talks about fresh coriander as if it had sprung from her very own heart. I would have liked to have talked to her about this but Queen Delia declined to speak. Am I being proprietorial? Yes, but only because the situation is unfair.

Asked about this, Nigel Slater, a delightfully candid man, first persuasively defended the fact that his book incorporates the best of Indian cooking. He believes that to grumble about white chefs 'taking' Indian recipes is retrograde. But he accepts that food writers often don't give due credit, and confesses he had not given much thought to why there are no Indian star chefs – 'I'm sure it will happen in time.' We can't wait that long.

Drew Smith accuses Indian food of being 'defensive'. Of course it is. We have had to invent two parallel cooking styles for a start. As Kochar says: 'Bastardised food was introduced here first by the British, whose memsahibs trained their cooks to make food which was tame and bland enough for their unadventurous palates. These cooks were sometimes brought here and this English–Indian cooking began.'

It worked, too. The punters are addicted to it even when (maybe because) the additives are four times the legal limit, as new research has shown. Now we are accused of not giving them authentic food. Well, they could have always had this if they had bothered to find out where we eat. Besides, ordinary Indian restaurants are doing what McDonald's does – provide cheap food that millions want and like.

Kochar takes a patronising view of' this: 'We must teach the customers better. And do it with confidence. They must recognise we are no longer meek people. We can perform and we can cook real and excellent food.' Slater agrees. Having been a victim of people feeding him bespoke Indian food tailor-made for an Englishman, he craves authenticity: 'The irony is that in order to draw in more middle-class customers, restaurants are turning themselves in to Conran diners. It feels still as if it is their idea of what a Westerner will like.'

The new-style Indian restaurants are still trying too hard to impress white opinion. There is a big difference between providing your best and mimicking those who are presumed to be better.

Adding on 'brasserie' or 'café' to Indian restaurant names is like Asians who change their names in order not to offend the English.

But are we being old fogies, Slater and I? This new British–Indian cooking can be very good, if we shed our old ideas about authenticity. I don't need to wear a sari to be taken as an authentic Asian. Our own children need places which replicate their modernity and are therefore authentic to them.

Change which comes out of increased confidence is good, says Wahab (whose restaurant, Cinnamon Club, opens next year with, alas, European decor, lobster somosas and even balsamic vinegar). 'What's the point of looking backwards? My manager is from the Ivy and my chef from a star Indian restaurant. That's the future.'

And the future is different, in other ways too, says Ward. 'All those waiters dressed up in red velvet are out of place. The customer now wants waiters who are their equals. They don't want to see an extra in a Raj movie or need to be genuflected to.' But must we let go of all the flocked wallpaper?

Those at the forefront of the modernising project certainly think so. The trendy London chain of Café Lazeez is metallic, with waiters in black clothes and moussed personalities. And business, says director of operations Samar Hamid, is excellent. Todiwallah's Café Spice Namaste is staggeringly successful and his book is published this winter. He is said to be in the running for the catering contract at the Millennium Dome.

Kochar is making no concessions – 'I will not be using sun-dried tomatoes. I don't need to, I will be fusing the many tastes of India' – but, his creations are so astounding they interrupt your dreams. These are not mice but supremely confident men who will not be stopped.

The best news is that places frequented by ordinary Asian people are getting more upbeat. I took a white friend to the Brilliant restaurant in Southall. The food was superb. A Sikh family at the next table sent us a bottle of champagne because they liked us. Another table sent over some birthday cake for my daughter. We all sang Hindi songs. It felt like a proper celebration of the end of an abject era for Indian food.

There is no racism in Britain

22 October 1998

As far as I can ascertain, there are no racists in Britain. I have been writing on race for twelve years and I have never met anyone who believes that he or she is a racist. I have had a colleague confess to me: 'I am not a racist but I wouldn't want my children to go to a school with too many Asians.' I have sat for hours clutching myself with fear as BNP supporters who had swastikas drawn on the arms of their babies explained they were not racists, only nationalists.

Politicians of all hues have described Enoch Powell as a great statesman and patriot, when what I remember is how in the green room of a Midlands television studio years ago, he ignored my outstretched hand and looked at me as if he would incinerate me with his flaming eyes.

We Black Britons are also constantly reminded how this country is not nasty Germany or violent, racist America. Only this week, ex-headmaster Ray Honeyford, who seems to be from another planet (if only), reminded us on *Heart of the Matter*, that it is those naughty 'race industry' people who create racism by talking about it. White Britons can carry out racist acts and discriminate against black and Asian Britons more easily than they can ever accept a description of what they are doing. So powerful are the denial mechanisms that those carrying out surveys on racial attitudes often ask interviewees about other people's prejudices rather than their own in order to gauge what is happening. Remember what Joseph Conrad – a writer tortured by his own xenophobic fantasies – wrote in *Under Western Eyes*: 'Words . . . are the great foes of reality.' And never more so than in the case of race.

This helps to explain Paul Condon's quibbling about 'institutional racism' – a term put about by Lord Scarman to explain what he found in Brixton. This term has created more confusion than clarity.

Institutions have no free will. They are managed by people, mostly white people. And in far too many key organisations these powerful

156

white people, instead of rooting out racism because it is morally repugnant, feel duty bound not to look the beast of racism in the eye.

The Met knows how racism and sexism are soaked into the fabric of the force. In 1983, David Smith, now Professor of Criminology at Edinburgh University, wrote a report on policing in London. After observing officers for two years, he found that there was a pervading culture of racism. The writer and film maker Roger Graef confirmed this in his book, *Talking Blues*.

But knowing something is not to accept it. No racist policeman has ever been sacked. Instead, millions of our pounds have been wasted on useless 'cultural awareness' training, out-of-court settlements and on endless campaigns to get more ethnic recruits, the latest of which was announced by the well-intentioned Jack Straw only this week. I would not join the force, as it is now, if I were paid a million pounds per annum. This culture of untackled racism is going on in many other state and private institutions too. And only a fool or a knave would now deny that racist violence and abuse seem to be blighting an increasing number of British lives.

What is so disheartening is that so many black leaders also misrepresent the reality of racism. They devalue the term by over-using it in inappropriate situations and fail to reflect the complexity of what is going on.

The recent controversial Commission for Racial Equality poster campaign was felt to be wrong by many, not because it was provocative but because it unduly simplified the issue.

I despair too when I hear (understandably) furious activists who bang on and on about endemic, all-embracing racism.

It is absurd to suggest that there has been no progress or that all whites are racist or that everything which happens to black and Asian people is because of this thing called racism.

This year British broadcasters excelled themselves with the unprecedented number of moving programmes on the *Empire Windrush*. White people have reacted to the case of Stephen Lawrence with feelings of anger and shame which have not been seen since the funeral in 1959 of Kelso Cochrane, a young black man who was killed by racists in north Kensington.

At a recent public meeting in Ealing I saw hundreds of white residents weeping as Myrna Simpson described the death of her daughter Joy Gardner in front of her four-year-old son as police taped her face up so she couldn't breathe.

The way to deal with racism is to name it exactly, shame it and where necessary punish it. Nothing else will work and nothing else will do.

The challenge remains: can we rid Britain of murderous racism?

24 February 1999

So the boil disfiguring the face of our country is finally lanced as the Lawrence Inquiry Report is published. It is hard not to feel relief as the poison oozes out and the wound is cleaned, bandaged and diagnosed by those we must trust. After all, they include a judge, a bishop and a doctor. But the carbuncle was only a symptom of something more endemic and treacherous, and this is, at least partially, recognised by Macpherson.

The public and the Establishment must accept that what the Lawrences started is the beginning and not the end of a long process of honest examination which implicates all of us in this country. To do this, three things are essential. First, we must remove from our minds the all-too-familiar faces in this drama – Doreen and Neville Lawrence, the five brutes who stand accused, the unsmiling Imran Khan, the theatrical Mike Mansfield and, up to a point, even Paul Condon, as people.

Second, we must not be conned by words of fine intent by those who know they are culpable. And finally, the government must be prepared to go much further than a report which, by definition, cannot go beyond certain parameters – although this one has gone further than was expected by making recommendations on education and race legislation. In fact, the most lasting benefits of this report may come from these broader proposals if, as is likely, they are taken on board. The dangerous anomaly in the 1976 Race Relations Act, which exempted crucial government activities such as policing, criminal justice and immigration in particular, is now to be scrapped.

Great expectations have been raised by this exercise. If there is any indication that the powers that be are trying to avoid radical steps, and that the politics of placation are beginning to play out, it will be intolerable to all of us black and Asian Britons, and to anti-racist white Britons too.

I see this already over the issue of whether Sir Paul Condon should go. Jack Straw says he should stay. The reasons given are unconvincing. If Sir Paul is as decent as his PR suggests, how can he bear not to go? Not only has this man presided over an investigation that the inquiry describes as 'marred by a combination of professional incompetence, institutional racism and failure of leadership'; he was the person to authorise substantial pay-outs (remember, it is our money) to black people complaining of racist treatment by his officers, who thus escaped punishment.

Condon was also in charge when Joy Gardner was killed when being arrested by police and immigration officers. We are in the middle of another set of complaints of bad policing by the families of Ricky Reel and Michael Menson. To keep Condon on is to make a nonsense of the 'shame' that Deputy Assistant Commissioner John Grieve says the force now feels.

Even more staggering is the news that Condon has decided to reappoint the Met race equality trainer, one Jerome Mack, who has been paid handsomely (remember it is our money again) over a decade, for providing training many black officers consider utterly pointless. As one of them told me: 'Mack just makes racist policemen feel good. That is why they have him.'

My concern, though, is not only with Condon and his power. Let us use this period of discontent to consider the wider effects of police racism and what we can do to make our forces more accountable and deserving of the reputation they would wish.

It is vital to start listening to the many other voices of those who have suffered racist violence; to scrutinise the media responses to what has been going on for half a century; to discuss how our education system has failed young black and white children alike and helped create the racists who killed not only Stephen, but Rohit Duggal (15), Rolan Adams (15), Navid Sadiq (15), Liam Harrison (14), Manish Patel (15), Rikki Reel (18), Imran Khan (15), Michael Menson (29), Ali Ibrahim (21), Ashiq Hussain (21), Ruhullah Aramesh (24), Panchadcharam Sathiharan (28), Donna O'Dwyer (26) and fourteen others who have been murdered in the United Kingdom during this decade alone.

God alone knows how high the figure would be if we went back further, to include murders such as those of Ahmed Iqbal Ullah (13) in Manchester by another child, and then added on the countless others seriously wounded, such as Mukhtar Ahmad (19), who was a pupil at the Bethnal Green training centre where I used to work, and who came in one day with a face like an Underground map and wildly fearful eyes.

Add to these victims the dozens of black and Irish people who have died of violence inflicted on them by the police while being arrested or in police custody (the Institute of Race Relations has been collating this information as has the Lawrence Inquiry. The list is long and frightening) and you begin to get a true sense of the true picture. If we don't take on the massive task before us, we put at risk the health of our nation.

It really does not matter what we choose to call it (I personally think that the term 'institutional racism' used in the Macpherson report is unhelpful, and is already creating more barriers to understanding because, to date, there are at least twelve different meanings of the term) but all the evidence we have before us in this report and many others shows that there is a pervasive culture of racial prejudice, racist assumptions and behaviour in all our public institutions from the army and police to the self-reverential BBC.

This does not mean that all white people are racist, or that there has been no improvement. But the idea that black and Asian Britons are interlopers, to be tolerated at best and killed at worst, is so deeply rooted in the culture of our institutions that it will take real political will and effective punitive measures to pull these attitudes out and grow something else in their place.

What is remarkable is that we have three political leaders for the first time in our history who are united in their determination to do just this. So I do have hope.

Stephen, you have become the son of this nation in a way that you could never have imagined. As you look down at us today, I hope you can see that nothing can ever be the same again for white or black Britons.

We will make a new country. Those who have been fighting for so long, will not let you down by selting for anything less.

Just how many porcini can you eat?

19 August 1999

Had a wonderful time in Tuscany and Umbria, since you ask. And not all my pleasure came out of knowing that, at last, I was up there with the chatterati and, of course, the Blairs, who were staying but a butterfly's flight away.

I loved the landscapes, the layers and layers of history and art (though I will not be seeking out any paintings of the Madonna and Child for a while) and the endlessly charming people, particularly Francesco, our landlord, who looked like Kevin Costner, especially when he threw off his shirt and walked around slowly fishing out wasps from the swimming pool. But, truth to tell, unlike all those other devotees of the region I found the food monotonous and ridiculously over-praised.

Just how many porcini mushrooms and tomatoes can you eat? And can we please agree that, unless it's drowning in good vinegar, mozzarella is the blandest cheese in the whole world?

Yes, northern Italian food is healthy and, when cooked well, tasty enough. But it does not merit the awe and reverence with which it is regarded by Italians and by upper-middle-class Brits. Together they have created an inflated reputation that does need to be debunked, however much the River Café foodies will rage.

In our local bookshop, I counted forty-seven Italian recipe books. It was, by far, the biggest category. Most of them read like books of religious revelation. Olive oil is the preferred drink of the angels, sings one, as it goes on for four pages about the properties of this holy sap. Our own sensible Delia quite loses her head in her summer collection, proclaiming that 'good bread dipped into fruity olive oil and tomato juices is the food of the gods'. Another writer devotes forty pages to pasta. Thirty of those have sauces where the ingredients are primarily tomatoes, olive oil and garlic.

In a restaurant in Florence we ordered antipasto that was described, in English, as 'the fantasia of perfect crostini and

162

bruschetta to make the tears of pleasure'. A very lovely, hand-painted platter (with angels, as it happens) arrived with tomato, olives, anchovies, mushrooms and cheese on toast. Our only tears were of rage at the prices we were charged for a plate of toast and bits. Another Tuscan dish that is hailed as definitive is bistecca alla Fiorentina. It is nothing more than a T-bone steak, which I have had better cooked in Texas where they at least add some piquant marinades to the meat.

We did have some exceptional culinary moments. Some small Tuscan restaurants, which were more earthy than heavenly, served excellent pigeon and other game birds. But on the whole, for a Londoner accustomed to great culinary variety, Tuscan and Umbrian food failed to impress, partly because it is so determinedly self-contained.

Even the French are more adventurous. At least they have taken to Vietnamese food. When I used to teach English as a foreign language, many of my students lodged with us. It was only the Italians who would not even try food that was not Italian. The effervescent Antonio Carluccio, in his best-selling *Italian Feast*, says without blushing that he has yet to find 'ethnic' cooking that is as good as Italian cooking. Instead of dismissing such culinary arrogance and bigotry, the British have for decades (since Elizabeth David, in fact) fallen over themselves to encourage these myths.

Perhaps I miss the point. Perhaps the attraction of Italian food is precisely that it is predictable and that it symbolises historical continuity, a kind of peace and simplicity. I can see how this might appeal to our metropolitan elite, whose lives in this country are now inescapably complex, diverse and ever in a state of flux. For a while they can feel connected to their old European ancestry and rural myths. No multicultural contamination here. No foreign bits that your grandmother would not have known.

This concentration on the old and abiding has other problems. It blinds visitors to other impressive aspects of Italian life that are to do with how the country is today. Municipal socialism in Umbria, for example, really works. It has given this once run-down area, which had a record number of emigrants (many of whom have returned), a sense of common purpose and confidence that is enviable. There is little evidence of what has become common in most parts of the world, the bloatedly rich towering over the eternally poor.

I love the way Italian families work, and the cross-generational respect that lies at the heart of their society. All this and more will compel me to return to that country. But not without my chillies, maybe some popadums, long-life methi parathas and home-made mango achars (or even Branston pickle).

The ordinary but brutal reality
of everyday racism

7 October 1999

A mother prays for rain every day after school so that her children won't ask to be allowed to play outside and then get abused and beaten up for being 'Pakis'. Which is what happens every time they play outside. So much so that her children themselves think that there is nothing exceptional about the abuse they suffer. A white mother of mixed-race children gets called 'Paki lover' and spat on when she hangs out her clothes. She now puts her clothes out in the dead of the night.

In another family, all the members have to plan out every movement of the day. The children go to the shops in pairs. They always have a phone with them. The house is never left unguarded and everyone has to give notice of where they are going because they have all been attacked so many times.

One woman has stopped growing flowers because racists destroy them as soon as they begin to bloom. A five-year-old child, who has become worryingly introverted, refuses to play on the swings in the local playground because she feels that she is being hurt – even though she is still too young to understand the meaning of the words that are always thrown at her.

These are just some examples from a new Rowntree report on racist victimisation. The authors, Kusminder Chahal and Louise Julienne, have gone out of their way not to sensationalise the material, and it is this feature that makes the blood run cold.

For page after page, the reader is confronted by dispassionate accounts of the everyday nature of such persecution in selected areas including Belfast, where Asian children are called both 'Pakis' and 'Taigs' as they are stoned.

As one victim says: 'How do you prove such abuse? These things happen so often that you can't run to the police every five minutes.'

Another victim remarks that everyone is now simply conditioned to accept this abuse as normal. And several victims report an overwhelming sense of shame that they can do nothing to help their children or even themselves. A number of them are on tranquillisers but have not been able to tell their doctors why they are so stressed.

What you learn from this report is that, for most of the time, racism is not a Rottweiler that draws blood and life out of you, but rather it is like an army of moths that quietly eats into the very fabric of your being, leaving you frayed and defenceless. Most perpetrators are not British National Party activists, but ordinary family members, including mothers with pushchairs, and grandmothers with false teeth and permed hair.

Another valuable report, by Rae Sibbett at the Home Office, confirms this. The British Crime Survey estimates that there are 130,000 racial incidents per year. Other estimates are double this. This summer, Lancashire constabulary apologised to Mal Hussein after failing to protect him and his white partner Linda Livingstone from an eight-year race-hate campaign on a council estate where he has the misfortune to own a shop. There is now documented evidence of more than 2,000 racial attacks by council tenants on this couple. But still people do not want to believe that such things can happen in our 'tolerant' country, where Trevor Macdonald is the nation's favourite newsreader.

In Tony Blair's own Sedgefield constituency, a moving Channel 4 documentary showed how one Muslim family has been tormented for so long (with words, graffiti, fire bombs and shouts of 'burn baby burn') that the daughter, fourteen-year-old Samina Yunis, has written to the PM saying that she will kill herself if it goes on. A reply from our morally valiant leader must surely be in the post. But his agent, John Burton, has been quoted – although he has claimed it was 'out of context' – as saying: 'We just don't have a problem with racism here at all – I know that... I think of this family, and I think that maybe they should just up and leave. They're obviously not getting on with the people in that area.'

Meanwhile, yet another scandal has erupted at Ford's Dagenham plant, where a wildcat strike has been called because workers can no longer tolerate the racial harassment which is meted out to non-white workers. In one case currently being heard by an employment tribunal, it has been claimed that an Asian man was put into a 'punishment cell' and told that he would be killed like the 'nigger Lawrence'. The company maintains that there is 'no major problem' of racism.

I thought, in these post-Lawrence times, that we were going to stop such insulting denials and get on with the business of making a just and fair country. Not a bit of it. All that seems to have happened now is that the blame for racism has been planted on despicable thugs, such as the ones who allegedly killed Stephen Lawrence, and on 'institutionalised racism', a hollow and deficient term which is chanted now like a mantra at endless conferences on the subject.

When will we face up to the reality that, although we have made great strides since the fifties and we have much to be proud of as a cosmopolitan society, we still have a frightening culture of racism which is so common that we cannot even see it? And what are our political leaders going to do about it? And will it make a difference to Samina's wretched life, Tony?

Why it sank my heart to see
the opening of the first Sikh school

2 December 1999

The first state-funded Sikh school in Europe opened this week. Jack Straw, duly garlanded with marigolds, I am sure, was at the opening, as were the many leaders and leaderenes who can talk so approvingly of 'diversity' these days.

This is the fifth faith-based school since 1997 to have been granted state funding. The others are the Mathilda Marks-Kennedy Jewish School in Barnet, the Islamia Muslim school in Brent, the Al Furquan school, also Muslim, in Birmingham, and the John Loughborough Seventh Day Adventist school in North London. April 2000 will see the opening of the Jewish Torah Temimah School in Brent. Asians expect there to be a state-funded Hindu school before long. Meanwhile, Church of England and Catholic schools seem to be applying ever more exacting criteria so that children from other faiths can be kept out, even if they make up a large section of the local community and rejection means they are relegated to some of the sink schools in the area. David Blunkett passionately backs these schools, believing they offer better choices to parents within mainstream education.

Unlike most other black and Asian Britons, my heart sinks into utter gloom when I hear about these victories and developments. For me, this is the end of a dream that has yet to be dreamt. It is educating children to separate themselves from others and to distance themselves from the core values that should bind the various peoples of any national entity. It is planning for the end of Britain as it has been struggling to become in the last fifty years.

And I mind terribly, because Britishness has only recently become a preciously acquired identity for many of us. From being a stamp of colonialism and snobbery, we fought to make Britishness into something else. Nowadays, many of us can say we are British without that abject insistence in our voices that we had in the past.

Remember that Goodness Gracious Me!, chicken tikka masala, Benjamin Zefaniah, London and Birmingham are British. They are not Scottish, Welsh, Sikh or Muslim. Yet today fewer and fewer people on this island (not including those on the rabid right who crave to go back to the past) seem interested in this essential, cohering identity.

A recent survey in *The Economist* showed Britain now commanding less loyalty than its constituent parts among the majority of the Scots and Welsh. Only a minority of the English were prepared to put Britain first. The forthcoming report by a high-powered commission on the future of multi-ethnic Britain, consisting of people such as Lady Hollick, Andrew Marr, Stuart Hall and Bhikhu Parekh, confirms that these identities are becoming increasingly more meaningful to vast numbers of people.

As the deeper effects of devolution begin to be felt, and the English get restive demanding their own parliament and territory, who is there left to fight for New Britain?

It seems that this responsibility now falls upon those black and Asian Britons who feel most passionately about the need to reinvigorate our dying national identity – something that will be discussed in a programme that I am presenting on *Analysis*, on Radio 4 tonight.

We have an important role to play in this regeneration. This is why I think it makes no sense to relocate within compounds, comfortable enclaves, which is what separate schools represent. When the first Muslim school obtained state funding in January 1998, I wrote that I was anxious that this would only make it easier for mainstream societies further to demonise and exclude us, and that there was also a danger that our children would not be able to avoid an over-developed sense of their own 'special' status and sense of grievance. They would never be interrogated about their beliefs and way of life, nor would they learn to do the same with Christians, Sikhs and others. All black schools contain the same dangers.

Today, I feel that even more is at stake, and that we have to think very carefully as a society about the implications of having any state-

funded schools that are driven by the desire to take future generations out of the complexities of modern multicultural Britain – and,
in effect, create tribes within the nation.

Of course, it is right and just that black and Asian Britons should
have the same rights to set up schools as Christians and Jews. But
while trying to remedy injustice, we may be ending up otherwise. I
have no doubt that these schools are excellent in many ways.
Looking at the delightful pictures of Sikh and Muslim children in
their own schools, you can see the confidence that must come from
the fact that they feel safe there. So many of our children are abused
or beaten up in playgrounds, or just made to feel ashamed for being
who they are. So I can understand why parents would want this
option.

The children will mercifully not be affected by white working-
class attitudes to education. This must be the only country in the
world where the poor see education as a threat to their right to
remain ignorant. They will learn respect, value the education they
receive and learn to be worthy inheritors of their particular religions
and ethical values.

My objections therefore are not those you often hear from virulent secular liberals, who despise the very idea of religion in schools.
Both my children have been educated at a Church of England
school, although with the younger one the battle to get her in was
exhausting. It is because the school has a good academic record, but
also because, as a Muslim, I wanted the children to learn about
Christianity so that they could learn that in the end there is but one
God.

But had there been another, equivalent school where all the major
faiths were taught, it would have been my preference – because that
is what integration should mean. And I believe profoundly that the
focus now needs to be on how we are to create integration between
the different and discrete British communities. The centre, else, will
not hold, and things will fall apart. And the people who will suffer
most will be us, the British people of colour.

Who wants to be an Asian millionaire? It's vulgar, demeaning – and dangerous

14 March 2000

I sit here with my head in my hands (metaphorically speaking) feeling shame and exasperation, wishing devoutly for this day to pass until the same time next year when yet again we will be presented with a list of the top Asian millionaires in this country. The respected and prominent Professor Bhikhu Parekh believes this obsession is vulgar and limiting. I think it is also demeaning and dangerous.

Would rich British Jews ever consider publicising their loot in this way? And do we Asians understand why they would not? History has taught us nothing. All groups who are victims of racial prejudice should know by now that they give ammunition to those who hate them if they are seen amassing wealth, however legitimately. Even in the new millennium, when the wealthy have acquired moral superiority over the poor, to be an obviously rich black or Asian is to invite the kind of attention a beautiful woman in a micro skirt would get in a rugby players' changing room. It may be unfair, but it is reality.

I thought we would learn this after our painful and humiliating expulsion from Uganda in 1972 by the appalling Idi Amin. What happened to us was not only because of one big, horrible, cannibalistic monster. Amin was supported by many ordinary black Ugandans because they envied and hated the affluent lifestyles of rich Ugandan Asians who never learnt the meaning of discretion, not even when their lives depended on it.

Unfortunately, then as now, all Asians (even the socialists) began to be seen as avaricious. Of course, whites and later black leaders had the biggest homes and bank balances. But they had power; we did not. Wealthy Asians believed that their money would protect them. Many still believe that here today. I am (too) often invited to dinner parties by my rich ex-school friends who hang pictures of Margaret

171

Thatcher over their Harrods dining tables. They mock me for not being rich and scold me for being too outspoken.

Samuel Johnson said: 'the insolence of wealth will creep out,' but I find it terrifying that my people so easily yield to it, forgetting that each time we get this kind of splash, a few more small and not at all rich Asian shopkeepers are attacked and robbed by those who have grown to believe that we are all worth it.

Sadly, it is the Asian newspaper *Eastern Eye* and Asian pundits who promote these images of the new maharajahs. This brainwashes our children (too many of whom already grow up in families and communities where making money is a religion), which is why so many young Asians featured in that other excruciating list published this weekend, of the fast-expanding band of young millionaires in Britain. So, gosh, here we have Ajaz Ahmed, 26, who is worth £12m already, and Avneet Kaur Sahni, 29, adding to her pile of $6m as we speak. Surely a lot to be proud of. Not a bit of it.

Black leaders are disturbed that this list of young rich Brits featured no black entrepreneur, which he puts down partly to discrimination and stereotyping and partly to a painful history which has made it difficult for black people to take risks. Thank your gods, I say, because a community consumed with material success becomes sterile, hollow and selfish. Black writers, artists, musicians, designers and public servants do not have to spend their lives begging to be taken seriously among their own, like too many of us Asians who are only valued in direct proportion to the money we make.

Family life suffers too, at times in grotesque ways. I had a very rich uncle in Kenya, whose favourite son, wife and twin baby boys were butchered in the sixties, and on 1 January this year, another son was shot dead in Kisumu as he left a bank. Money had everything to do with this violence.

In his new collection of short stories, *Equal Love*, Peter Ho Davies, who is half-Chinese, describes the burial ceremony of a Chinese newspaper magnet. The son makes sure that he burns a big car, house, lots of money – all made of paper, all for the afterlife. As he does this, you find out the emotional destruction caused by the acquisitive father.

Asian wealth worshippers care little about how money is made. Despicably low wages and poor working conditions in Asian-owned businesses are not uncommon. This is captured beautifully in *Balti Kings*, a heartbreaking new play recently staged at the Lyric Hammersmith. The actress Sudha Bucher, the co-author, told me how angered she was while researching this play in the back rooms of a number of Indian restaurants. There have been questions raised in India about the business dealings of at least one of the richest families. Friends of mine operate in East European countries with the business ethics of a pack of hyenas.

As for the use that Asian millionaires make of their money, ask any Asian artist or community group how much they have ever had from them. Unless there is something in it for them – a peerage preferably – most do nothing for the community. They adore the Majors or the Blairs, turning up for some expensive bash where they can have their pictures taken with the powerful. But they still do not see that they could make an enormous difference by becoming more socially and politically aware. For starters, they could fight on behalf of asylum-seekers or warn the government that there will be no more garlands or cheques unless it withdraws its policy of demanding bonds from visitors from the subcontinent.

I know I am being hard on my own; it is because I care more about what they are and what they do. White millionaires can be just as selfish and destructive. I hate living through this historical period when money is so overvalued and culture, education, service so undervalued by everyone.

British society is becoming one big, dirty rat race. But groups that are already targets of hatred should think about how they wish to be perceived and should understand the implications of being admired only for being good little millionaires. And I am truly sorry that in saying what I have said I will have encouraged in some bigots the very prejudice I fear.

'We are black men.
That means we make babies'

Guardian, 13 April 2000

This has been an extraordinary week for Patrick Augustus. His auto-biographical novel, *Baby Fathers*, has been optioned by the BBC. It is a bold move because the theme – young black men who have children with a number of women and wear this as a badge of honour – is usually left well alone by anxious white liberals and radical anti-racists who ate always wary of 'encouraging' racism.

The deal is worth nearly £1m and Augustus, himself a father of five, is delighted if a little bemused. He is your proud, black, urban man with all those subversive traits that are irresistible to many women and deeply threatening to white men. Last winter he brought another baby father, Victor, to talk to me about his children.

There was, said a weary Victor, the problem of the new black woman who no longer indulges men like him: 'They're changing, man. Three strikes and you're out. They want their BMW man who will come home bringing flowers, a happy-ever-after life. Most black men can't provide this.'

Patrick, a local hero among south London lads, believes that men who womanise are victims of circumstance and of wily women who know exactly how to exert power using their sexuality: 'There is a lot of animosity between black men and black women today. Black men reject intelligent black women and go with young girls who look up to them. You know, give them comfort because it is hard being a black man. Sad to say, what starts as a dance or a flirtation, ends up as a baby. And let me tell you, there are a number of men who never agreed to be fathers. It was the girls who decided and who went ahead.'

This may well be the case sometimes. But again and again and again? What about personal responsibility, what about restraint? And the boasting which we have both heard from baby fathers about their big and small babies? Is this not living down to the worst stereotypes of black men?

Yes and no, says Paul, 23, a computer programmer who 'visits' three baby mothers at the moment, two black and one white: 'Yes, we are doing what society expects. Just like Darcus [Howe] once said. We are black men, that means we make babies all the time. I try to buy them nice things and I would break anyone who tried to harm my kids. But try to go inside out heads. We are kept out of everything. The one place we know we can win, where the white man is no good, is in bed. This is where we can be kings. That is what I thought when I was young. All my children were born before I was 21.'

It is essential not to see this only as a 'black' problem. Young white men have as many partners and children. All around us there are black fathers and partners – Sir Herman Ouseley, Paul Boateng and a host of others – who are role models for all, of society. Writing in *Black British Feminism*, the academic Tracey Reynolds rightly criticises the dangerously simplistic way this subject has been dealt with in the media, but you only have to read the *Voice* to see that it is now perceived as a major area of concern.

The 1991 census recorded that 49 per cent of Afro-Caribbean families are headed by alone mother compared with 14 per cent in the general population. Some are high achievers who have made the decision to go it alone, partly because they cannot find the man and relationship they want. These are self-determining baby mothers rather than gullible victims of baby fathers.

Others are lone mothers as a result of death, divorce and other 'normal' events. But a substantial number are young, poor and emotionally vulnerable. But even these women do seem to be getting more sussed.

Sadie, 19, has two children by two men who are friends: 'I am stupid. I thought they were the coolest guys, and I was so lucky. They were great dancers and they look at you and you melt. But now I just want to look after my boys. I don't want them to grow up like their dads – all talk and nothing else.'

Donna finally decided to throw out Wayne, the father of her child and another by her arch-rival in school, Aimee: 'I think Aimee and I both had babies as a competition for a man who was never worth it.

Then he started beating me up and said he would go off to her if I complained. And just to keep face I said nothing. Now some third woman is expecting his child. I will not let him near my child.'

A number of other women have multiple partners themselves so that they are not dependent on the goodwill of one baby father. Patrick despises such women: 'They want one man to fix the house, another for sex, one to take them partying. They use children as weapons and I have seen men crying over the way they are treated.'

He has started a pressure group for men struggling against women who are becoming a little too much like baby fathers themselves. White baby mothers are, I think, less trouble. I spent, an evening with a group of them recently and they were indeed desperate to be understanding. They talked about the effects of slavery on black men, and explained how it was possible to live with betrayal and double standards. Lust was high on the list.

As Susie, 20, put it: 'White men are boring and safe. A lot of white girls think black men have great bodies, like D'Angelo, and we want to have their babies because they are so beautiful. I like a cool, tough guy, you know.'

Yet, according to research in progress by sociologist Ravinder Barn, these beautiful babies of white mothers are increasingly ending up in care mainly because the women find it so hard to cope. These women are isolated, disapproved of by both black and white communities, often abused. If they find a white partner new problems can arise with the child and the baby father. Many do not want their children to go, but feel they have no option.

There may still be some women willing to oblige, but even Patrick now accepts that the good old days seem to be coming to an end for the baby father. He is worried, though, that his fame and fortune will make him a victim of an ambitious baby mother instead.

Why multiculturalism has failed

Daily Telegraph, 23 May 2000

Nothing is for ever. Progressive ideas that are right, bright and appropriate at one historical moment can, in time, fade and decay or become defensive in the face of further progress. I believe this is what is happening to policies promoting British multiculturalism today. We urgently need ties that bind – and multiculturalism isn't delivering them. It risks building barriers between the different tribes that make up Britain today, rather than helping to create a new shared sense of Britishness.

Few would deny there has been progress on race relations in recent years, but racism continues to blight many lives. I feel profoundly British, but experience has taught me to put a bucket of water under the letterbox when I go to bed and, just last week, a London cabbie refused to let me into his taxi because of the colour of my skin. I have fought against racism for three decades, and will always support uncompromising action against overt and hidden discrimination. However, our multicultural policies, with the emphasis on ethnic monitoring and on special provision for black and Asian communities, seem increasingly divisive and irrelevant to a new generation of young people, and are out of touch with the way our world has moved on.

We do not have the optimistic and integrated society we all hoped for. It is not just Scottish and Welsh nationalism that threaten British identity. In these post-devolutionary times, multiculturalism is pitting all communities against each other. People who used to think of themselves as black are now retreating into tribal identities – demanding attention and resources for their particular patch. White people have no stake in multiculturalism, either – it is seen as something that black people do. The English are understandably disgruntled that their ethnicity is denied while all other identities – Welsh, Scottish, Hindu, Caribbean and the rest – are celebrated. Young white kids celebrate Diwali in schools without any sense of how it links to their own identity.

The cloak of multiculturalism has been worn by those with no interest in integration. Treating black people differently has enabled white institutions to carry on as if nothing substantive has changed since the arrival of the *Windrush* from the West Indies. As long as 'ethnic minorities' were given some money and space to play marbles in the ghetto, nothing else needed to happen. Whether you look at the BBC or the top FTSE companies, the multicultural answer has failed to transform anything very much. Talking to the teenagers who have grown up with multiculturalism, I found that many young people – black, Asian, white and mixed race – are impatient with the whole ideology. They reject the traditional categories which multiculturalism tries to shoehorn them into.

Their notions of diversity go way beyond a love of curry. Although most feel connected to the values of their parents to some extent, their identities are changing in unpredictable ways. Young white men absorbing urban black ways of life (Ali G is really out there) and young Asian girls refusing forced marriages show how cultures cannot remain static or settled whatever purists may wish. A young black man said, simply: 'I think this kind of thinking is for sad old people.' A young Asian man was equally scathing: 'Multiculturalism is a boring word. It is grey and small and domestic. It does not include Europeans. It does not include internationalism. It is like an old cardigan knitted out of different coloured scraps of wool.'

Others felt that multiculturalism merely has pernicious effects. So community leaders use it to justify human rights abuses in their own backyard. Police and social workers are often reluctant to intervene where they suspect domestic violence in case they are accused of racism. An Asian girl I interviewed said she was 'treated like a Paki' both by white people and by her own family who forced her to marry a man who then repeatedly raped her. She said: 'Their multiculturalism is just a cover. Some Asians use this to hide what they are doing to the girls in the community. Leaders and politicians let them get away with it.' So whose multiculturalism is it, anyway?

The out-of-date term ethnic minorities is an obstacle to integration. It is based on the ludicrous assumption that there was once a large, homogeneous, white majority surrounded by 'ethnic minorities' who were just too strange for words. These measures are even less defensible in a complex, diverse society grappling with devolution, globalisation and integration into Europe, American domination, collapsing values and fragmentation at every level.

My criticisms have nothing in common with the views of those who resent these policies because they regard this as a white Christian country that must resist diversity. More than ever we need a national conversation about our collective identity. We need to concentrate our energies on the ties that bind us and use this to create a new British identity. Diversity is an inescapable condition of modern life and respect for this is essential. That respect will have to apply to everyone, black and white. But respect for different ways of life cannot be allowed to destroy any sense that we live in the same country.

Once multiculturalism has been laid to rest, we can concentrate on developing a strong, diverse British identity rather than retreating into ever-smaller tribes.

Priest's murder exposes a world of gay hatred

28 October 2000

Harish Purohit, 42, a married man and devout Hindu priest in Leicester, was found murdered last week. By all accounts, he was much loved by his family and enormously respected by his community.

But he also had a secret life. By night he socialised with gay and bisexual men in local gay venues. His young widow, Anjana, is suddenly having to cope with this as well as the shock of the brutal killing. Mr Purohit was not being hypocritical. This is what most Asian and black gay people have to do because of rank prejudice against and ignorance about homosexuality.

White gays also face rejection and discrimination but they can be themselves more easily because most are not part of cohesive communities. Whether Mr Purohit was himself gay is not the issue. He must have felt that if he openly mixed with gay men he would be ostracised and condemned. And he was right to fear this.

When I wrote a column about the campaign to keep Section 28, a deluge of letters from black and Asian Britons, followed. Some were outpourings from homosexuals experiencing intolerable pressures. Others were from homophobic people who had no sense of the usual codes of verbal restraint which you now see even among the rabid right.

Gay people were 'the Devil's children', 'deviants', 'an abomination, products of the debauched, godless West'. A Mr Anoop Patel said that he 'wished these poisonous monsters a terrible afterlife'. A Mr Singh advocated castration and forced 'retraining of the mind, body and soul'. Tony, a black boxing coach, announced that gays were the damned which is why the footballer Justin Fashanu, 'that sinful pervert', had committed suicide. What they said about Aids cannot be repeated. They riled against the films *My Beautiful Laundrette* and

East is East where one son turns out to be gay ('No true Pakistani can be bloody gay').

Manjit Roopra, of the Naz Project which works to educate South Asian communities about HIV, says black and Asian homophobia comes coated with that pietistic paste of self-righteousness promoted by many community leaders, Hindu, Sikh, black Christian, Jewish and Muslim. 'We cry racism when it hits us in the face yet we oppress gay people in our own communities,' he says.

Shariffa, a pharmacist who was educated at a private school and went to university, comes from a middle-class British Muslim family. Her mother is a lawyer. When she turned twenty-two, the family told her to choose her own husband, but to make sure he was a Muslim. A year later, she told them she was in love, but with a woman. She was packed off to Karachi and there a young uncle raped and burnt her on her breast with an iron, telling her he was 'saving her'. She was so traumatised she has been unable to contact her partner and lives alone, acutely depressed and unemployed.

Suresh, a part-time model, was thrown out of the house when he announced his homosexuality. The only son in a very traditional Gujarati family which owns a supermarket chain, he says: 'I found it almost amusing because they were weeping and cursing the day they came to this country. They were not going to get the dutiful bride and dowry or the grandsons. Tough shit I thought.'

Then his mother tried to kill herself and ended up in a coma: 'They accused me of being a killer. I turned to drink and became addicted to Valium.' Four years on, the family refuses to respond to his monthly letters.

Ali, who works at the Naz Project, has chosen not to see his Muslim family for fourteen years. At twenty-one, Ali tried to stay within the fold and got married. But he soon left, having made sure everyone knew the marriage was not consummated. Why has he cut himself off? Is it shame? Not really, he says. It is more a sense of responsibility. His sisters might not find husbands: 'It took my family so long to feel safe... What right do I have to kick all that to the ground? I miss them a lot, but this is what I have chosen.'

Richard, a black musician, used to love dancing until one night, in a club, a black gang beat him up for being a 'faggot'. They crushed his ankle, leaving him with a limp: 'What was hard was that the black brothers were doing this to one of their own. They just saw me chatting up this mixed-race guy who is openly gay and they thought they would teach us a lesson.' Richard was brought up on the infamous Broadwater Farm estate in Tottenham, north London. He described how he created an aggressive macho persona to protect himself.

Research by Big Up, the only British organisation for black gay men, found that more than half of those interviewed felt isolated from their own community. Research by Naz among south Asians replicates these findings.

The homophobia has other, deeper roots. Black men have responded with masculinity to a long history of systematic emasculation. For Rudolf, a black teacher in Manchester: 'Whites are gays because they have been feminised. They are failures, fairies who have to bugger each other for comfort. Black men are real men.' Religion is used to justify these prejudices. Rudolf is an ardent gospel singer.

The Reverend Christian Weaver, of the Pilgrim Church in Nottingham, believes that, hard though it is, all religious institutions must lead people away from homophobia. 'Everyone must be treated with respect and have the right not to be maltreated. I would stand with gay people on a picket line on these issues,' he says.

For victims of racism, furthering the line and community cohesion is a defence against annihilation, even among liberal Jews. Gay Asian men often marry and produce children and lead a promiscuous under-life, subjecting their wives to terrible physical dangers.

Rajinder, a businessman, says: 'I told my wife I was gay after our marriage. Now I am HIV positive and although she is not, I feel like a thief who stole the life of a lovely young woman.' Rani is HIV positive and her gay husband died of Aids after three years of marriage. It took days to find a priest for the funeral.

Stars such as the actors Meera Syal and Art Malik are getting involved in campaigns to change these practices and the shocking death of Mr Purohit has finally brought the subject out into the open, something that is welcomed by Naz and others.

Do not assume all racists are white

5 December 2000

Damilola Taylor, a newly arrived ten-year-old Nigerian, bled to death alone in a filthy stairwell in Peckham because some young men stabbed him and cut open an artery. Those young men are thought to be Afro-Caribbean. They may not be, but indications are that they were. They probably did not mean to kill him, but the wound was in the wrong place on a boy who was the wrong kind of black child in the wrong place at the wrong time.

What do I mean by the 'wrong kind of black child'? Damilola was African, and I have no doubt that this was a central reason why he was picked out by the black British kids who bullied, humiliated and frightened him. A few media interviews did venture to suggest – ever so carefully – that there is evidence of damaging prejudice between Africans and Afro-Caribbeans, and that this could be one factor to take into account, but these voices were soon overwhelmed by a chorus of exculpation.

Ministers emphatically claimed that the problem was wholly to do with general bullying, social deprivation and anti-social behaviour. Michael Eboda, the editor of the excellent *The New Nation*, claimed that people were attempting to 'create a conflict where there is none', and said that after talking to young black kids of all backgrounds in the area he is convinced that 'any barriers that were there are almost gone'. The tragedy came about, says Eboda (of Nigerian origin himself), because there are too many kids with knives around.

Now the police have thrown their new, more sensitive selves into the debate. Sir John Stevens, the Metropolitan Police Commissioner, said on London Weekend Television: 'What is being said is that there is a certain amount of tension between racial groups. We must not deny it but we must not build that up into a situation where there's more violence.' And most of the other vast and detailed reports have concentrated on the problems of inner-city life. All these are important arguments, but they should not be used to conceal some hard and heartbreaking realities.

White racism is the biggest bully out there, but prejudices between the various people of colour are also creating tensions, terror, brutality and daily victims on the streets and in the school yards.

If you could magically get rid of white racism tomorrow, the lives of many black and Asian people would still be blighted. Sikhs, Muslims, Hindus, refugees, Afro-Caribbeans, Ugandans, Nigerians, mixed-race people, all know well the traumas of having multiple points of conflict in their lives. Some battles are to do with their rights in a world dominated by white power. Others – equally painful – come out of how the 'other' is defined by distinct non-white communities.

In the past six months my life has been made hellish, not by white racists – who do what they do and I know how to deal with them – but by a small number of Muslims who think I am 'not a correct Muslim' (last year they issued such serious and concrete threats to me and my children that I had to withdraw from conferences I had agreed to speak at), and by black and Asian individuals who are consumed with envy and a savage hatred for what I write. Yet we may never openly debate these hatreds because it is considered too risky to do so.

In 1998 I commissioned a survey for a report on race and politics which looked at white attitudes towards different communities as well as racial and ethnic attitudes between groups. Some activists denounced the report as 'racist'. Yet those who make the strongest public rebukes know better than most what is really happening out there. But they have joined the culture of denial which pervades so much of public life today. They are fooling nobody and only make it easier for white racists to point out the dishonesty of their rhetoric. On Radio 4's *Today* programme, an outspoken Nigerian woman, Chief Mrs Lola Ayorinde, quite rightly pointed out this humbug to William Trant, who represents a West Indian community organisation. Her words fell on deaf ears.

Eboda is right to say that large numbers of young black Britons think of themselves as people of this country with none of the baggage carried by their parents. But he fails to point out that in every area where previously there was unity and understanding between non-white groups, relations are now falling apart.

This weekend I bought my first ever original painting. It is by Shema Ladva, a brilliant young British Asian artist, who graduates today. Her paintings – some of which are on show at the Waterman's Art Centre in Brentford, west London – are based on what she has observed around Southall. You can see the pain, the turmoil, the claustrophobia and yet terrible separateness between young Muslims, Sikhs and others.

Others, too, are speaking out. Many West Africans are cab drivers for the various broadcast channels. I talked to six of them this week and they are quite upfront about the splits between them and Afro-Caribbeans. It is a difference in values. Africans worship education and self-improvement, obsessively so, they say, and can be arrogant. They feel too many Afro-Caribbean men waste their lives and leave school without qualifications. As one driver put it: 'I am not saying there is no crime among us. But at least Nigerians are educated criminals.'

Afro-Caribbeans, in turn, feel resentful and put down by these 'superior' attitudes. Two of the drivers had had Afro-Caribbean wives, but it did not work out because of chasms between expectations. Afro-Caribbeans I have spoken to feel it is time to stop pretending all is well with the rainbow coalition. In fact some of the funniest black stand-up comedians and of course the characters in the long-running Channel 4 sitcom *Desmond*'s – set in Peckham, ironically – exploit these tensions.

Challenging a culture of denial is never easy, but you can see how it is beginning to happen, and what the gains are, even when we are dealing with deep emotions. Take slavery. A few years ago, one could not mention that slavery was a partnership enterprise that depended on the robust participation of African slave merchants – entrepreneurs who had no qualms about what they were doing because their only concern was profit. Arabs had been carrying on the Saharan slave trade for decades before the white man arrived. The sheer scale of the Atlantic slave trade would not have been possible without tribal wars and the greed of white and black traders.

A number of African academics featured on BBC2's *Timewatch* programme on Sunday night spoke openly about this. Black traders, including women, came to Liverpool to negotiate and get the goods they wanted. You saw African-Americans weeping and kicking the walls of the slave prisons as they heard this side of the story. The same 'truer' story can be told of the Raj, which again needed greedy 'native' collaborators to prop up a system where the powerful were seriously outnumbered by the powerless.

You don't tell these past and present stories to allow white Britons to pass the buck. You do it in order to change things. Those of us who have to struggle against racism know how hard it is to fight people who reject there is racism in this land, which they say is replete with tolerance and decency. Yet we insist on the same paralysing denials when it comes to inter-ethnic prejudices which can also kill our children. Oh no, it is proclaimed, there is no such friction, no such prejudice. Maybe the death of Damilola will finally force an end to these pretences.

Unless we condemn all gang violence, our anti-racism is a sham

13 February 2001

Mention the possibility that violence between ethnic minorities may be as bad as white racism against black, and that such conflicts have been denied too long, and the so-called 'ethnic minority leaders' will accuse you of everything from ignorance to irresponsibility. Yet that is the obvious and unspoken implication of a succession of recent assaults and murders, including that of Damilola Taylor.

Nobody doubts that Damilola, a recent arrival from Nigeria, was victimised by gangs that included black British children. If he had been bullied by young white thugs and then found stabbed to death (allegedly) by one of the bullies, these same leaders would be doing the rounds, ferociously insisting that the crime was racially motivated and not the inevitable result of bad schools, violence in society and too many knives in circulation – the three explanations we have been given so far by various representatives and spokespeople in Peckham.

They insist that there is no problem between the various 'black' communities in the area and that there has been a wonderful swell of renewed unity as a result of this terrible death. I remain sceptical. If this is true, why are the killers being sheltered by those who know them?

The same protection surrounded a gang of Asian and Afro-Caribbean youngsters who viciously attacked a group of Somali students in Southgate in north London in 1999. Bodrul Miah, an Asian, repeatedly stabbed eighteen-year-old Abdul Osman, a bright student at the local college. The gang members were convicted last month, but the police, local MP Stephen Twigg and the college principal still insist that ethnic difference was not a key motive for the attack.

Local Somalis beg to differ. One said to a reporter: 'We believed it was a race murder. The Somalis are a different culture, a race apart, and they were picked on by the Asians. Nowadays when a white man kills a black all hell breaks loose; a black kills another black and it is an embarrassment.'

This weekend, news broke of Asian gangs in Oldham who have been attacking white people. Many anti-racists will find this even more of an embarrassment. In their eyes white people can only ever be perpetrators, never victims of anti-white violence. It is true that serious assaults are mostly committed by white thugs, and that white racist gangs have been as busy as ever, terrorising black, Asian, mixed-race, refugee and other groups. But we need to move our attention to the increasingly brutish behaviour of young men in other communities too.

In west London, particularly in higher education establishments, simmering rivalries periodically explode between Muslim and Sikh gangs, and these only ever get reported in the local papers such as the *Ealing Gazette*. A young Muslim female barrister tells me that the courts in Birmingham are full of Asian members of criminal gangs. A violent gangland culture is emerging across the races.

Gangs are not new in this society, nor is the violence associated with them. What is worrying is the spread of this behaviour. There isn't a single community that can afford to remain smug or superior. Gang members unite under a common identity, real or invented. So white kids beat up 'Pakis', 'chinks' and 'black bastards', who in turn retaliate or victimise refugees or other newcomers.

Ethnicity is only one of the fault lines. You also get gang battles within groups, a point that is well made by Home Office minister Paul Boateng, who this morning launches 'Young, Gifted and Dead', a poster campaign in London's Harlesden area, where drug and turf wars have left eight black men dead in the past eight months.

But whether it is inter-ethnic rivalry or drug-related criminal activity, surely it is time to address these developments? We have a vast amount of credible research into race discrimination, but barely anything on these new problems. Funders are squeamish about such research because of fears that such information will make white racism worse.

First of all, white racists need no convincing that we are a thoroughly bad lot. Sure, right-wingers will rush around 'proving' that all social problems are caused by immigrants and their offspring. But they do this anyway, with or without evidence. The Home Office, universities and think tanks need to take bold decisions and begin some serious research that can then be used for social policies.

We need to know exactly what is going on, and to make the information public. The causes are likely to be multi-layered and diverse. These gangs flourish in places where, for years, all public amenities have been eroded by market-led cuts. Oldham is one such area, as is Southall, where once there was a well-equipped leisure centre (now a supermarket), youth clubs and cinemas. Maybe the young people are displaying tribal tendencies as a response to a homogenised world, and they are undoubtedly feeling the alienation of all young males who have little self-esteem or prospects.

In some Asian communities, economic deprivation used to be managed through strong family bonds. Asian families are more solid than many others in this country, but there are signs of disintegration and conflict. Third-generation Asian children are Thatcher's children; they cannot communicate with their parents, and seek out gangs to make new bonds. We must find out how racism and religious discrimination makes beasts of victims.

I remember a young Bangladeshi student of mine in Bethnal Green who was horribly mutilated by a gang of white neo-Nazis. After the attack, he became so violent himself that we had no option but to expel him. Black boys may be underachieving in schools partly because of an internalised sense of hopelessness, which they have picked up by observing how racism ground down their parents. And we may hate what they stand for, but we should invest more money in finding out more about the thoughts and lives of young white racist gangs too.

This does not mean that I think we should busy ourselves understanding antisocial behaviour without passing judgements. We must condemn gang violence, and condemn it whatever ethnic group is involved. Unless we can weep equally for black and white victims of these outrages, our anti-racism is a sham.

All these angry young men need
to escape from their ghetto mindset

26 June 2001

So it's Rochdale, Burnley this week. Where next? I hear Huddersfield is a bit quiet, and that no cars have been burnt so far in Dewsbury. And when next will we see their dazzling performances at cricket grounds which sent one *gora* (whitie) steward off to hospital and the rest of us (including most other Asians) into despair? Lots of scope still for free media attention to give their mean little lives a little status.

They say that the widespread racial prejudice against them – which is undoubtedly there, and proven by independent sources – gives them the right to behave as badly as you wish and to victimise others. I too have a son who is a young adult, and he too faces racism. But he would not disgrace himself or me in the way they do their families.

They don't give a damn that for the first time in a long time, according to a Mori poll for the UN last week, race relations worry people in this country more than standards in education or that the British National Party has found a new lease of life, or that many British Asians now want to call themselves something else so that can dissociate themselves from thugs like them. And doubtless they have no interest in a finger-wagging old bag like myself.

For what do I know of life in impoverished ghettos? Or what it feels like to be a hot-blooded young male (I notice that the sisters are not out kicking ass) never allowed to belong, not by Powellites and Tebbitites in white society and not by community patriarchs, the fathers, uncles, politicians, priests. They have kept him restless and uprooted; his passions have deliberately been conscripted into subcontinental politics or an idealised religious diasporic project.

Islam in particular. Several young British Muslims have gone off to fight in various 'Islamic' conflicts around the world. Dr Yunus Samad, from Bradford University, found that 'Islamic icons and

190

metaphors are easily deployed by young men who have barely any knowledge or interest in Islam but use the metaphors to express their anger and hostility at being excluded.'

He may wear the word PAKI defiantly cut and dyed on his scalp, but he has known the pain of this word as it was hurled at him on the streets, in school playgrounds and by punters who regularly assault Asian minicab drivers. The latest riot this weekend in Burnley was triggered by one such attack, which left a cab driver with a broken cheekbone.

These young Asians are not torn between two cultures, a favourite cliché. Their world is crowded with circling vultures who pick at disaffection and create open sores which fester and infect. Pundits and leaders say this is youth gone bad, and/or too much Westernisation and/or the lack of jobs and resources and/or racial conflict, all of which matter but don't always lead to mayhem. These conditions prevail in areas of London too so where have all the riots gone there? Most Asians used to say that black rioters were giving them a bad name and that Asian children were raised better. But go to Tottenham or Southwark and see for yourself. Crime is high, drug crime in particular. Violence too stalks the streets, but you do not get the old scenes of streets erupting.

Young Asian troublemakers (only a tiny minority, remember) are breaking out in this way because their mutant identities are increasingly detached from the so-called 'community leaders', the Frankensteins who made them in the first place. For all their hollow bravado, the troublemakers would never move to the Indian subcontinent because theirs is a manufactured attachment, lacking the genuine links of their parents and grandparents.

They say they are Muslims, but this is obvious only by day. Their undeclared activities – involvement with drugs and prostitution for some, or more harmless nightclubbing – takes them into a strange nocturnal other life which the elders are anxious never to acknowledge. Their relationship with women (all except their mothers, who are unquestioningly adored) is cruel and controlling and at times physically abusive.

The last time I was in a cab in Leeds with an Asian taxi driver, he stopped his car and slapped a young girl who was with a girlfriend because she was laughing too freely in the street. These men are often forced to marry cousins from back home with whom they have little in common, and a large number of them have drink and marriage problems. Added to this is the reality of racism and consequent low self-esteem. A thoughtful mullah (British born, unlike most of the others who are imported from Saudi Arabia or Pakistan) believes these men 'are the product of sick nationalism and narrow culture on both sides. Whites who think their nation is still white so they do not accept these men. And families and leaders who say they must be Pakistani or Indian or Bangladeshi and should never be British.'

All residents are denied in deprived areas; racial explanations and brutal nationalisms divert people away from that important truth, and nobody gains. I have said before that we need to promote interdependence and a sense of shared purpose between the tribes of Britain – white, black and brown. Northern Ireland may have much to teach us about how this can slowly be built, preventing an easy resort to militancy. A shatteringly effective school video of *My England*, a play which examines national loyalties in football, is launched later this week by the ARC Theatre Ensemble. Some 80,000 children and young adults have already used this material which has been shown to change young people's attitudes towards diversity and citizenship. We need much more of this kind of education.

Finally, these young men need to choose and make their own leaders who will get them out of the ghetto mindset which is making them so unstable and dangerous at present. This worked in London. Go to Southall, Newham, Brixton and you will find innumerable projects and campaigns run by young black and Asian Britons who have empowered themselves enough to realise that burning cars and shops is a dead-end life which gets you nowhere – unless of course, nowhere is exactly where you wish to go.

Just see what Africa has done for us

27 August 2001

More Africans (350,000) than Bangladeshis (234,000) live in Britain today. I mention this because in all the flip-flapping over girls doing better than boys in the exam results other important comparisons have gone missing.

Figures from the Department for Education and Skills have provided little useful information so far on how the most recent grades break down in terms of ethnicity. But over the years, Africans have consistently been among those with the highest qualifications. A study by the Policy Studies Institute in the mid-nineties revealed that 40 per cent of 16- to 24-year-old Africans had A-levels or equivalents compared with 33 per cent of white Britons and 36 per cent of Indians.

I thought it important to share this precious information because I am sick already of the number of conversations floating around again – since the abominations currently perpetrated by Mugabe – about how Africa is beyond redemption, essentially barbaric, truly the heart of darkness, a basket case, incapable of embracing modernity, is too uncivilised to understand democracy. The words flow easily in my presence once people realise that I am an exile, one of those East African Asians thrown out by Idi Amin thirty years ago (goodness, has it really been thirty years?) next year.

The people voicing them assume that, as a victim of one of the worst of these rulers, I will agree with these views. How contemptibly wrong they are. Yes, sure, since independence, African states have produced an endless stream of villainous, murderous, autocratic leaders who never want to give up power. Some, it has to be said, were actively encouraged by Britain, France and others. Idi Amin was helped into his position by Israel, the US and Britain because President Obote, who came into power in Uganda after independence, was moving too dangerously close to the Soviet Union. This British complicity has never really been told to the British population.

Meanwhile, Jean Bedel Bokassa, aka 'Emperor of the Central African Empire', was a lifelong friend of France, which knew he was killing thousands of innocent civilians and, like Amin, snacking on bits of them too.

Charles Wheeler's series on leaders who changed history on Radio 4 this summer revealed how even the good leaders, Kwame Nkrumah for example, became excessively self-regarding as time went on. And that tradition continues with Moi of Kenya, Mugabe of Zimbabwe, and the various military dictators around the continent. When judgemental non-Africans look beyond the brute leaders, their panicky eyes alight on images of illegal immigrants, Aids victims, Nigerian fraudsters and bodies strewn across the streets and jungles, images which are real enough and sadly not figments of fevered imaginations.

The tide of pessimism can overwhelm, but that would be missing the staggering contributions Africans are making all around the world. Among the most (perhaps the only) respected politicians in the world today are Mandela and Kofi Annan. Don McCullin, the legendary photographer who has been exhibiting photos depicting the reality of Aids in Africa, shows the profound humanity of ordinary Africans. They give the dying the kind of physical contact which most are denied in richer countries where fear of contamination keeps away all but the truly nearest and dearest.

People are always startled and disbelieving when I tell them that Uganda had a brilliant education system and that Makerere University, where I did my first degree, was among the finest in the world. Going into the smug and unexciting world of Oxford after that was an awful comedown. If you don't believe me ask Paul Theroux, the novelist, whose childhood was spent in Kampala. Paul was part of a vital, live, innovative iconoclastic intellectual movement in the sixties.

I have just managed (God bless the internet) to find copies of a brilliant magazine, *Transition*, which was doing in the sixties what *Prospect* magazine is doing today, providing sharp, intelligent counter-intuitive analysis of politics, society, art, literature, the empire, black leadership and even Hollywood. Martin Luther King wrote about the death of Kennedy. I discovered James Baldwin, V. S.

Naipaul, and the African novelist Chinua Achebe through this magazine. *Transition* has been revived in Massachusetts by the renowned
writer Wole Soyinka who was also involved in the original venture
which was set up by an African Asian, Rajat Neogy, a man who knew
no fear and often found himself in hot water with emerging black
politicians who wanted only to be worshipped while they bled the
land and the people.

I don't believe in role models, but Neogy (whose personal life was
a mess and who died alone and lost in the US in 1995) was an inspi-
ration. He captured the spirit of that age, youthful, hopeful, full of
dreams which could not even be dreamt before. The sixties in this
country was nothing compared to the sense of liberation we felt
then.

African intellectuals honestly appraised Nkrumah and Nyerere,
debated single-party states, the pill, the tendency of Africans to
blame outsiders for their problems. Theroux was excommunicated
by whites after writing a storming essay condemning the white
Tarzans still in Africa. Sadly, most of these people who could have
made the future great for the continent were either killed or fled
here, to the US, France and elsewhere.

Other Africans with aspirations too started moving out or
sending their children abroad to get an education and a future.
Hence the qualifications and many success stories of Africans
abroad. We have gained what the continent has lost.

Just look around and you soon see just how many successful
Africans we are privileged to have here. Some names are well known,
Ben Okri perhaps. But others are subsumed under the 'black' label
so that the African heritage is all but wiped out. Let me end with a
brief list of Africans who prove just what Africa is capable of. There
is the gloriously well-connected showbiz correspondent Baz
Bamigboye; Diran Adebayo, the pacy novelist, and his brother
Dotun who is a publisher and much else. Ekow Eshun, the smoothie
culture critic, Ozwald Boateng who has turned Saville Row into an
exciting place, Zainab Badawi, the journalist, the artist Chris Ofili,
Seal, the singer, Bishop Sentamu who sat on the Lawrence Inquiry
and is as wise as Rabbi Hugo Gryn. Chiwetel Ejiofor, the actor who
played Romeo at the National last year, is thought to be one of our

best young actors today. David Oyelowo was an utterly credible King Henry VI at the Barbican last season. Mixed-race people with an African parent would add dozens more names and would obviously include Paul Boateng who is rising up the ministerial ladder fast.

My intention is not to provide a testimonial on behalf of Africans who can do this perfectly well for themselves. It is to temper the thoughtless vilification of Africa and Africans which I know will get worse as white Zimbabweans become the victims of a ruthless African ruler. Just remember that some the highest achievers and contributors in our society are Africans and show just a little respect for where they come from.

Did anti-racism policies lead to the death of Victoria Climbie?

4 February 2002

The Laming Inquiry into the tormented life and death of eight-year-old Victoria Climbie would have ended today if there hadn't been yet another cock-up by the inept, bungling, self-serving social work department of the London Borough of Haringey.

The council suddenly presented seventy-one documents to the inquiry on Friday. These papers, first demanded last May, were pronounced lost by Haringey. Now they have been found at the bottom of some drawer. No, I don't believe a word of this either. Lord Laming, the inquiry chairman said he was 'absolutely furious' – not usually the sort of words to emerge from a cautious, former senior civil servant.

This is one of those investigations which shows us how uncivilised our society still is, unable and unwilling to protect the most vulnerable from monstrous cruelty. Listening to Victoria's bewildered parents on Radio 4 yesterday it was impossible not to weep. They entrusted their daughter to a relative because they wanted her to come to this 'great' country. They played 'eeny meeney miney mo' to choose the lucky child in the family who would get to go. Victoria was the lucky winner.

Her smile is what gets me every time I see the pictures of her, with the ribbons in her hair (her great aunt, Marie-Therese Kouau, who beat her, burned her, tied her into a garbage bag, froze her to death in a cold bath, still thought it was important to make the girl look nice), her face covered in wounds, and with that grin as if to say she is all right really. Perhaps this is why the social workers, doctors and others too turned away from her and did nothing to save her life. Or perhaps it was because the child and her abusers were black.

A new racism in the public services offers non-white victims of abuse less protection and lower standards of care because of an institutional commitment to anti-racism. In this Monty Python world, black children at risk are left at risk because it is considered 'insensitive' or 'Eurocentric' or 'culturally imperialist' to intervene. And when there are black or Asian professionals involved the problems become even more intractable. Many are denied the right to interfere by white bosses who prefer to avoid confrontations with ethnic-minority families. Others aggressively promote the ideas of black cultural norms which must always be respected.

It is my view that these attitudes and practices may have contributed to the neglect of Victoria Climbie. Angela Mairs, a social work manager, left the inexperienced case worker, Lisa Arthurworrey, herself black, to make flawed and dangerous judgements. Was she just negligent or did she exclude herself from the case because she was white? Suspected sexual abuse was never followed up.

Ms Mair denied and then admitted that she had decided no further action was needed on the morning of 25 February 2000, hours before the child died of 130 injuries, injuries which nurses had drawn attention to previously when Victoria had been to hospital. Her body was so covered in cuts and burns and blows that the nursing staff could not lift her to give her a wash. She was sent back to her killers who finished her off.

The National Society for the Prevention of Cruelty to Children, very good on equal opportunities, failed Victoria too, for all the right reasons I am sure. Worst of all was the queen of 'black culture' and born again Christian, Carole Baptiste, who was supposed to but didn't supervise Ms Arthurworrey, who was often absent from work, who failed to turn up at the inquiry, who then arrived to put up such a reprehensible performance of self-pity that I remember thinking that in a sane world such a person would not have been given responsibility for stray dogs.

Beyond the rage we all feel, we are entitled to know if race is going to be discussed when we move into the next phase of the inquiry when prevention is on the agenda. Once upon a time, black and Asian families were misjudged and had their children taken from them because they were thought to be inferior people. Now black and Asian families are presumed to be wholly on the side of angels and their ethnicity is all that is considered when decisions and judgements are made. There are black and white parents who are average to excellent nurturers and black and white parents who cannot parent or who destroy children. Simple facts these, but they seem beyond the collective wit of social workers.

Estimates suggest that over 11,000 West African children are living with informal foster parents in this country. Child asylum-seekers and thousands of black, mixed-race and Asian children are living with adults who match their ethnic backgrounds. Most, I am sure, are well looked after. But when problems arise, are social work departments going to hamper staff from doing what is necessary and what they would do if it was a white child? Most social workers are excellent and we all owe them. But they are confused about what they are allowed to do in cases involving non-white families because of cultural relativism.

I could give you many examples of how this creates special perils for non-white children who need protection. Take two: an inviting leaflet is produced in a Yorkshire town with many black and Asian children in care. It is meant to attract more 'ethnic' foster and adoptive parents. It says: 'Black children need you. You do not have any special qualifications; you do not need to be a house owner; you do not need to have a spare bedroom; you do not need to be in employment. What you need to have is – soul, patience, understanding.'

This is no different from the expectations many teachers have of Afro-Caribbean pupils, that the pupils should dance and drum and run and not bother with middle-class stuff like science and literature. A couple of readers, teachers, from a shire county which I am sorely tempted to name, emailed me gruesome details last week about a young Bangladeshi girl who is being physically and sexually abused and who they say is not getting help from nervous professionals.

Unless this latest nightmarish case forces us to re-establish the idea of universal standards and rights for all children in Britain, the Laming Inquiry will have been a waste of money, time, hopes and expectations. That would be as unforgivable as the needless death of Victoria Climbie.

The secrets and lies of Britain's Asians

15 July 2002

Elders, they are the keepers of our secrets, Asian men and women with withered and merciless faces who have walked the hard journey of life without revealing pain or complaining, burying tragedies along the way. They were taught from childhood that the only things which matter are conformity and *izzat* (public reputation). And they have enforced respect for these with ever more vigour, afraid that they had ended up living in a society where such values had long gone and where racism was always on the prowl, looking to wound and maim them.

To get yourself a bad name is worse than death, which is why suicide is a common form of exit in many Asian families. As Mr Kotecha, who knew my clever but wayward father, once told me: 'Beti, remember never to talk about your family or friends, never tell the truth, because your duty is to protect your loved ones. Better to jump into the sea than speak about your beloved father. Don't even ask the questions, just put on a happy face and say only nice things.' Some parents pretend their children are dead or weave long, elaborate stories and updates to conceal that their sons or daughters have married out. Others refuse to talk to young people who come out as gay.

Some traditional values do still serve us well. I, for example, would never want to acquire the so-called freedoms of modernism and post-modernism, which create distorted, hedonistic, never-satisfied individuals. Respect, obligations, an understanding of consequences and mutuality are central to a fulfilled life. However, the stifling of all personal aspiration, and often the truth, is cruel and wrong.

Behind all the jolly good shows of Asian family life lie thousands of people whose lives are trapped by excessive caution, by lies, secrets, deceptions, whispers, threats, dissimulation and inhumane oppression. And the pressure not to talk is becoming stronger.

Reports this weekend revealed frightening details of drug addiction and trafficking among young Asian men and the devastating effect this is having on neighbourhoods. Not supposed to talk about that. Alcoholism is a serious problem, not only in Hindu and Sikh families but in a substantial number of Muslim families where, of course, nobody drinks. Domestic violence? What, washing your blood in public now? Incest? Child abuse? Rubbish, such things never happen in our families. Homosexuality? Another Western bloody disease. And so they go on, the custodians of virtual virtue.

They hated the film *Monsoon Wedding* because it touched on child abuse within an outwardly and enviously happy extended family. They also wanted to lynch Ayub Khan Din for his 'dirty' story, *East is East*, and Hanif Kureishi after *My Beautiful Laundrette*. And from the threats and curses I get, and will get again today, they would like to staple my lips together too.

Meanwhile, the problems simply grow to devour everything. Indeed this may well be happening in some of the northern towns and in the East End of London which the local MP, Oona King, has described as the 'heroin capital' of the country. God help her for simply saying what has been obvious for years. Nine years ago when I used to teach young adults in Tower Hamlets, east London, I saw the problem with my own eyes. My baby's childminder lived on the fifth floor in a block of flats. On five occasions I saw young Bangladeshi boys and men comatose on the stairwell, with syringes around them. Once, one had passed out in the small lift and was lying there smelling of urine as the lift went up and down. It was frightening but when I mentioned it to local Bangladeshi luminaries, I was told it was something 'the community' was dealing with.

I have also met Asian women who did many years in prison (some middle-aged) because they were forced by their husbands or brothers to operate as mules carrying drugs to and from the subcontinent. In one case, heroin in small plastic pockets was sewn into a quilt that was wrapped around a six-month-old baby. Most of the women have since been divorced because the family did not want a woman with a 'bad name'. This April, a thirteen-year-old girl from Bradford was found carrying heroin worth more than £1m. Last week, the Southall Black Sisters (SBS), a campaign group fighting for better treatment of women within families, challenged a coroner's decision not to hold an inquest into the death in Bradford of Nazia Bi and her two-year-old daughter, Sana Majid Ali, who were burned to death in a locked bedroom. The SBS claims 'the family and wider Asian community closed ranks and did not want a public hearing'.

Drugs, criminality and violence are obliterating the already fragile bonds of black British families, too. Where were the community power brokers when street crime increases were causing such anxiety last week?

You can also see the same demand for silence among British Jews. Jewish people who are prepared to speak out and act against the Israeli Prime Minister, Ariel Sharon, are attacked both by Zionist fundamentalists and by moderates who agree with them but feel that to be openly critical awakens anti-Semitism, always a light sleeper.

I understand the dynamics of racism, anti-Semitism and Islamaphobia. Problems within communities are relished and used by white racists. But what is worse: racist gloating or the collapse of families, hope, principles and entire localities? People who proclaim that they are protecting the communities through discretion know well how much young blood is haemorrhaging away from the hearts of those communities.

But expose these issues and the reactions are louder and more threatening than ever. I have watched with incredulity as groups and individuals, passionate anti-Islamaphobes and anti-racists have tried to discredit the painstaking reports on the northern towns by Sir Herman Ouseley, Ted Cantle and the Keighley MP, Ann Cryer. The last is much admired for her honesty by young Asian women who no longer feel able to sit tight and bear it all.

The objectors would rather point accusing fingers at white people than their own. Poverty, social exclusion and discrimination create conditions for crime and a drug culture. But these problems are only going to get worse if they are forcibly concealed. And racism cannot excuse domestic violence, sexism, child abuse, forced marriages or black and Asian pimps who think it is OK to ensnare vulnerable white women to work as prostitutes.

At last, it appears, more people are taking up these challenges. Projects have begun in Southall, Rotherham, Birmingham and elsewhere to get families to deal openly with issues that previously were locked up. Idealistic young Muslims are getting together and influencing peers with self-destructive lifestyles. Better funding for women's groups is making them stronger. And government ministers are becoming less afraid of causing offence to black, Asian, Muslim and Jewish Britons.

The 1990 Trust, an umbrella organisation bringing together voluntary black and Asian groups, recently said some black and Asian communities were 'imploding'. I agree. If we don't stop this, if we still pretend and lie, racists will be the only winners.

The countryside is a no-go area for black Britons

23 September 2002

I was on the Nicky Campbell programme on Radio 5 Live last week, discussing the countryside demo, a march that seemed to me to be about just about everything. These people seem to be marching about a very long and unrelated list of grievances: the hounding of foxes, dying post offices, rural wretchedness of a vague kind, petrol prices, city tourists, demands for unlimited sympathy and subsidies for rich and needy farmers, banks, house prices, milk maids, fear of crime, fear of annihilation, the right to life and liberty and maybe, somewhere in the back of the march, is some group defending the doily, part of a way of life in danger of extinction unless the government provides rescue funds for it.

Hundreds of thousands of true sons and daughters of this great nation stormed into London to sound off about how deprived they are and how they feel victims of prejudice so bad that, according to the Prince of Wales, they are even worse off than blacks and gays. How intolerable! My heart breaks at the thought of those poor, flushed apple cheeks of country Brits as they watch us blacks and those queers overtaking them in the gallop to privilege.

If the reports are to be believed, Prince Charles has written a letter to the Prime Minister making just this point. The heir to the throne apparently also claims in his note that the government is 'destroying the countryside'. This is ridiculous, even for a spoilt man prone to strange utterings. First, what is he doing participating directly in politics? It is one thing for his mistress to let her views be known, but for Charles to intervene in this way shows monumental arrogance and ignorance of the unspoken things the march also represents.

Has he given the slightest thought to why it is that the countryside remains such a no-go area for most people of colour? Hundreds of thousands of black and Asian Britons have farming in their blood, and are the descendants of tillers, but have you ever seen a black or Asian farmer or farm worker? Does Charles really not wonder that there might be a coded message is behind all these 'way of life' complaints? You don't see any black or Asian people on these marches (if anyone did spot the Devon Council for Racial Equality banner or the Jamaican Fox-Hunting Society do correct me), and often extreme nationalist groups are in there with their repulsive ambitions to claim back Britain for whites.

Now sure, all demos have their crazies. During anti-racist demos you always find yourself with some strange companions, campaigners fighting for yak farmers or whatnot, but the Prince didn't bother to make careful distinctions. He should have. There is an important difference between the real problems – the needs of some farmers enslaved by supermarket giants, the wages of farm workers, environmental protection – and campaigners who want to exclude outsiders.

That is what they mean when they go on about their 'way of life'. Now Charles, Prince of Equal Opportunities, gives these exclusionists succour. Oh I hear you yelping all right. You will accuse me of tainting good people by calling them racist. To name racism these days is considered a far worse crime than to act in ways that directly or indirectly discriminate against black and Asian citizens. But I say this again, may we not speculate that the march is in truth making a stand for the kind of country this was before all us darkies arrived? Could it be that the number of Countryside Alliance supporters has swollen because the Tory Party seems in danger of abandoning this agenda, what with all this talk of learning to embrace gays and blacks and Asians into the party? John Major flirted with this, being a Brixton boy, and then succumbed to old Tory fantasies of village greens and warm beer. Now, although Iain Duncan Smith turned up on the march, he is also aggressively promoting tolerance in his party, even appointing an Asian vice-chairman. And the green wellies don't like it one bit.

On the Radio 5 programme, I was challenged to justify my views. Are those who object to my thinking absolutely sure that the Countryside Alliance really would like multiracial Britain to invade its pure little village? Would they welcome a beautiful temple or mosque to stand with the small church spires if a substantial number of us did manage to sneak in by cheating estate agents? No-stupid, that is precisely what would destroy their way of life. They already have all those other townies buying up the barns that they sell to them at exorbitant prices and food inspectors interfering with what they feed their pigs and cows. Yes, they can handle one Mr Patel in the paper shop, a Mr Khan running the local Taj, maybe a doctor or two, Mr Chou with his Chinese takeaway, but more than that you are talking cultural genocide, can you not understand that? Otherwise, keep them in Birmingham (or Manchester, Liverpool, London, Bradford), as they said in one report on rural racism.

One officer at a rural Race Equality Council wrote to me recently saying most people are in heavy denial: 'We know racism is there, but we only hear what we want to hear in the countryside. We shoot the messenger or we ignore the evidence.' *Challenging Racism in the Rural Idyll*, a study published by the Citizens' Advice Bureau, even found that researchers faced abuse during interviews. Major racial incidents have come to light in Yeovil (Paddy Ashdown came to the aid of an Asian waiter who was attacked and then faced months of harassment and threats), Norfolk and rural Wales, and a number of enchanting localities with wonderful trees and bluebells have NF, Combat 18 and BNP cells. And as a few more black and Asian Britons move out of the cities, the resistance to their presence gets worse. Most shameful of all have been the recent outbursts over asylum centres in countryside locations. We have seen howling mobs who wanted to scare off human beings who have risked everything to find some place of safety, some place where they can have half a chance. Yes, city people may resent them too but you don't see us gathering en masse to hound them out.

Sadly, the organisations that are pushing for ramblers and wildlife and ecoloaical issues, such as Friends of the Earth, are no better at making sure they open their doors to Britons who are not white. BEN, the Black Environment Network, does stoic work in the face of such problems. They prefer to use goodwill. I think a much more demanding approach may now be needed. With the Countryside Alliance wielding such influence, the environment groups and the

National Trust and all those others have got to wake up to the new danger symbolised by this march.

I don't accept any group in this country has the right to demand that their cultures should be protected from pollution, not Rastas, not Orthodox Jews, not the mullahs of mayhem. However, people of all backgrounds, including the English, must have the freedom to be who they are and to take pride in this without being labelled barbaric or racist. I say this in an essay in *Reclaiming Britishness*, the book that also features Blunkett's controversial arguments for learning English. But that is very different from demanding that the British public must pay for and forever put up with the disagreeable demands and dubious values that so many country people feel wedded to. Down with you, I say, and stay out of our mixed cities.

Black history should never be safe history

7 October 2002

Those who care for such things know that this is Black History Month. Across Britain, local authorities, schools, universities, broadcasters and arts organisations will be finding new stories or retelling old ones in an endless struggle to get these transfused into the bloodstream of this nation, just as they have for many years now. The idea was started by the late, black Labour MP Bernie Grant and others as a response to the long, miserable period of Tory rule. Margaret Thatcher's vision of Britain was narrowly English, imperialist and essentialist. Remember, she started her reign in 1979, the year after my son was born, with comments on how we (blacks and browns) were 'swamping' this country. In 1990 she said, in Bruges, that Britain should be proud that 'we conquered and, yes, civilised the rest of the world'. Those who voted for her loved this, from their very own Boudicca.

Black history events were then a rebellion, a declaration of defiance against this sort of monstrous, narrow nationalism. Anti-racists, the Inner London Education Authority and the GLC found small ways of keeping warm the alternative truths about slavery and colonialism. We met in cold, dusty halls, empty school classrooms and kept our hopes up. We knew we were seen as dangerous by the state and this was one reason that the axe came down on the GLC and ILEA.

In Mr Blair's inclusive Britain, Black History Month has been mainstreamed. It is everywhere. The V&A Museum, for example, has an event on surrealism and its appropriation of Caribbean imagery, and another one this week showing the startlingly live work of the photojournalist Neil Kenlock who worked for *West Indian World*, Britain's first black newspaper. On Thursday, English Heritage unveils a plaque to the great Paul Robeson, and so it goes on. Many of us have been invited to deliver lectures in prestigious halls with vast organs and dressed-up footmen, and it should all be satisfying for the thousands of us who have fought for such acknowledgement for so many years.

It is and it isn't.

Don't think I am not grateful. It is wonderful that my daughter is getting so much validation of her right to be born. I salute the establishment figures who have opened such doors. But a part of me is now also getting worried that the real challenges, the urgent revisions needed to tell the true history of this nation are still being avoided by the powerful. Take Prince Charles's witterings this week in Devon about British children lacking knowledge of proper history and heritage. Whose history? Whose heritage? These are the obvious questions long asked by the poor, by women and, most passionately, by black and brown Britons.

History is a dangerous business – many vested interests are involved in telling certain stories and silencing others. I doubt whether David Starkey and, say, Simon Heffer (who wrote a thousand-page book on Enoch Powell without speaking to a single black Briton) will be participating in Black History Month. These are the men whose views reassure millions of white Britons that all is still well with their world. This is a type of psychosis which other countries are prone to. Australia today under the right-wing John Howard is similarly disinclined to look at its vile history truthfully, and India's leaders have embarked on a mission to recast that nation as one where all Hindus are saintly and much put-upon by savage Muslim interlopers. But in this, my country, I do feel the responsibility to ask how long this can carry on.

Black History Month has become too safe perhaps. Worse, it has had little impact on the popular consciousness. Just look at the results of the poll carried out by the BBC in their search for the hundred greatest Britons (a television series based on this survey is about to start). Thousands of people voted and not a single person of colour appears on the list. Not even Magdi Yacoub, the brilliant heart surgeon, or Mary Seacole, whose nursing of the wounded in the Crimea was so effective that she was more valued by soldiers than Florence Nightingale. For a country still consumed by the two world wars, they didn't even rate Noor-un-Nisa Inayat Khan. Who? I hear you ask. The beautiful daughter of one of the men who founded the Sufi movement and an American mother, she volunteered to join the British secret service. Under the code name 'Madeleine', she went to France and worked as a vital link until she was arrested by the Gestapo, tortured and then shot dead at Dachau.

I have other misgivings too. The Black History Month has tended to focus mostly on Caribbean stories – reclaiming the black label as meaning only that. Why are British Asian stories kept to a minimum? Yes, slavery was confined to Africans but, after abolition, Indians were taken as indentured labourers to places as far-flung as Fiji and South Africa. And, to be truly daring, the month should also include the histories of asylum-seekers. We have a fine body of work on Jewish exiles and it is right that we should forever be reminded of the Holocaust, but with such obnoxious attitudes fostered by the press and politicians against those seeking refuge, Black History Month should have made these narratives the core of the programmes.

With such a focus, we might have reminded ourselves that Robeson was a victim (as was Charles Chaplin) of the most vicious persecution in the US because of his political views, and that WH Auden knowingly agreed to a marriage with a German woman so she could win the right to live in the UK. I would have liked more controversial debates about the terrible harm that was done by the Empire and the role played by black and Asian people to keep this enterprise going for as long as it did. West Africans in Britain should be discussing the part played by their ancestors in the slave trade and the failures of their nations to address this. Television and radio should have arranged ferocious debates between the children of the rulers and ruled, instead of sanitised documentaries on the Empire. We should have a hot controversial event about the history of Iraq. As Professor AG Hopkins of Cambridge University argues in *Globalization in World History*, you cannot understand many modern trends without reference to the old empires.

We need histories which show the love that can emerge between old enemies and the threads that bind us all. The splendid new book, *White Moghuls*, by William Dalrymple, is a joy because it shows the attraction between white men and Indian women during the Raj. The central story is almost unbelievable – a love affair, encouraged by her family, between a teenage Muslim princess and General James Achilles Kirkpatrick, a soldier who arrived to dominate and ended up a slave to love.

Much is at stake, particularly as memories – short and long-term – are being washed clean by some efficiently engineered cynicism. Blackpool was a frightening reminder of this. As delegates fell over, palpitating before the gods, Clinton and Blair, hardly anyone seemed to recall Clinton's deadly foreign policies or the achievements of post-war British socialists. If such recent living memory can be so easily edited to suit, how much more fragile and susceptible to manipulation is faraway history? We are now a mature and diverse democracy; we deserve a more truthful story about how we got here.

Who wrecks the hopes
and dreams of black boys?

9 December 2002

The black British poet Linton Kwesi Johnson is one of my greatest Britons. Still a fighter for justice, his raw energy, anger and integrity run through beautifully crafted poems, making them blaze where other poetry merely shines. Sue Lawley was knocked off her chair this weekend when he chose Vivaldi to take to his Desert Island.

'What?' You could almost hear her cultivated mind panicking, 'a black street man like you? Are you sure? What about something more suitable, you know, Rastaman stuff, or soul, sounds to remind you of what you really are?' She was well placated when he did go on to choose Marley.

A black man in Britain – with a handful of exceptions – has his identity thrust upon him every single day by whites and blacks alike. There are templates they must fit, roles handed down by history, negative assumptions which remain stubbornly in place even in the twenty-first century, when the first black Cabinet minister, Paul Boateng, has arrived, the nation's most trusted newscaster is Trevor McDonald and Bill Morris has risen to exert extraordinary influence in the trade union movement and beyond.

Individual successes like these have made no impact on the way society perceives black men.

They are feared because they are expected to be into drugs, crime and violence, and for their sexual incontinence. They are assumed to be feckless and careless about family responsibilities. They are seen as genetically programmed to excel at sports, dance, music. They are thought to know how to pull women and have unbeatable prowess in bed. They have to be super-cool and have beautiful bodies. And weren't we just reminded of this when the BBC plastered huge posters all over town of four perfectly formed black bottoms of the talented cast of the series *Babyfathers*?

212

If only these were only dreadful and racist stereotypes without much substance. Depressingly, life imitates these images more, not less, as time goes on. And the worst effect is that they infect the lives and aspirations of young black boys. Afro-Caribbean boys are three times as likely to be excluded from school than any other group and their exam results are too often abysmal, leaving them drifting and susceptible to destructive choices.

Today, a conference organised by the National Association of Schoolmasters Union of Women Teachers will attempt to address this problem yet again, but this time the talk will go beyond the most common explanations given thus far – racism and poor teacher motivation. Both of these do still bear some responsibility for the catastrophic outcomes we are witnessing. But Tony Sewell of Leeds University School of Education (who is black himself and has researched this area better than anyone) has conducted a study which will make simplistic anti-racists very twitchy.

After studying 150 black fifteen-year-olds in five secondary schools, Sewell concluded that peer group pressure was a bigger threat to the progress of these children than racism or a lack of role models. Four out of five interviewees cited this as their main barrier to achievement. It is uncool to get good marks, the hard workers are 'dissed' and the leaders of the pack pride themselves on how many girls they can pull and how easily they can threaten teachers, especially women.

In their excellent study, *Young Masculinities*, published earlier this year, Stephen Frosh, Anne Phoenix and Rob Pattman found that in school Afro-Caribbean boys were expected to be super-masculine, super-virile, tough and promoters of authentic male style. They were positioned by others and positioned themselves as hard and therefore superior to white and Asian boys. This then led to greater discrimination against them by authority, ending in exclusions.

I wonder what chubby, tone-deaf black boys go through, or those who are anxious about their sexuality, or lads who want to go to church, like most of their parents and grandparents did. In what are euphemistically call the inner cities, such boys have no freedom to be or do what they want. They are pressed to conform to the tough subculture. Just last week the mothers of victims and perpetrators in

Peckham, south London, had to change their plans to march against this violence because of serious threats from the gunfighters who value nothing and want everything.

These nihilistic peer group values are just as damaging for white working-class children or young Bangladeshis, Sikhs or Muslims. But the problem is at present most acute for young black men and boys, particularly of Afro-Caribbean and mixed-race origin. To watch them live and die in the way so many are doing at present must break the heart and hopes of the entire community.

Just imagine what it must feel like to be born a nerdy black boy with a passion for physics and dreams to be the next Stephen Hawking? There must be some. Lots more bright, black boys could become bio-technologists, doctors, psychologists, poets like Johnson and the equally admirable Benjamin Zefaniah, painters, painstaking carpenters of beautiful furniture, sitar players, primary school teachers, space scientists, ballet dancers and all those hundreds of other occupations which young black boys can't even imagine as they think about themselves and their lives.

Racism disallows dreams. And that doesn't change whether you are a newspaper columnist or a renowned actress or a swank Lord in crimson robes. But these days, for black boys, the dream is wrecked by their own companions and heroes.

There are thousands of black boys around the country who will be thwarted by the twin evils of racism and peer group bullying unless they are helped to resist both, and this too is something Sewell and others are advocating.

It seems to me that we also need to pour some money into finding out what helped to make the difference in families from the Caribbean which, in spite of racism and other pressures, have produced fine and highly successful black men, men who have become beacons like Tony Phillips, the respected Radio 4 producer, and his brother Caryll Phillips, the novelist; Trevor Phillips and his novelist brother Mike. There are many, many more such clusters of achievement. Maybe it was easier then because the drug culture hadn't penetrated every aspect of life and parents could have more influence on their children than any of us has today.

The saddest truth is that if Stephen Lawrence had not been

murdered, he would have been a misfit in many a gang of young black men. He was ambitious for a career as an architect. His bloody death has made him a hero, but he would have counted for nothing in the hard crowd had he lived. Among the street cred, true blacks, Stephen Lawrence the architect would have been a sell-out, a coconut, a bounty bar; brown coating, white on the inside.

The Lawrence Inquiry ensured that racism in Britain was finally acknowledged. We now have new race equality laws to challenge the prejudices and cultures of schools and other institutions. Next April it will be ten years since the death of Stephen Lawrence. Time now, I think, to tackle that other massive problem in our society – black on black violence, external and internal.

My little pink Queen and her dreadful brood

2 June 2003

By mid-morning, the heat had already turned my skin to what felt like rancid butter. I was scared that it would soon turn black and upset my mother who, like all proper Asian mothers, worked hard to keep my skin fair and untouched by the Stygian colour of damnation. I was with some nursery school children and thousands of other older kids lining the streets of Kampala, capital of the British protectorate of Uganda. It was 2 June 1953, and we were marking the crowning of some pink queen far away, whose face was on the wrapper of the small bar of Cadbury's milk chocolate we were given as we stood there. The melting chocolate spread on pristine uniforms, faces, legs and ribbons, and many of us started to cry.

For people in the UK that day was obviously altogether more meaningful – especially as the coronation coincided with the arrival of television, making royalty more intimately accessible than ever before. In his well-written, elegiac (and sometimes blimpish and a tad too nostalgic) book, *The Shadow of a Nation*, the Radio Four journalist Nick Clarke confesses that, like many others in that post-war generation, his first memory belongs to the young Queen's coronation. Royalty then, he says, was an essential symbol of national self-assurance, real pride, continuity: 'Everyone knew where they were and who they were, back in the fifties.'

I am trying to imagine what this certainty and loyalty to the monarchy must have felt like. It is the least I can do as a republican, on this day fifty years ago when young, lovely Elizabeth was crowned. The unexpected rush of royalism in the country last year as millions came out to mourn the Queen Mother and to celebrate the golden jubilee did show that the old country still stalks and shadows the new, more raucous, disorderly, questioning,

216

demanding, irreverent, creative, equal, incredibly confusing nation we are becoming. Maybe that is all it was, a temporary, joyful retreat into an irrecoverable past. It appealed precisely because that class-structured, predictable white Britain has vanished and we will never again witness the whole country rejoicing in the crowning of a British monarch the way they did in 1953. Not even for sultry blue-eyed, golden William.

Look back at the gush during the jubilee and you cringe. David Cameron, a Conservative MP, wrote: 'The events of the past few days show the broad and continuing support for the monarchy as an institution.'

No they didn't. They made Britain look like an old folks' home where only selective remembrance meant anything. We are more than that now, much more, and we should resist this slide into dementia. To watch the drooling, the prurience, the tragedy of a people prepared for ever to defer to and pay for a second-rate brood is unspeakably depressing. Oh sure, the tourists love it, but they don't have to live with this shame. Do you really believe that the Americans, who so adore our royal Britain, would take it all off our hands? No dynamic country would wish for such a burden.

As Roy Hattersley wrote last year: 'A monarchy, based on the hereditary principle, encourages the nation to look backwards to its glorious past rather than face an uncertain future. It promotes values that a civilised country should abhor' – values that institutionalise the idea of inherited class superiority. What is this handed-down superiority? All I see is inherited stupidity among many in our revered Royal Family.

William's face appearing on the stamps only made you understand the horror of such a burdensome heritage: he will be stuck to the throne whether he wants it or not; he will be expected to raise the royals back to celestial spheres, this murky, greedy, unattractive family that seems unable to see how spectacularly it fails itself, let alone the benighted nation.

This is the view of crabby republicans like myself. But as time goes on I wonder if, secretly, royalists are getting ever more incandescent at the parade of palace follies and brazen infidelities and the twittering middle-aged Charles who needs (at least) four palaces to perfect his life of son-of-the-soil simplicity. Fiercely committed royalists must surely be very miserable today that this lot is letting down the whole edifice.

But here comes news of more 'modernisation' from St James's Palace. Charles wants a job description laid down in a Prince's Charter, outlining his rights and responsibilities. He is so modern, he has asked his officials to make up the charter instead of getting his public involved. He is also trying to pay a bit more tax on the money made by selling gifts given by well-meaning people around the world. The charter, he hopes, will give him clear rights to interfere even more. He wants to poke his aristocratic nose into politics, policy, architecture, farming. Every time he does, he reveals his instincts – he is an anti-progressive reactionary who finds the modern world distasteful. And so he should, for the distaste is reciprocated.

No, Sir, too little, too damn late. These manipulative gestures may still fool some, but more and more Britons are finding it hard to put up with this expensive farce and what it means for the nation that they love.

Sikh separatism is a problem, not a solution

15 September 2003

This weekend thousands of Sikhs gathered in Wolverhampton to attend a national convention to launch a new 'political party' with the explicit aim of pushing for better Sikh representation in key British institutions and more state-funded Sikh schools. Where greasy opportunism beckons these days, hopeless Tories rush towards it, and so it was at this convention. Oliver Letwin with his beatific smile praised the event, the organisers, the nice day, Sikhs, their contributions, probably their pets and well-kept gardens. Three-quarters of the people he was addressing vote Labour. Maybe a dozen or so will be kind enough to switch to his party. Oliver works ever so hard for so little reward. New Labour and the Lib Dems will no doubt have sent in their blessings too.

British Sikhs are only following what British Muslims have been doing for a decade, and before them British Jews. They observe politicians sucking up to the Board of Deputies of British Jews and increasingly the Muslim Council of Britain. They want to get in on the act. This is no different from the battles that Roman Catholics have fought to gain more rights and the interminable struggles for greater power between the two Christian factions in Northern Ireland. British Hindus are quieter and work more skilfully behind the scenes. (A senior MP told me recently that wealthy Hindu businessmen had considerable influence in all three parties and that some of them were supporters of the Hindu nationalism that today blights India.)

Of course, while the Church of England is massively privileged in our unwritten constitution and Parliament, other faith groups in this multifarious society can only respond competitively, using valid arguments of equity. Meanwhile, the English too get more covetous and evil-tempered as they watch devolved Scotland and Wales. They complain that the Scots are everywhere. The media is full of them

219

and all the political bouncers employed by New Labour, from John Reid down, seem to have threatening Glaswegian accents which make dainty English dispositions quiver with fear. They are also most mistrustful of the EU and the euro. In Wales and Scotland, anti-English opinions are de rigueur and there is much loose talk about who can be accepted as 'real' Scots and Welsh and about the preservation of cultures.

I despair of these developments. I detest the politics of community and singular allegiances, forced or stipulated. They imprison us and hold back our nation from the demands of life in the twenty-first century. In his exceptional book, *On Identity*, Amin Maalouf is rightly repelled by 'the notion that reduces identity to one single affiliation and encourages people to adopt an attitude which is partial, sectarian, intolerant, domineering, distorting their view of the world as it is'. Just as our collective lives are meshed together, as the nation state loses definition, as globalisation begins to show itself as more than merely nomadic capitalism, as identities and values become more complex and mixed, we get the rise and rise of ethnic, religious and nationalistic politics which, instead of being marginalised, are promoted by the powerful.

Did you know that, in August, a ministerial steering group was set up to consult faith groups on public policies? Why do we need this? Most religious leaders are men of a certain age. Far too many of them have intolerably retrogressive views of what God wants women to be and believe children are possessions of adults. What are the implications of this for the progressive agenda? I have faith. I hold some imams, priests (Christian, Sikh, Hindu), bishops and rabbis in great esteem and often seek their advice and views. In many ways they are more empathetic acquaintances than rampant, fundamentalist secularists. But I no longer support single-faith or race-based schools and the special dispensations that they seek and get. They are just as detrimental as all-white institutions: places where people who share the same values reinforce each other and their own exceptionalism, with nobody to interrogate their presumptions or unsettle their clubbiness.

Academic results, discipline and self-motivation can be excellent in these schools, and we could consider state-funded schools that offer serious education about all the major faiths, and an alternative stream of positively secular education, as a better alternative to existing arrangements which are so out of date and sync with our fast-moving times.

It is disturbing how pervasive have become the ideas of 'strong communities'. Pundits have successfully sold the idea that these are per se a desirable goal because they have cohesion and that American import, excellent 'social capital' or mutuality. Who can argue with that? Post-industrial societies broke those bonds, and we should remake them to enable people to feel more secure, nurturing and productive. But we need to do this across imagined boundaries, not inside them.

Take Neighbourhood Watch. In many ways it was a good thing which brought people together to fight crime. But where I live it quickly became paranoid, with neighbours panicking every time they saw a group of black men or people who looked like 'asylum-seekers'. Getting diverse people to develop local ties that bind is quite different from fostering exclusive and excluding identities. That is remarkably difficult, but unavoidable if we are to belong in this small, spirited island.

There are other reasons why we should reject the politics of ethnicity and community. They are based on the idea that culture stands, or must stay, still. Young people are stifled by such assumptions. Third-generation Sikhs, like Muslims and others, are agents of change in the transforming of modern British sensibility. Why should they be directed into new ghettoes? This is a game that gate-keepers love to play. It helps keep power 'hideously white', as Greg Dyke memorably described the BBC, which has just announced an 'Asian' season with exciting programmes on Asian millionaires and Lawrence Llewelyn-Bowen telling us about curries. Ho hum.

What the world needs today more than anything is to foster a sense of obligation towards people to whom we owe nothing or who are utterly unlike ourselves, what that humane sociologist Richard Sennett describes as 'the act of turning outwards . . . a new relation to other people as well as to shared symbols like those contained in a religion'. Community loyalty militates against that kind of generosity or understanding.

Last week I said on television that I was terribly upset by the murder by a suicide bomber of a twenty-year-old Jewish woman who was to get married the day she died. I received dozens of e-mails denouncing these sentiments. What was I doing feeling sorry for an Israeli, when Sharon does such wrong? Is compassion to be based on ethnic/religious/political loyalties. If a young Orthodox Jewish woman was being assaulted on our streets, should a Muslim or Christian not rush to help?

If Sikhs are now to think of themselves as only Sikhs and not Asian, black and inextricably British – and the same goes for Muslims, the English, the Baha'i and the hundreds of other tribes of Britain – how will the centre hold? How will that change the unyielding British Establishment?

The BBC's penitence makes
it difficult to defend

2 February 2004

I too am gloating, though obviously not with the swag and swish we have just seen in that model of virtue and honesty, Alastair Campbell. He, who used exquisite S&M techniques to titillate and humiliate political journalists, who once thumped a senior journalist for dissing Robert Maxwell, who gave us that dazzling dodgy dossier on WMDs, is exultant that his version of events has been totally vindicated by Lord Hutton. He told us so, he crows.

I also told you so, in these columns. As the Hutton inquiry began, I wrote that the investigation would help to keep Tony Blair in power. Here are my exact words: 'We will have a good many more years of Tony Blair, the man who believes that all he does is right and his right to do. Something is rotten again in the state of Britain and this time it is a Labour Prime Minister, the willing inheritor of Margaret Thatcher, who is responsible. This is why I have only limited interest in this inquiry and why I am exploding with frustration.'

That frustration – shared now by millions of British citizens – has grown and grown and grown this past week as the incredible conclusions of the Hutton report were being ingested and thrown up, smelling foul. The government and intelligence services are declared spotless. Dr Kelly is criticised and the BBC is wholly damned. Hutton has become a guard dog and used his bark and bite to warn off any future sorties into the fortified enclosures which protect our manipulative political masters.

He could have emulated his betters. Lord Scarman, looking into the Brixton riots in 1981, upset all expectations by going deeper and further than he was directed by Margaret Thatcher, who wanted punitive retribution on those she considered 'the enemy within'. Scarman, considered and fair, highlighted the causes of these riots.

Lord MacPherson's report into the Stephen Lawrence murder again refused to stay within any remit. This Scottish judge, no race expert, changed our landscape by exposing the racial inequality that still prevails in too many British institutions. Hutton has taken us back to the dangerous old days when judges like Lord Denning and Lord Widgery carried out inquiries which ensured the Establishment was always protected.

Tony Blair and Tessa Jowell want an 'independent' BBC which is as 'independent' as they allow. This reminds me of what Idi Amin once told a journalist: 'Yes you have freedom to say what you want, my friend. But this is a free country, so I am free to cut off your tongue if I don't like it.'

And at this perilous moment in our democracy with the government acting so perfidiously, how does the BBC react? With never-ending penitence and bloodletting; with such pusillanimity that it is disabling those of us who want to defend the institution with vigour.

Even yesterday, when popular opinion and most of the press were coming out against the report, on the *World at One* (Radio 4) the BBC was inviting criticism of its news coverage and asking if the corporation deserved its licence fee and special status. Rupert Murdoch's *News of the World* had carried a survey which showed that more than half the respondents didn't want the licence fee. This, said the presenter, showed the days of the fee were over. Like the poor misguided man who allowed himself to be eaten by a cannibal in Germany, the BBC is now cutting off its own joints and feeding them to its enemies. What do they think they are doing?

The governors, in particular, have shown themselves to be contemptibly inept. (They're like Chicken Little, who had an acorn fall on her head and thought the sky was falling. She got so scared, half her feathers fell out. She alarmed her friends, who all fled with her, until they met Foxy Loxy. He invited them to his safe den and ate them all up.)

Not one governor appeared on the *World at One* to defend their actions or the BBC, even at this crucial time. These people, there to protect our interests and that of the institution, have failed and should all go. Gavyn Davies, an impressive man whom I have met a number of times, should never have departed when he did, though at least he left with his self-respect, refusing to bow to the howls from 10 Downing Street which wanted abject capitulation. (They got this fast enough from the eager genuflector Lord Ryder, standing in as chairman.)

Davies should have stayed and taken his own time to respond to the biased report and the government. Key changes had already been made by the BBC to ensure that there would be no repeat of that one, small, slightly flawed, dawn report by Andrew Gilligan.

Greg Dyke had no option as he was pushed. But I hope he carries on making a stink. Unfortunately, he too is guilty of pandering to this government and its paid tyrants for too long. He now tells us that Campbell was vicious over the build-up to the war and demanded 'balanced' coverage, meaning a stream of pro-government propaganda. Dyke says he had to ensure that some programmes were weighted to suit this demand, among them the *Question Time* programme.

I complained bitterly that this appeared to be the case when I was on with Geoff Hoon, Oliver Letwin and Charles Kennedy in London. Nick Passani, the producer, was livid and argued with me passionately that I was slandering their reputation. I said I would take their word in good faith and that maybe I was wrong to cast such aspersions. I am happy to reiterate my allegations, now that the ex-DG himself says such doctoring was going on.

There was also a concerted effort to back the government's abominable policies on asylum-seekers. As any playground monitor will tell you, give in to bullies, try to please them and they will attack you more.

The danger is that the cowardice is getting worse. According to a diary report, Tariq Ali was disinvited by *Any Questions* this week because of fears around the Hutton report. I have been told by insiders that some of us are considered too hot at the corporation. A concerted campaign by Zionist extremists to disallow me on to key programmes is apparently having an effect. The *Today* programme and *Newsnight* are under considerable pressure to get tamer.

My love for the Beeb is not blind. There is much that is wrong with it; it too can be arrogant and celebrity-driven. Black and Asian people are still not treated as equals to their white counterparts and the dumbing down is real. But when you look at the whole, it is a bastion of excellence with values which are deeply civilised and journalism which is admired the world over.

The institution is now in terrible danger as the Charter renewal beckons. The deceptions over the WMDs are set to create further fury and it is no accident that as this debate begins to boil, the Hutton findings have slashed into our public service broadcaster. The wounds are not yet fatal, but they will be if the BBC does not rise with force to defend itself from this mendacious government and its other foes.

The pathetic BBC board of governors won't do this. They are ready to let their organisation bleed to pale weakness. But some of the biggest BBC brand names – Joan Bakewell, Jonathan Ross, Jeremy Vine and others – it is said are set to fight this assault. I hope they succeed. Otherwise the corporation will not be worthy of the support it has had from all of us this week.

Reform
Islam

Ordinary Muslims worldwide are today caught in the middle of two ruthless forces; we are squeezed and crushed in the war between them. *Western powers, led by the US and its satellites, are embarked on international and domestic policies without rules, without a moral compass and the targets are Muslim people and Muslim states, these days frequently described as 'terrorists'. The 9/11 attacks have created a madness which will not subside. Muslim states and too many individuals are corrupt and violent often towards their own. Islamic networks are proliferating and some have an anti-Western and a Stalinist agenda. And every time they blow up places and people, all Muslims stand accused. This collective culpability and collective punishment is abhorrent and counter-productive. It drives too many young Muslims into the arms of fanatics and conservative Islam (not the same thing). They ask, and they have a point- why are suicide bombers worse than sophisticated US, UK and Israeli weapons which pulverise babies and their mothers? The politicisation of the hijab is another issue dividing Muslims. I will never wear one and am only answerable to Allah for all my decisions. But such dissent from literalism is now harder than ever before. Most Western Muslims feel their voices are silenced and they are fearful for their children and the future. Just as so many in the US and the West are too, but for the opposite reasons.*

The impasse has got to be broken. After centuries of intellectual stagnation which followed periods of greatness, Muslim thinkers are now embarking on an evaluation of their cultures and discussing a reformation. Not before time. Muslim autocratic rulers are finding new

pressures coming from below for open and more accountable gover-
nance. Human rights values – universal surely – have got to underpin
the practice of our faith. At the same time Islam is the fastest-growing
faith in the world, including the West.

Challenges to US hegemony are necessary and some of the most
erudite challengers come from Muslim backgrounds. For this the world
must be grateful. American and British lies, propaganda, arrogance no
longer have the impact they once did. Iraq is a lesson I hope will not be
forgotten. But much is rotten within Muslim cultures and families and
this is not getting the attention it must. These pieces attempt to grapple
with many such impossible complexities. I am proudest of the column
which asked Muslims to condemn the Taliban. It was published the day
before the 9/11 attacks.

Satanic betrayals

New Statesman and Society, February 1989

Zaheera is a young Muslim teacher who left home in Bradford to escape a coercive family life. She has read The Book (Salman Rushdie's *The Satanic Verses*) and is deeply offended by some of the contents, by its mockery, but most of all by the repeated failure of the white community to understand how Muslims in Britain feel about their religion and their lives.

Zaheera is not one of the Ayatollah's fist-punching fanatics. She is very critical of some aspects of Islam life, particularly the invasions that have been made into the lives of Muslim women all over the world in the name of religion. She talks calmly. I do not want to see Salman die – that is immoral and wrong, and anyway not what the majority Muslim population here would want. I don't even think the book should be banned. But right from the beginning, I have felt that everyone was treating the Muslim protest as if it was completely crazy. This freedom of expression – why do we have pornography and libel laws and a law of blasphemy which only applies to Christianity? How can that be fair? How can they say this is a multi-racial country when there is one law for Christians and one for Muslims? And what hurts so much is that one of our own, someone I really used to admire, someone who stood up on television and told the white British how racist they were, has let us down so badly.'

The interviews with young Muslims carried out last week in Bradford, Southall and elsewhere by intrepid *Independent* reporters once more going forth to discover what the ethnics do/say/eat clearly indicated that however 'Westernised' the youngsters appeared to be, they feel hurt and humiliated by Rushdie. The intensity of their feeling was overwhelming and hard for a Westerner to comprehend.

Something has clearly happened to the Muslim community in the last few years (and possibly in less vociferous ways to the other Asian communities) which has made them defensive, uncompromising and at times separatist. During the crisis in Bradford in 1985 over the dismissal of Ray Honeyford, the headmaster who criticised anti-racist education in schools, one of the Muslim leaders who campaigned to have him removed. C. M. Khan opposed the moves taken by some Muslim parents to create all-Muslim schools in the area. He said then, 'We persuaded parents that to live in a mixed society they should bring their children up in multiracial schools.' Where do people like him stand now on this issue?

So what has gone wrong? One school of thought is that there is a global assertion of Islamic fundamentalism and that this episode is a part of that grand movement. But could there be a domestic explanation? – political pressures and tendencies within Britain which have created an atmosphere where the present Muslim campaign was inevitable? Pundits are now beginning to deliver their wise words. The august Peregrine Worsthorne opined, in a piece considered worthy of publication in both the *Sunday Telegraph* and the *Evening Standard*, that the fault lies with those wet liberals who glorified multiculturalism and multiracialism and got this country saddled with 'a million citizens who take religion, quite literally, with deadly seriousness.' Ignoring the slight inaccuracy of numbers, Worsthorne clearly believes that multiculturalism, a thoroughly bad idea to begin with, has gone too far. He would like to forcefully, incorporate the minorities into the British way of life.

This is also the opinion of people such as Ray Honeyford who said in 1985: 'The price to be paid for immigrants to live in Britain is the price immigrants have always paid, the pain of change and adaptation'. It is surely a sign of the time that BBC television is repeating a series entitled *The Triumph of the West*. There seems to be no recognition that all the communities that live in this country have to temper and change their cultural and religious positions and this includes the white population.

But the assaults on multiculturalism have also come from liberal sources, civil libertarians appalled by the Rushdie episode who feel that unacceptable behaviour is being tolerated under the cloak of multiculturalism. But It is hard to accept that argument on the Rushdie affair. Hugo Young who has written so well on the curtailments of freedom in this country should start from some of the same assumptions and reach the same conclusion as the leader writers of the *Sun, News of the World* and the *Star*. They all believe the motherland is a terribly tolerant country (give or take an Ireland of course). It is a glowing view that many black Britons may not share. Religious and cultural fanatics say the papers, can go to Iran. The *Star* even offers to pay for a one-way ticket.

The opposite point of view is represented by those who say that the growth of intolerance in some of the ethnic communities is the result of this country never really embracing multiculturalism, which entails a true recognition of equality and diversity and mutual respect. Roy Jenkins's call in 1966 for the creation of 'equal opportunity accompanied by cultural diversity in an atmosphere of mutual tolerance' was never seriously implemented. What happened was more of the 'sari, samosa and steelband' variety of multiculturalism. Institutions and laws never backed the principles up. This is why we can have the kind of illogicality which has infuriated the Muslim community – blasphemy laws for Christianity, and not for Islam. Meanwhile, the country has got harder and more indifferent to the plight of its minorities.

The real danger is that the actions of Muslim extremists allow the assault on multiculturalism to steam ahead. Teachers in schools can at the moment hardly teach about Islam as the faith which taught the West to revere wisdom and beauty, says Keith Ward, professor of history, and philosophy of religion at Kings' College, when it now comes in 'bearing gifts of fear and violence.' It's certainly clear that those who want to break multiculturalism are backing the separatist Muslim and anti-Rushdie campaign. Tory MP Nicholas Fairbairn, hit out at Rushdie last week, and the group which supported the white parents in Dewsbury are reported to be backing the all-Muslim school. And bit by bit the ghost of Ray Honeyford is being resurrected by those who want to do away with the gains made in multicultural awareness – the *News of the World* this week virtually canonised him.

The backlash has started already. Little Jeya, an eight-year-old Asian child next door, has come home crying three days in a row saying they call her a dirty Muslim. The teacher says it is the first time in her memory that Muslim has become a word of abuse.

God's own vigilantes

12 October 1998

'I don't shake hands with women.' says Rehman. 'Are you a Muslim anyway? Didn't your parents teach you nothing, like" I tell Rehman, who is one year older than my son, that his mother would be horrified to see him showing such disrespect to an elder. He comes down slightly from the edgy, hysterical heights he has been perching on. His intense brown eyes, though, still dart about reacting to every sound and imagined disturbance. He is thin, dressed in a baggy tracksuit with a face which reminds me of Jeremy Irons.

'Sorry, like. But you know it makes me very angry that our Muslim sisters are losing everything Islamic. Like you, why don't you cover your hair?'

I ignore this fresh insolence. After all, we are alone in a graveyard somewhere in a small town in Yorkshire. It is the only place Rehman could think of where he felt able to meet and talk. He has reasons to be scared witless. It has taken weeks of making contact, sending messages and patient groundwork to locate someone who will admit that he goes looking for runaway girls and women. Anonymous phone calls and off-the-record conversations confirm that Rehman is one of a large network of men. But they have gone underground even though, as Rehman says, they are doing God's work acting as moral vigilantes.

'I am a community investigator I help families to find their lost children. Those who are being stolen by the whites – like they stole black children before and adopted them and like they do with Aborigines in Australia. They are brainwashing our girls. I tell the families where they are hiding so that they can bring them home and show them the correct way.'

He shows me a rusty knife which he claims he used to slash off the hair of a cousin who came home with a perm. Does he get paid for this community service? He would not say but instead broke into another deeply felt speech on the poisonous spittle of the big, bad, Western wolf. Then he gets cross again.

'Don't write shit. I'll find you if you do. And don't say I'm a bounty hunter. I'll get into trouble like that Taher and Smiler.'

Taher and Smiler were featured on programmes about bounty hunters on Channel 4. Taher – a bald, fat, unpleasant chap – proudly went about breaking into women's refuges and 'persuading' distressed young women to go back to violent husbands or families. It was all for money really but carried in brown paper bags of sanctimony. After the broadcasts, local Asian women disguised in Talibanesque chadors, beat up one of these heroes. What a sight that must have been. He also lost his job. Apparently, Taher received death threats for shaming the community not by what he was doing but by bragging about it on television. Distorted lives bring such distorted values.

The programmes also showed the clients. One man, handsome like Al Pacino, wanted to reclaim his abused wife after she left him. His father spoke with moving dignity about how marriage was central to the Pathan way. He advised his hothead son not to fly into a rage but to be kind. And then, without changing his voice, added: 'Get her back. Then we can do what we want. You can set her alight.'

Other stories were just as chilling. All the while Taher is grunting on about how girls have no *izzat* (shame), no idea of family honour. Just like Rehman, only there is something about Rehman which redeems him, even as you feel the urge to throw him to the ground and place a stiletto heel over his neck until he apologises to womanhood. But merely to despise such men would be easy. We need to know them and learn why it is that in Bradford, Kirklees, Leeds, Halifax, Dewsbury, Huddersfield, Manchester and beyond they have made the control of young women in the community the focus of all their passions.

Rehman came here from rural Pakistan at the age of one. His mother is a widow. His father had a heart attack in the park and died alone in 1988. Rehman and his brother have two GCSEs between them. Their sister Samira – married off at sixteen in Pakistan – has seven GCSEs. Rehman says I can talk to her to see how the girls learn to be happy. We call from a cheap and cheerless international phone call shop with him hidden behind a Palestinian scarf. Samira sounds lively enough: 'I'm OK. Nobody spits on me here or calls me a Paki. My cousin's husband is a really nice person. But most of the other UK girls are so sad. Some have died, you know. They get beaten because they are too independent.' The call has to be terminated because Rehman has no more money and as a man he cannot let me pay.

The next day I get to meet other such men. Again they treat me with a mixture of contempt ('I don't care about those fucking Jewish-owned papers that you write for') and genuine regard granted automatically to someone older. This protocol has travelled down their ancestral bloodstream. I realise that like the young black men who give life meaning by becoming flash hoodlums, these men have created a role for themselves which gives them (dubious) status. Spectacularly failed by the education system and their parents who could not equip them for the world, they have fallen upon this dangerous option. The other is driving cabs. The two are intricately connected.

I spend three expensive hours cruising with Mahzer, a singing cabbie. He cannot read or write but can tell you exactly everything about every female pedestrian. Once or twice we reverse ominously as Mahzer tries to reassure himself that young women we have just passed are not up to mischief. Another taxi driver – with a *tasbi* (Islamic rosary) hanging down – tells me that, if it wasn't for them, all girls would be prostitutes. I learn later that he is a pimp who only deals in white girls. I feel sick with claustrophobia. Everyone knows everything about you here. They can find out your NI number, your refuge, the relevant benefit offices, or where you are within hours.

And this is one of the key reasons why so many girls and women are running away from home these days. Some 132 of them asked the police for help in 1995: by September this year the figure was up to 202. The post-seventies generation is dramatically over-represented. I met twenty of them. Most of all, they just wanted to be trusted and to have some choices. They wanted not to be watched for twenty-four hours – even when asleep. They were not craving the freedoms of their white peers. Only two had boyfriends. Seven had run away from newly imported husbands. Many had been badly beaten and emotionally depleted. One fifteen-year-old was kept isolated for three years in her bedroom. Sometimes all they want is higher education. Legends keep them going. Like the true story of a runaway who is now a graduate and successful businesswoman.

Philip Balmforth, Bradford police's community officer, is the indefatigable local scarlet pimpernel who rescues these girls and who arranges new lives, new identities. I once saw him confronting an Asian youth who was pacing the floor like a furious beast. He wanted his sister back. She was thirty and had been his prisoner for months. As a teenager, she had got pregnant and was then whisked off to Pakistan. After giving birth (the child, she says, was burnt alive in front of her) she was forced to marry a widower. She now has two daughters and is in this country refusing to go back. There are so many such stories in the women's refuges. Those who have fallen in love face the worst fates. Even if they get married they are recaptured through promises or threats and they 'disappear'.

Independent investigations have revealed that since abolition of the primary purpose immigration rule, forced marriages are rising. Home Office figures show that applications for visas for husbands have increased from 255 in 1997 to 1,132 in 1998. Many are perfectly legitimate marriages: some are cruel coercions. Desperate women, Muslims and Sikhs mostly, often contact me. Many more approach the High Commission or officials here. And yet this is not seen as a serious enough issue by our government. Because of dual nationality rights, British-born girls who end up in Pakistan are not considered our problem. What would happen if white British women were being brutalised abroad? Girls are dying and going mad on the subcontinent and here. Many are choosing suicide. But officialdom has retreated into silence. Balmforth is not allowed to talk to the press any more. Men threaten riots to stop his wortk. The Coroner's Office refuses to release any information about suspicious deaths of Asian women.

The good news is that key pillars of the community are now speaking out. Ishtiaq Ahmed of Bradford's Community Relations Council feels the pain of parents who fear cultural loss and family disintegration in the moral-free society which is what Britain seems to have become. But why are young men like Rehman so authoritarian? 'This is one way they can prove their loyalty, their value,' Ahmed says. He is clear though that none of this should condone inhumane behaviour. And he uses the words of the great religious leaders to explain to families that their actions are ungodly. 'We are giving our young people no choice but to reject us. Our good values will disappear.'

We Muslims must decry the Taliban

10 September 2001

Any Muslim trying to discuss in public the evils that the Taliban is doing in the name of Islam finds himself deluged with angry mail. You shouldn't be writing about the Taliban, say my co-religionists indignantly because 'it encourages stereotypes' about Muslims, or because it distracts from the issue that they regard as the only one worth worrying about, namely Islamaphobia in the West, or because they believe the Taliban has nothing to do with 'real Muslims', which, of course, they think I am not.

They will carry on denouncing me and others like me, as they do week after week, and meanwhile another horrific chapter unfolds in Afghanistan. The Supreme Court of Kabul in the Islamic Emirate of Afghanistan is about to decide on the fate of eight aid workers – four Germans, two Americans and two Australians – who have been accused of and tried for preaching Christianity. They have had no access to the basic rights one would expect if this was any kind of just process. Meanwhile, thousands of Afghanis are appearing as asylum-seekers around the world to be humiliated, perhaps even to die, a reminder of just what life is like under the Taliban.

Just before the farcical UN anti-racism conference in Durban (which thankfully ended this Sunday) I argued that I did not agree with this expensive, inflated and useless event. I felt it would force an ugly competition between the oppressed; groups would reproach each other without reflecting on their own failings and that it would not or could not deal with the most pressing injustices of our time.

For me, these are, without question, the latest Palestinian crisis and the brutish Taliban regime in Afghanistan. The first detonated, spreading yet more bitterness and hate among delegates in Durban, and the second was barely mentioned, in spite of the presence at the conference of some of the most powerful Muslims from Europe and the world who used their influence to great effect when calling for an end to Islamaphobia.

It could be argued that the Muslim delegates did not bring this up because the Taliban is not their responsibility. The regime is not truly Islamic. And, anyway, the panic generated about the Taliban is really best understood as yet another 'American phobia', an argument you will find running through September's *Impact International*, a serious monthly publication for Muslims worldwide.

Let us unpack each of these. Anything done in the name of Islam by self-identified Muslims must be the concern of all Muslims. We cannot be held responsible for these actions – as we so unfairly were when the Ayatollah Khomeini issued the fatwa against Salman Rushdie – but Muslims are brought up to think of themselves as members of a worldwide community, or *umma*, diverse in many ways but bound together through the basic beliefs of their faith. We have no right, therefore, to opt out of any situation which embarrasses us or which we find difficult to confront when it is happening in the name of Islam.

The second excuse is no more sustainable and yet it is used ever more readily to obfuscate the issue. Mention any of the evils which go on in the Muslim states (and evil goes on in all states, here as much as anywhere else, but is that any reason not to talk about particulars?) and you get these standard replies: 'Ah, but that is not what the Koran says.' 'Islam does not advocate that.' 'These are political battles, not the fault of religion.'

Let us accept these protestations as made in good faith; although if you took them seriously enough you would have to condemn the rulers of Saudi Arabia, Iran, Iraq, Afghanistan, Pakistan, and various other countries which, for example, wilfully violate all the human rights of women, even those guaranteed in the Koran.

But is it right or wise to ask you that you should be judged only for the theory, the most idealised thoughts and principles of your religion? Surely what matters is what Muslims do, how they behave, not how they might behave if they knew better? If committed Muslims really do believe that Islam can be a force of good in the world, why do they choose to ignore those people and regimes who corrupt this potential?

As for Uncle Sam, it is true that the US uses the Taliban and Iraq's President Saddam and others as excuses for its dangerous foreign policies. The Taliban is the bastard child of the Cold War in Afghanistan and, even now, I hear that eager Western moneymakers are happily doing business with it. But I still totally condemn the regime. It is responsible for a desolation which, says the veteran broadcaster John Simpson, is leading to an outflow of people as massive as the vast migrations of the Dark Ages. Most of these people are seeking refuge in Pakistan and Iran, but new Home Office figures reveal that Afghanis now make up the biggest group of asylum-seekers in this country.

Girls and women are being beaten, oppressed, denied health and education, hanged and stoned for the smallest transgressions. There are stories coming out of women's resistance groups which fight on and pay an unimaginable cost when they are found out. There can be no trust between the people any more. Spies and their threat to survival ensure that. The very fabric of that society is being burnt. What religion forbids the game of chess? Or old fables and songs? Joy itself is banned as it once was in Cambodia and also in China during the cultural revolution. Hindus and Sikhs have been forced to wear marked clothes to identify them.

This is not new in our history. There have always been major conflicts, the rise and fall of various interest groups in different parts of the world. From Moorish Spain to the Iranian revolution, cleansers have come forth to get rid of those they consider too lax and worldly. Even Engels (who was, in common with others of his time, quite openly racist about Orientals) wrote perceptively about this 'periodically recurring collision'.

But this latest virulent purification is happening in the twenty-first century, in a globalised world where the inalienable rights of men and women are becoming universal and non-negotiable.

As European Muslims we could, and must, do much more to push for these than we choose to do. The Muslim Parliament, the Muslim Council of Great Britain, Lord Ahmed, Baroness Uddin, Lord Patel, Mohammad Sarwar MP, *Muslim News*, all have considerable influence in the world today. So much so that Tony Blair has told them he carries a copy of the Koran as well as the Bible with him everywhere he goes.

So let us start publicly condemning the Taliban and call for the British government to stop deporting Afghanis who have fled here.

Why don't prominent British Muslims start collecting money and names for a full page newspaper advertisement to announce this? I'll put in £200 to start the ball rolling.

This fireball of fear and loathing

14 September 2001

'Anything done in the name of Islam by self-seeking Muslims must concern British Muslims, but we cannot be held responsible for these actions.' This is what I wrote in my column on Monday. How was I to know that, barely twenty-four hours later, Muslims around the world would be swept up in a fireball of fear, confusion, shame, anger, pity, sorrow and loathing for those who have again put us in this position where we are all now suspect, judged as terrorists or sympathisers of terrorism, as depraved curs who are determined to tear out the heart of modern civilisations?

And this is before we have any proof that the grotesque attacks on key American buildings were carried out by Muslim fanatics. If they were, we know we will all stand accused in the hearts and minds of millions of non-Muslims. The wave of sympathy we feel for the victims and their families (innocent Muslims may well be found among the many victims) and the fury rising in our communities against these violators of life and faith will not be noticed. Instead Islamophobia will once more erupt worldwide and be legitimised by some political leaders.

It is OK to hate a Muslim again. Already Russians are strutting about claiming vindication for their inhumane destruction of Chechnya and Israel is looking decidedly smug, expecting no more condemnations of its increasingly ruthless actions against Palestinians. Hindu fundamentalists have started e-mailing their anti-Muslim messages around the world and I have just heard that here a group of young Sikhs spat on and threw stones at some Muslims girls walking home from school. They were shouting abuse and accusing them of giving Asians a 'bad name'.

What will make the next months even harder is that the lunatic and murderous factions who call themselves Islamic will be encouraged by the power of their methods, and those who are brought up to hate the West (a hatred that too often works against them) will rejoice, and this, too, will add to our burdens. Living in the West we will be seen as the enemy within by both sides, and we now know just how this will press in on our lives.

Jewish and Irish Britons will understand what a difficult balancing act it is to walk that tightrope where you are furious and indignant for being held responsible for the evil actions of others, but you know you cannot claim absolute disconnection. Every time the IRA bombs mainland Britain, Irish Britons find themselves under suspicion. Jewish Britons these days are frequently asked to pronounce on Sharon as if they have to make constant pledges in order to remain on the left side of liberalism. None of us caught in this can avoid thick and steady guilt that soon overwhelms, especially in the aftermath of truly horrific events.

It is far, far worse if you are a liberal Muslim or a Muslim whose faith lives comfortably with the values of the West. Most American and European Muslims would say this about their lives. They have many justifiable complaints about discrimination and the hatred that they face, but many of us now see ourselves as people of Europe, not just Muslims who happen to be in Europe. That is not how we are perceived by the West, and there are many Muslims who abhor this integrationist position.

I have already heard from young Muslims who defend the Taliban and burn with anti-US sentiments. I share some of these. US policy in Iraq and Israel upset the mildest of us, but, no, we would not kill American citizens to avenge these, nor would we make excuses for those who do. But who cares about these distinctions? All Pakis are now terrorists and so fair game. So we brace ourselves again for a period of bile and beatings and hate mail and furious writers who will take no time to reflect but will decry Islam and Muslims. Remember the prophetic pronouncements of Bernard Levin after Oklahoma? 'Do you realise?' he thundered. 'In half a century, no more, fanatical Muslims will be winning wars around the world and Oklahoma will be called Khartoum on the Mississippi.' The newspaper *Today* had a picture of a fireman holding a baby with the headline 'In the name of Islam'. It turned out to be all-American white boys who had plotted this barbarism but the prejudices remained intact.

I presented a documentary for Channel 4 in the aftermath of the Oklahoma bombing. In the US, Senator Dave McCurdy and Jeff Kaymen, a Washington writer, were both responsible for careless and emotive outbursts against Muslim extremists they say plot and live in the US. They were unrepentant when they found that they were wrong. In that time and space between blame and truth, Muslims in the US lived through hell. Their children were abused and attacked in schools, homes were stoned and mosques shot at. One Iraqi woman I interviewed, a refugee, had a miscarriage at seven months in front of her three-year-old after she had to barricade herself against a mob throwing stones outside her small house. It will be much worse this time because it looks as if it just may be 'Muslims' who carried out the atrocities.

It has begun here too, although there is a real shift in unexpected places. In the *Sun* yesterday, there was a 'map of evil' giving information about Muslim regimes and troublemakers around the world. But, and this is astonishing, the editorial across two pages said that it is wrong to malign Islam and Muslims every time such evil actions erupt. Quite right too. We don't say that Christianity is to blame for the ugly scenes outside the Holy Cross school in Northern Ireland. The *Mail*, too, was surprisingly measured. Tony Blair has been brilliant, using his emotions and language with care and precision so that he doesn't appear to be condemning all Muslims for what has happened. But people don't always take much notice, and, anyway, you can't undo years of demonisation with a sudden outbreak of reason and caution among the influential classes, welcome though it is.

Muslim women friends of mine have today stopped wearing hejab and my mother has told me not to wear shalwar khameez but saris over the next few weeks. People have been phoning saying they are too terrified to go out. One mother in Halifax says that her child was kicked in the playground and called a terrorist. Muslims at university tell me that they are being picked on by their peers and accused of being members of militant groups.

I was in Newtown, in Birmingham, on Tuesday at a conference on gender equality. The Muslim mothers left early because they were worried about getting their children indoors before sunset. One of them, a youth worker, said: 'What can I do to show them that I am not a killer of Americans? Can I give them my blood, can I write to somebody, what can I do so they don't hate me and think I hate all white people?'

On the way to the station from this impoverished area, I saw graffiti that had already gone up to strike at anyone who might try and comfort themselves that these were phantom fears: 'Go home fucking terrorist islames (sic) or die. Revenge is coming.' It was signed 'BNP'.

Don't tell me how I should worship

15 October 2001

With the entire world whipped up, anxious and alert, questions are being asked by Muslims which would never have arisen before. Through internet networks they are feverishly discussing the war, why Muslims are so despised and the shame (deeply important word this for Muslims) that so much corruption, violation and authoritarianism is found in Muslim countries and communities across the globe.

This last issue, especially, has taken on an urgency and honesty I have not seen before. Perhaps it is because more of us realise that our lives depend on confronting these ugly realities. We Muslims can only survive onslaughts, both real and ideological, if we become more astute and less defensive.

A fortnight ago, on a special Jonathan Dimbleby programme about Islam, Dr Ghada Karmi, a respected Palestinian academic who describes herself as a 'cultural Muslim', pointed out – with great bravery I thought – that Islam had never gone through a reformation, implying that this had to be the next step. I agree.

But first the many caveats. I don't mean we must jump on the liberal high horse that would have their own values as superior to anyone else's. As Richard Webster pointed out in his indispensable little book, *A Brief History of Blasphemy*: what the most extreme liberals are advocating, whether by intention or default, is the right to proclaim the superiority of their own revelation and to abuse the gods who are worshipped by other, supposedly inferior cultures. During the Rushdie crisis this army took up words (their arms) to reassert this message and worse. I look back at the hundreds of cuttings I collected then and even now feel shaken by the names, the tone and the content of what was hurled at us all, all Muslims.

Michael Foot proclaimed that Islam was 'the great persisting threat to the world'; Roy Jenkins regretted that so many Muslims were allowed to settle in this country; Hugo Young ordered us to go back where we came from; Connor Cruise O'Brien declared Islam a 'sick' religion. These were not right-wing ravings but the words of eminent people, habitual advocates of equality and justice. But then the founding fathers of liberalism believed utterly in the superiority of European societies.

J. S. Mill thought non-Europeans were 'backward' and incapable of self-regeneration and self-analysis. Today, other such voices reveal their true distaste of Muslims (many are seen soulfully clutching abridged versions of the Koran as if a couple of days' reading will get them up to speed and help fine-tune their attacks) and this time they are louder and brasher because of the horror we have just witnessed.

Enlightened Muslims have an almost impossible role, but it is one which must be taken up. We must continue to rebut the foolish claims of fundamentalist liberals and remind them of the distressed, atomised and utterly lonely society which they have created through aggressive individualism, where the habits of obligation and duty have been obliterated. But whatever our feelings about this and the failures of the West in Afghanistan, Iraq, Palestine, or colonialism and the unbearable US hypocrisy and hubris, we must act to stop the rot within.

I understand the pressures of this strange war but this is not the time to suspend such self-interrogation. There is an urgent need to start up a dialogue and momentum which will help reform Islamic societies to stop the descent into a new dark age.

This could be done in two ways. The first, perfectly respectable, has already been embarked upon by Muslim clerics and scholars. Dr Zaki Badawi of the Muslim College and Rana Kabbani and Sarah Sheriff, two writers, have gone back to source to painstakingly explain the meanings and metaphors in the Koran. This may, they hope, deter those easily led to wild and unholy acts by barbaric mullahs who want to take us all to hell. In her book, *Women's Rights in Islam*, Sheriff reminds Muslims that the Prophet said: 'Whoever had a daughter and did not bury her alive, nor insult her nor favour his son over her, Allah will enter him to paradise.' Muslim women were also given the right to sexual satisfaction and education. The reformation therefore could be to promote the 'truth'.

I prefer a second way or perhaps another parallel route to create a progressive force within Muslim communities. This would take a historical rather than theological approach. We need to demolish the idea of a uniform *umma*, the worldwide community of Muslims supposedly identical and unchangeable. Yes, we have these threads which connect us and they are the five eternal and immutable principles, belief in Allah, prayers, fasting, *zakat* (charity) and pilgrimage to the holy cities. But beyond these there have always been differences, disagreements, various political and cultural alliances. In Pakistan, Sunnis, Shias and the different factions with are facing growing friction as the boulder of the Taliban's demanding, hardline Islam begins to smash them.

Two Muslim sub-groups, the Ahmedis and Ismailis (my community, which has adherents in Tajikistan, Afghanistan and which has built hospitals, universities and schools across Pakistan), have already experienced these pressures. I find it ironic that Muslims who insist that Western countries should respect diversity ignore the way hegemonic Islamicists are crushing all diversity within. I have never worn hejab; nor did my mother or grandmother. Our imam in the fifties told families to stop the practice and to educate their daughters. Now, Muslim men and women accost us in the streets and instruct us to submit to the hejab. I find this intrusive and contemptible. Who are they to tell me how to worship?

We should learn from the periods when Islam was quietly confident, open, culturally promiscuous and just. The city of Sarajevo, for five-hundred years, was among the best of what we were capable. So were Granada, Delhi and the Persian cities. A civilisation cannot survive without diversification, evolution, change, cultural and technological trade and cooperation. Most British Muslims would not be able to live in Pakistan or Iran now because British values are too deeply inside them. There is no conflict between modernity and Islam and the many successful yet faithful Muslim intellectuals, professionals (Dr Magdi Yacoub for one) and techno-wizards will tell you so if you care to talk to them and not the maniacs who want to kill the West or the rambling Francis Fukuyama who believes in the clash of civilisations.

Our reformation must be built on human rights which are not 'Western' but universally agreed. Please explain to me how the five pillars disallow equality, rule of law, democracy, freedom to choose, and personal autonomy? We are doomed unless we begin this process. In 1970, the relatively unknown British poet Basil Bunting wrote: 'Sooner or later we must absorb Islam if our own culture is not to die of anaemia.' Now we have the same fears about Muslim cultures. We will haemorrhage, bleed, spill blood and surely die of that loss unless we now learn to absorb the best ideas in the world.

We British Muslims must reclaim our faith from the fanatics

5 November 2001

For the past few years, well-intentioned Muslims have backed an annual Islam Awareness week to disseminate positive images of Muslims in this country. Like Black History Month, the aim is not to be too controversial but to inform and educate those who are wilfully or otherwise ignorant about the faith at its best and its millions of blameless followers – a PR exercise and one that was felt to be necessary because of mounting Islamaphobia.

This week it is upon us again, but in the choppy, howling world we suddenly find ourselves in today, the original good-news agenda appears tawdry, self-deluding and inappropriate. A tea party in the trenches is not a good idea.

Polite discourse on the nobility of Islam will do nothing to stem the sickening racial prejudices that are re-emerging with a vengeance. Bigoted white Britons (of all classes) now think they have right on their side and so they crush and demean Asian Britons because brown-skinned people are all damned Pakis who support terrorism that kills their sweet American brothers and sisters.

Do-good platitudes will not discourage alarmist reports in the media, now possessed by fears of enemies within, real and imagined. Yesterday a newspaper claimed that its poll of 1,170 Muslims (the first such survey to date) showed that one in ten Muslims approved of the attacks in the US and 40 per cent backed bin Laden. We are not told precisely where this 'random' sample was carried out, and there is obviously a lot of scope to prejudice results by choosing certain sampling points, and the questions were designed to entrap. But my English mother-in-law and her neighbours in Sussex will not know that, will they, as they read this paper of authority?

Those frantic suddenly to know the truths about Islam don't need this awareness week, either. My dears, you can't take a teeny step in

248

any direction in our press these days without being accosted by learned white journalists delivering detailed sermons on the Koran (Blair and Straw are also experts on this suddenly) or on various manifestations of Islam and ever more obscure cults and charismatic leaders. Thanks to these newest of Islamic scholars, I have discovered Deobandic Islam in India that forbids the use of chairs and Sayyid Qutb, 'the father of modern Islamic fundamentalism', an Egyptian whose loathing of the West was triggered by a drunk American woman who tried to seduce him on a liner in 1948. So all this is her fault then!

Or it could be Wahhabism, the uncompromising form of Islam that dominates in Saudi Arabia and that has been successfully exported all over the world. I even learnt that, until recently, Muslims could openly (not secretly, like some do now) drink alcohol and that many traditional medicine books recommended wine. With so much information sloshing about, why waste the week on awareness-raising?

It is impossible today not to feel that a little less 'Islamic awareness' would be a very good thing for those al-Morons who daily pronounce on the evil that is the West and who call upon all Muslims to fight for the Taliban, whose exemplary Islam has destroyed one half of Afghanistan's population – the mothers, sisters, wives and daughters – and incarcerated them in the world's first mobile prisons.

They didn't go to fight the Serbs when the Muslims of Kosovo and Bosnia needed all the help that they could get. No, because those European Muslims represented modernity and cosmopolitanism, not the barbarism that calls itself Islam and is on the ascendancy today not only in Lahore and in Kabul but also in Bradford and in Birmingham.

We British Muslims, with all our diversities and conflicts, are more in crisis today than ever. The fanatics have taken over the asylum, and quiet moderation may no longer be enough to reclaim the faith. Time now for the brave among us to say that we do not wish to be united with the extremists just because they are Muslims. Name them please, the mullahs in mosques, the Muslim and non-Muslim local and national politicians who have in part created the monstrous men we see on the streets who want the Taliban in Westminster.

Let us reflect, too, on how this crisis is affecting other visible groups and, indeed, ask how Hindus, Sikhs, Buddhists, Jews, Baha'is and Jehovah's Witnesses manage to retain their faiths without bullying this nation? They too face discrimination and fear assimilation. But they see themselves as part of a Western democracy, not against it and against everyone else.

In recent years, too many young British Muslims have rejected anti-racist groups and other communities in the name of their superior Islam. They write to me mostly to tell me that I identify too much with Asians or blacks. True. My Islamic identity is above all humanistic. This is the message that Islam Awareness week could usefully try and impart to the too many xenophobic Muslims we have around us today.

We might also begin more open discussions about the forced marriages (a new government report this Tuesday will show how many of these are found mostly among British Muslims), drugs and degeneracy that are destroying Muslim family life. Women and men are running away because they cannot surrender their free will to cruel authoritarian elders.

This awareness week needs also to launch more media rebuttal networks – we already have some very good ones that are making an impact. We must imprint on the national consciousness the complex views held by moderate Western Muslims about the war. Most want the bombings stopped immediately because we are killing innocents who have suffered enough. They abhor bin Laden and extremists and those (whoever they are, because I am not sure I know) responsible for the carnage in the US.

They do not trust the US government to do what is right and resent the rhetoric of Western political leaders, which implies that American lives are infinitely more valuable (so we must remember them and evoke them in our hearts) than all those Afghans we are killing and than those Iraqis who are now abandoning their babies because they cannot bear to watch them die for lack of medicines and other basics. Such a radical agenda would make the awareness week make sense. Otherwise I can't see the point.

Ramadan's true spirit is threatened

19 November 2001

Normally Ramadan, which just started, would see Muslims around the world willingly laying down their many differences, even enmities, to submit to the tough discipline of fasting, one of the five pillars of Islam which binds them together. The month should bring greater empathy with the poor and oppressed, honest introspection, kindness, peace and sublimation.

All hardships – internal and external – hurt less for a while and even among the most deprived British Muslims, a temporary but important confidence and renewed faith settles in. The most defective and deficient Muslims (and there are many of us) feel drawn to the vast canopy of Islam at this time. We are always welcomed in by our less flawed brethren, who know that after Eid they will once more have to show their disapproval of our maverick ways.

The war and 11 September have torn through all of that. Now this sense of warm universal belonging is constantly interrupted by the desperate desire to disconnect from various vocal Muslims and their dangerous rhetoric which threatens to subsume us. Every day dozens of Muslims are contradicting these spokespeople and asserting their own independent views. Never in my life have I seen so many well-articulated and argumentative letters in the newspapers from ethnically diverse British Muslims – men and women, old and young, middle class and working class, Sunnis and Shias – all expressing a vast variety of opinions on the situation.

Networks of young Muslim professionals have emerged as an energetic and dynamic rapid rebuttal force. They respond, positively and negatively, in numbers, to journalists in the mainstream and the Muslim media. They managed recently to push off course an incendiary Kilroy programme which was to star big-name Muslim fanatics.

Moderates are finally emerging from the shadows because they know that if they don't, the extremists and the unthinking, already

251

too much in evidence, will push forth their indescribably hateful views and make us all suffer the consequences. Attacks and verbal abuse suffered by people with brown skins have risen by 30 per cent since the catastrophic attacks in the US and every time Omar Bakri and his gang speak out, this gets worse still. Asian taxi drivers get beaten up, Muslim women are spat at and shoved off pavements and our children get kicked and taunted.

The bad news is that the media shuts the door on British Muslims with diverse, intelligent, unconventional ideas. I can't tell you how many calls I have had from television or radio programme researchers asking me if I am anti- or pro- war. When I explain that I support intervention and am wholly against the Taliban but that I oppose the wild bombing and am afraid of what comes next, interest evaporates. They need someone who takes 'a clearer line' and is 'representative'.

Most editors only want to hear Muslim interviewees who either sound violently anti-Western (because it is always so exciting) or those who will say that Blair and Bush really really love Islam and therefore must be supported in all that they wish to do.

Another kind of Muslim voice which is becoming popular is that of the bloke (one a day, it seems lately) on the *Today* programme or other flagships who cannot communicate well in English and can therefore be patronised or ridiculed. Producers would prefer us to present ourselves as cut-throats, clowns or blockheads. All three exist in abundance among British Muslims, as they do among all other groups, but it is a travesty of democracy to exclude the millions of Britons who are trying to deal with their responsibilities as Muslims and who are now permanently in the West, and not just camping here in Bedouin tents.

Because of effective protests against this deliberate manipulation of expressed opinion, we have now been given 'scientific evidence' which allegedly shows that most British Muslims are against the war and that large numbers back Mr bin Laden. First, a newspaper gave us survey results to prove that Muslims are 'unpatriotic'. Four out of ten Muslims believe 'bin Laden had reason to mount war against the US' and that British Muslims should fight with the Taliban. It turns out this study was carried out by enthusiastic reporters outside targeted mosques on a Friday and in a few known Muslim residential areas. The questions and answers were twisted to suit a pre-set agenda.

Next came an ICM poll of five-hundred Muslims commissioned by the BBC which was, at least, carried out by reputable pollsters. But look closely and you discover only 31 per cent of the interviewees were over 34 and 69 per cent were men. This explains why 80 per cent oppose the military action in Afghanistan and 57 per cent do not believe Tony Blair when he says that the war is not against Islam.

We are not the enemy within. I have not met or heard from one Muslim who thinks 5,000 plus people deserved to be turned to ash. What I have heard is that the US has become too arrogant and self-serving; that it supports intolerant regimes which have destroyed liberal Muslim voices in the Islamic world; that the West has always exploited the rest of the world and needs a new enemy after the Cold War; that the Taliban and Mr bin Laden were monsters created in part by the West.

I have also heard, time and gain, that it is vital for Muslims to use this moment to rethink their futures and to stop the pressure to conform to one, imposed, ruthless, joyless, political Islam; that Israel has blackmailed the world long enough; that the West is killing Iraq slowly; that it is foolish to say that our young people should fight for the Taliban to defend Islam, seeing as all Afghanis, including the Northern Alliance, are Muslims; that the bombing was wrong and was used to satisfy the bloodlust of angry America; that unless Muslim women are given their rights, we will not deserve any respect; that we must fight to keep diversity and critical conversations alive.

Complicated positions about values also confound clever-dick headline writers. I love my Western freedoms and rights but I hate the excessive booze-and-sex popular culture which is threatening to drown us all, black and white. I'm trying to teach my children to respect older people and learn the importance of self-sacrifice, self-restraint and prayer.

I will never, ever (even if Mr Blunkett detains me indefinitely), say that the West is the centre of civilisation. We, the children of the Empire, know well the barbarisms, past and present, which have flown from Western ambitions and greed. But the West has given us technological innovations and invaluable principles to build good societies and almost all post-colonial Muslim leaders have stamped out lives, rights, aspirations and dreams.

All these thoughts, contradictions, cross-currents of pessimistic anger and optimistic determination are invading the spirit of Ramadan. American Thanksgiving this weekend, once a simple affirming occasion, will feel even more charged and emotional. Everything did change on 11 September.

The beauty secrets of Asian women

26 November 2001

Two separate stories, seemingly unconnected but actually entwined, emerged this weekend, each in its own way questioning the idea that Muslim women who wear hejab or the burka are serene and content with the way they look, untouched by the punishing pressures of media-generated beauty myths which have left most of the rest of us unable to live in peace with our faces and bodies.

Story No 1: a study published in the *International Journal of Eating Disorders* reveals that the veil does not protect women from those compulsions and anxieties which flow from feeling physically imperfect.

The study, by Tracy Mann, a professor of health psychology at the University of California in Los Angeles, compared female Iranian university students in Tehran with those studying in Western universities. Professor Mann wanted to find out whether attitudes to beauty and body shape differed significantly and to test whether media images were causing higher levels of eating disorders and anorexia in Western countries.

The results were startling. Women in Iran were just as obsessed with their weight as those in the West and were as likely to suffer from eating disorders. What's more, they felt they needed to lose twice as much weight, on average, as their Western counterparts.

Story No 2: news is emerging, so my human rights friends in Pakistan tell me, of how the Taliban tortured women in prisons for disobedience to their menfolk, for alleged immodesty or adultery, for being suspected of political activities and for being interested in make-up and ornaments. In the women's prison in Kabul, they have found lipsticks, bangles, perfume, even stockings, all evidence, apparently, of the depravity which the regime wanted to stamp out. So behind that moving shroud (And please don't tell me women must want the burqa because they have not all thrown it off to dance semi-naked in the streets. They can't give up something that they have lived under for so many years without fear and they don't trust the men from the Northern Alliance not to violate them). these women still felt the need to adorn themselves, even when they knew that it might lead them into a torture chamber. In two cases, my informants tell me, their husbands reported them to the Taliban because they hated the women making themselves look beautiful, even though they were seen only by other women, mostly in the family.

There has been much argument this week over whether Cherie Blair was right to say that the burka worn by the women of Afghanistan symbolises utter degradation and oppression. Perhaps it is to be expected that those for and against this position have argued loudly and with immovable conviction. Uproar on both sides. Feminists and liberals wholly applauded her statements while devotees of the hejab hated her presumptuousness and felt she had no business attacking religious and cultural practices which she knew nothing about. Did she not understand that covered women had greater freedoms and equality than Western women?

In her book, *A Glimpse Through Purdah* (1999), researcher Sitara Khan, who works in Yorkshire, found these views were widespread among the Muslims she interviewed. One reader's letter to a newspaper captured what I have heard many times over: 'I wear the burka, and would want my daughters to because this frees us from the horrible looks and wants of men outside the family and also makes us happy to be what we are. I don't need to diet, or to colour my lips. My husband likes me how I am and always will. Non-Muslim women [have] nervous breakdowns because they must be young for ever and look like film stars.'

As ever, the truth is more messy and complex and I hope the stories I alluded to will lead us to reconsider the bland and brash statements we have all been making on the lives and desires of women in veils. I am convinced that Western ideas of beauty have been stamped across the world and that it is hard not to be influenced by them. I cannot look in the mirror without feeling a failure because the whole world is thinner, younger and indescribably lovelier.

Bollywood actresses were once plump and pretty and of all ages. Now they all look like Cindy Crawford and seem always to wear green contacts to hide their dark eyes. The same is true in Africa and elsewhere. Maybe the Iranian women are simply reflecting this other pernicious kind of globalisation.

But it could be that these anxieties are worse for Iranian and other veiled women because they are so desperate to get some kind of control over their lives, some kind of autonomy, in an existence which offers so little personal freedom and choice. I wonder if being forced to wear the veil (as happened to educated women in Iran during the revolution, when they were imprisoned and beaten if they refused to cover themselves) made them start to focus inwards. Denied the right to be attractive in public places, perhaps they become obsessed with attractiveness in private places, inside their cloaks. Professor Mann found that Iranian women in Tehran craved empty stomachs and hard exercise regimes.

Remember, too, that these societies, which allow men so many more rights, may be making women fearful that they will be easily discarded. Mary Wollstonecraft was right when she wrote in *A Vindication of the Rights of Women*: 'Taught from infancy that beauty is woman's sceptre, the mind shapes itself to the body and roaming round in its gilt cage, only seeks to adorn its prison.' I know many Arab women who wear the burka and who spend a fortune on make-up, expensive perfumes and fabulous underwear and who queue up in Harley Street for cosmetic surgery, especially when they get to their thirties and begin to fear that their husbands will dump them for younger wives. But maybe it is subversion which motivates all this beautifying and ornamentation. This may be how Afghan and Iranian women reclaim some power. Even in the worst days of Taliban rule, secret beauty salons in the backs of houses still permed, hennaed and waxed hair and had fun little make-up parties where they could defy the powers and regain some joy in their bleak lives.

I met a student from Afghanistan in April who is studying beauty and hairdressing in London. She chooses to wear the hejab but this, she tells me, is 'nothing, just a scarf. Doesn't mean I don't like make-up or nice things like you'. She can't wait, she told me, to get back to Kabul. 'Women here are so busy they have no time to look beautiful. At home they have so much time so they sit all the afternoon making their skin and hair look beautiful, to make fashionable clothes, not for the men but each other. This is important for us, so please understand and don't just think we are stupid like quiet cows under a stick.' One day, perhaps, such activities will once more be possible and my friend will go back and open her salon. I accept that for her and others this beauty business is empowerment. But I fear that for others, like the anorexic Muslim women in Tehran, it is an expression of self-doubt and desperation. And we should all be concerned about that.

Taking the wrap

23 October 2003

There have never been so many covered heads among British Muslim women. It is a trend that is blazing its way across neighbourhoods, schools, colleges and workplaces. Even the Metropolitan Police, despite its present difficulties with racism, has recently adopted a uniform scarf. Go to any big store, use any public transport, or visit almost any public place, and you are as likely as not to see headscarves, in all shapes and forms, an accepted feature of our multicultural landscape. People are now so used to seeing female workers with their hair wrapped in the 'hijab' that they barely notice any more.

Karen Allen, a 28-year-old scheduler for Sky TV, speaks for many when she says that, after an initial period of jibes when she first converted to Islam and the hijab, 'people are fine now. They say things like: `That's a nice one you're wearing today."

But there is also a sense in which the hijab has never been more controversial. In France, the suspension of two sisters for wearing headscarves at their Paris school last month has rekindled a fierce debate over the nation's commitment to secularism. In Germany, an Afghan-born teacher was barred from wearing a headscarf at work in a Stuttgart school. Last month, Germany's highest court decided that the school's authorities had acted illegally, but ensured that the controversy will rumble on by ruling that, in future, federal states should have the final say in such cases.

There are similar arguments raging in Oklahoma and Quebec, where hijab-wearing schoolgirls have also been ostracised by the authorities.

Meanwhile in Britain, at the end of this month, committal proceedings will take place in the case of Hazel Dick, a 42-year-old science teacher from Peterborough, who has been charged with religiously aggravated assault after allegedly forcing a Muslim pupil to remove her hijab – a charge which she denies.

If Dick did object unreasonably to this garment, though, she was out of synch with British society, which has not reacted towards the hijab with undue nationalistic panic. Apart from some unbending commentators who loathe it, public attitudes have shifted over the last two decades towards acceptance.

Among British Muslims, however, the hijab continues to occupy the most contested of spaces. I spent several days this spring talking to British Muslim women across the country, old and young, about their lives and the future. They had thought deeply about the many challenges facing their faith, especially since the attacks in America in September 2001 and the more recent crises over Iraq and the Middle East.

They all agreed on global politics – the lies told about Iraq, the Palestine situation, the immoral foreign and trade policies of the West, shameful Muslim regimes. But there were almost unbridgeable divisions between them about what makes a good Muslim. The hijab usually embodied this rift.

First, the arguments against.

Zarina, a primary school teacher, told me of her experiences on the streets of Birmingham. 'I wear a *shalwar* [a long tunic] but no head covering. Twice, young Muslim men have stopped their cars to abuse me, spit at me and one even came out and slapped me. Who do these people think they are?'

I have seen this with my own eyes: religious vigilantes threatening and hitting women in the streets because of what they are wearing, or not wearing.

Rumy Husan, of the Leeds Business School, says: 'Who sets the limits of acceptability and on what criteria? The practice of veiling is foisted on women and girls often through coercion and emotional blackmail.'

For Muslim modernists, Islam was born at a particular time and in a specific location. It cannot be seen in ahistorical terms. Many of the directives in the key Islamic texts were relevant to those days. It is not incumbent upon women to shroud their hair and bodies, they say; the only compulsion is to dress with modesty. Ultra-modernists argue that one can be a faithful believer in the shortest of skirts because what matters is how you feel inside.

260

For literalists, on the other hand, every word in the old books must be followed to the last letter. Interestingly, though, these 'true' Muslims don't ride camels through the streets of our cities (because that is what the Prophet did) or demand that British law should recognise polygamy and stoning for adultery. They, too, have moved on – but not with regard to the hijab.

Leila Babes, a Muslim sociologist in France, writes persuasively about the right of all Muslims to interpret texts personally without the 'faith police' telling us they know best. Such new thinkers are important for Islam as it struggles with modernity. The revelations in Mecca focused on eternal spiritual messages, but subsequent legal rules are open to debate and interpretation.

Some Muslim intellectuals believe veiling applied only to the Prophet and his family, to protect them from petitioners. But there is a directive in the Koran for women to 'pull close together to themselves' part of their dresses when with men, and to 'draw their headdresses over their bosoms', and it is these directives that are cited by defenders of the practice. Technically, they are completely in the right. But then again, a man is also given the right to chastise his wife (physically) if she fails to comply with her conjugal duty, and no Muslim woman I know would ever comply with that today.

According to Rana Kabbani, author of *Imperial Fictions*, the practice of hijab-wearing was adopted by Muslims during the Byzantine period, when affluent women covered themselves to avoid hungry looks from the rabble. Another theory is that the garment was made obligatory when wars had created many widows and rape was rampant. (This is why women in rural Afghanistan refuse to shed their chadors.)

Politics has made and unmade the hijab throughout history. After decolonisation, powerful Muslim women threw off their veils to follow the secular road to selfhood. The shah of Iran, rulers of Turkey, Tunisia and others dictated that this was compulsory progress, together with education for the females in their domains. It was an uncritical emulation of the West, but women were unquestionably given roles and opportunities they had never had before.

Their daughters later threw the veil back on to show their contempt for the West and its secular values, in the first instance in Iran during the Khomeini revolution.

In Britain, the revival gathered pace in 1989 when the *The Satanic Verses* furore erupted and Muslims felt their faith and identities were under unfair attack.

The revivalists were also rejecting the servility, silence and unnecessary gratitude they had seen in their own parents who had settled in this country and carried on quietly in spite of years of racism. Like black pride in previous decades when afros were proudly worn, the hijab was a defiant sign of reclamation. But even as this garment was being embraced in Britain, women and girls in Algeria, Afghanistan and Iran were being beaten and imprisoned for resisting their enforced veiling. Some are still dying for the right not to cover themselves.

There is no doubt that many women make the choice to take the hijab, but nobody can seriously claim that this is true of all those who cover their heads. What do committed hijabis say? I sought out dozens of them. Some refused to speak to me (one told me she only spoke to real Muslims, not fake ones like me), but the rest were happy, persuasive and thoughtful (though some preferred to remain anonymous). And some were radiantly lovely, with the hijab framing perfect faces.

'Why don't you try and wear a hijab, see how wonderful it makes you feel?' said one sister, a lovely woman, S, with a bright smile enhanced by glossy lipstick.

'No, I don't want to,' I replied.

'Just try it for one day, just for me, and see how free you feel.'

'But I do feel free.'

'See how much respect you will get from everyone,' prompted her friend, F, who was also a hijabi.

'I get respect from around the world whatever I wear.'

'What will you do if your daughter wants to wear one? I am the only one in the family who wears hijab, not my mum or sisters or aunts.' S, again.

That one got to me. For, truth to tell, although I don't want this for my daughter, I would never try to stop her.

Samia, a science undergraduate, chose the hijab because, 'men are weak, men have no control over their physical needs. We must therefore not give them the occasion to think these thoughts on the streets.' She talks with the slow speed of a sage. But they think them anyway, like most other men, I argue. For religious police in Saudi Arabia, even shrouded women are deeply lascivious. They want to ban women from public spaces altogether. And anyway, I ask Samia, Nusrat, Layla and others, how dreadfully unfair is this to Muslim men, to believe they are not capable of self-control? And does this then give them licence to disrespect and fantasise about the majority of women around the world who do not wear the hijab?

'No,' says Layla, who looks exactly like the younger Audrey Hepburn in *The Nun's Story.* 'We are only helping men to become better Muslims. And anyway, what is making the bigger problems in our society – half-naked teenagers who get drunk and pregnant, or us hijabis?'

An excellent question that all of us must answer. Muslim families are exerting what Lord Parekh of Kingston upon Hull calls 'moral self-defence' against the chaos and liberal tolerance of anything that people choose to do in private and public. They have the same worries as the readers of the *Daily Mail*, but they respond by putting up a barrier between their girls and the 'dirt' all around them. I can understand this as my own sense of fear grows for my daughter. Besides, as a wonderful book, *Veil: Veiling, Representation and Contemporary Art* (edited by David Bailey and Gilane Tawadros) reveals, the hijab does not necessarily thwart the creative spirit of Muslim women.

Then there are the obvious hypocrisies in our societies.

I went to Barcelona a few weeks back to talk about immigration and national identity. A curator of a Catalonian museum asked why Europeans are so disgusted by the hijab, yet respect nuns on their streets and Catholic women who wear headscarves. From the pictures of the Madonna to the most extravagant bridal outfits, West to East, the veil is loved, painted, written and sung about. It makes your sexuality sacred. Do liberal secularists ever rage against these images? Or protest that the veil lifted in church for that first kiss with the bride is an affront? The catwalks, too, are replete with the veil as a symbol of beauty, enticement and femininity.

Other pro-hijab arguments are much less compelling. Hijabis say they are free from the pressures of the beauty myths which debase women. This is true up to a point. But research shows that women in Iran suffer from more food disorders and body-image problems than Iranian women in the US. I have seen rows of anti-cellulite cream in mosque shops, and many Muslim women are as terrified as the rest that their men will get younger wives.

As for capping male desire – I wish. Haleh Afshar, an Iranian intellectual, told me once that a white policeman begged her for photos of veiled women. I, too, have such letters from white men, saying it must be like unwrapping presents, and others who want utterly to own a woman.

The fact remains, also, that many of the proudest Muslim women in the world, from Baroness Uddin to the Nobel Peace Prize-winner Shirin Ebadi, are not hijabis. If they go to hell I hope I am with them.

And what are we to make of those subversive hijabis who beautify the scarf with lace, or CK logos, or wear bright, bold turbans designed to turn heads? Or those who use it strategically? Shazia Mirza, the stand-up comic, wears one to add a frisson to her show (she does not wear it on the street), Jemima Khan when she is expressing her Muslim identity. There are still situations where the hijab is enforced as a mark of control. Too many young girls believe they must cover themselves, and the pressure is getting worse. Among some British Muslims, the hijab is now considered inadequate – you have to cover your whole face. That is the next stage of this ongoing veiling drama.

As Ahdaf Soueif, the novelist (unveiled), writes: 'The veil, like Islam itself, is both sensual and puritanical, is contradictory, is to be feared; it is concrete, and since cultural battles are so often fought through the bodies of women, it is seized upon by columnists, politicians, feminists.'

Feminism, Family, Football and Fornication

F amily values have too long been associated with the WI and grey (plus hypocritical) Toryism. Since the sixties people left of centre have moved in the direction of social libertarianism and the doctrine of personal fulfilment without looking around them to see just what devastation was following these massive social transformations. Much good has come out of the sixties. The freedom to be an individual, the end of deference, women's equality, children's rights, the new father (he does exist) and so on have brought privileges to most of us in the West which we would not readily surrender. Societies which remain locked in past gender and family assumptions – some live here in the UK – are not only hideously oppressive, but are being left behind economically and in terms of the quality of life. But excessive choice and personal gratification combined with an untrammelled consumerism should cause us concern. Relationships breakdowns, the most reckless drugs, smoking and drink culture in Europe, shameful levels of teenage pregnancies are causing internal and external havoc. Popular television, the worship of stars, the commodification of sex have coarsened our society unimaginably and there is no going back, unless the centre left begins to take these new problems seriously. If it can get away from the insane idea that only right-wingers mind about these trends sweeping through the UK.

But to bring up these concerns is to be handed the crown of the joyless Mary Whitehouse. She is now gone. We are in different times and we must address the way we live now.

I'll take each game as it comes

20 February 1995

Like many others, I was outraged when I saw the bewildered, frightened face of a young boy as a group of bestial English football fans created havoc during the Ireland/England international last week. But my outrage was directed at the parents for taking a child to an event that everyone knows is likely to be full of heaving, sweaty, pent-up men looking only to let rip and draw blood. These views or prejudices are based partly on one personal grievance, partly on what I have gleaned from the media and partly on the irrational fears that grow in the dark recesses of the mind.

The only time I had been to a football match was in 1972. I was taken as an act of atonement by the one I then loved because he had shouted at me for screaming out in agony after I had accidentally poured boiling water on my foot. He was watching football, you see, and it happened to be a key moment. He thought he could show me how much he cared and also why he had behaved so grotesquely by spending money we didn't have on going to see George Best playing for Manchester United. Forgiveness was withheld. Seventeen years later, when casting around for excuses to leave, this event was brought up as an example of how we were never meant for each other.

After all this time, this Saturday I ended up going to the Tottenham vs Southampton match at White Hart Lane – this time with my teenage son who shares his father's ardour for the game and for Spurs. I have often thought that I longed to do this, particularly when I was raising him on my own to compensate for the loss of a man in the house. I also wanted him to think I was cool, which he did on Saturday, at least until I asked him whether one wore lipstick and earrings to a football match and what words of encouragement I should shout.

But such trite questions covered up deep and genuine anxieties. Some of these were simply feminist rumblings about whether this was encouraging in my son the kind of macho bonding that has generally done the world no good at all. But others, more seriously, were concerned with our safety.

Hardly any Asians play professional football or go to games. The main reason is fear of violence. My poor mother was convinced that my son, who is big, bold and uncompromisingly Asian, would be dead by Saturday evening. She would try to pray for the entire afternoon, she told me. Compared with the numbers of black football players, few black supporters appear at matches. Why should anyone pay good money, only to be surrounded by constant racial abuse?

What is even more disheartening is that until recently, when the Commission on Racial Equality started highlighting the racism endemic in English football, the problem was accepted as an integral and inevitable part of the game.

But could this be only a small part of what actually goes on during fixtures? Rough calculations indicate that more than half a million people attend matches across the country every week. Are people like me guilty of middle-class ignorance which we cover up with an aggravated sense of apprehension?

We were about to find out. Covered up with enough clothes to stop a bullet, overexcited and agitated, I set off with my son Ari. There was nothing volatile about the hordes hurrying towards the stadium, in spite of the foreboding presence of policemen in vans and on horses. Not all fans, I realised to my shame, wore ugly expressions (some looked like beatific pilgrims) or carried beer bottles, though there were a few self-conscious toughies walking backwards in the middle of the road, trying to get themselves noticed.

One man, wearing a black leather cap with earmuffs, was walking with some difficulty and was offered an arm by a young woman in a miniskirt. Her boyfriend walked on, leaving her to it. Friendly blokes approached us – probably because I looked so gormless – to ask if I wanted to sell my ticket. Everyone was relentlessly nice, including the chain-smoking skinny woman at the reception who was talking on two telephones while trying to help me get an extra ticket for our photographer. Her promise came to nothing, but she made me feel good.

We went into the stadium just minutes before the game was due to start. It was a blindingly sunny day and I was startled by how physically thrilled I was at the vibrant colour and the sight of thousands of people. The roars that went up and down, the exquisite chanting and songs, some with the depth of hymns – the sheer power of that moment gripped me with an intensity that may have had something to do with the fact that it was so unexpected.

We were in the front row – the kind of vulnerable spot where an irritated footballer might try to kick your face in if you said unkind things about his mother. On my left was boy with no facial hair but a booming voice that resonated in my ear hours afterwards. Next to my son was a woman who looked like the actress Miranda Richardson at her most desperately vulnerable. A fat man, bald at the top and with the rest of his greasy hair tied in together, was trying to get comfortable in a seat that was too small for his ample girth. He found this unbelievably funny, as did the line of seven giggling, middle-aged Chinese men wearing white Lycra gloves and Spurs scarves sitting behind us.

I could see no other Asians or black people, but there was no antagonism directed towards us. In fact, our section was full of couples and families. A doctor sat with his eight-year-old son next to an Irish family. Both men said they loved bringing their children to matches and that what happened in Ireland was nothing to do with football and everything to do with politically motivated extremists. 'This can't stop us,' said the doctor. 'It is something my father did with me, and something I want David to do with his children. It is part of our family life, it is a continuing tradition and we have so few of those in our country.'

It is certainly true that you saw all the generations together, sharing something powerful and in a way that you couldn't see anywhere else. The women were young and old, some on their own, most with their men, none looking out of place. This was completely different from the possessive male account that Nick Hornby gives in his brilliant book, *Fever Pitch*.

As the match progressed, the rituals – when you clapped, sang, screamed, moaned, put your head in your hands – began to take shape, though I didn't dare join in because I lacked the care and real commitment of the others. Alas, my caution went too far. I failed to rise with joy when Spurs scored the first goal; this would, Ari thinks, have rendered me dangerously conspicuous had he not hauled me to my feet to cheer.

The Chinese men were screaming in their own language. Once they did shout 'Come on, you Spurs', but it sounded odd. Once or twice they landed blows of pleasure and excitement on our heads. They would have been mortified to realise this, so we did not complain.

There were some disagreeable moments – when a black player on the Southampton side was called a 'fucking animal' or when (especially foreign) players were injured and both sides called for their instant deaths. There was also the hostility expressed for the referee every time he did his job. And what was I supposed to say when my son laughed out loud at 'jokes' about the sexual practices of female relatives of Southampton players? I am not a sad prude, but did I really want to laugh at these obscenities? The slightest whiff of real trouble and the officials and police moved in to kill it before it got anywhere.

Although I did get involved in the game, and even found myself lusting after the gorgeous legs of the players, I was the outsider in this community where, even as rivals, for a while people shared values, pain and pleasure, and related to one another in a unique and important way. So little else these days allows us to feel that connected.

It also seemed to me that when it works positively, the tribalism that football encourages might be an important counterforce to the empty, fragmented lives that people are forced to lead, devoid of hope and faith in economic well-being, political solutions or religion. English people have also had their sense of identity corrupted by history and political misuse. This must be why so many turn to hating those who are culturally more confident and distinct. And while football may be giving them more scope to vent these nauseating sentiments, it may be providing others with a much needed sense of group identity. And even the worst displays of xenophobia by English fans do at least show us that, as Mark Twain says, 'white men are no less savage than the other savages'.

PS: on the way home we had a fantastic cab driver, a football fanatic who told us that he regularly throws racist fans out of his cab: 'It's not on. Football is a decent game and it should be for everybody.' The day was complete.

Cruel Britannia

Community Care, 16–22 April 1998

My mother always said that Britain is a great place to be young in but a frightful place to grow old in. She is right. Unlike most other countries, even in the Western world, older people (unless they can arrange to have the looks and money of Joan Collins) are seen as a burden, a problem, even an embarrassment.

Although it has been wonderful to watch older people, especially pensioners, getting more vociferous in recent times about their rights – as we did with their response to the recent Budget – the sense that such people can have no place of pride in our society is only growing and getting worse. Cool Britannia is relentlessly youthful, alas. Age discrimination is getting worse and is now considered perfectly acceptable.

This is what we need now to address. It is the underpinning attitudes towards old age that need to be transformed if the many excellent policy suggestions from the Centre for Policy on ageing are to take root. But here is where the muddle begins. What messages should we try to communicate? Is the message to be that you can still wear a sexy bra or run the marathon even if you are over fifty-five? That the old can be young too? That is simply, giving in to the pressure that the only worthy human being is one who can look or act young. What happens to the rest?

Respect for old age needs to come from a sense of reciprocity, and obligation. Older people might be sprightly, active and young at heart. Many are; others are not. Most older people have valuable experience and the temperament to inform, advise and entertain. Others are depressive, grisly, and are losing their skills and competence. They all should matter to us equally, for collectively they are the reason we are here today. If we don't accept this broad-based contribution we will get a hierarchy of the older people we value and those we discard.

So deep is our fear and rejection of old age (how many reading this would tell people their real age after they are forty for example?)

that we cannot see that it is a preferable alternative to early death and a priceless reservoir of lived experience and survival. How did we lose our awareness of that? There must have been a time in recent history when old age, even in Britain, was celebrated – because life expectancy was so much shorter than it is now.

I grew up in the colonies and we were fed endless images of old Englishmen in dressing gowns reading to their grandchildren and drinking Ovaltine. Memories of the war kept a national sense of gratitude going for a long time then too. Then came the 1960s, bringing a spirit of iconoclasm. This was good, but it also carried into national consciousness the arrogant belief that the young were better than the old.

The fragmentation of extended family life that took place as urbanisation gathered pace and increasing divorce rates have had a negative impact too, as has middle-class individualisation. In their excellent book, *The Communities We Have Lost And Can Regain*, Gerard Lemos and that most amazing of old men, Michael Young (who has had a child in his eighties), argue for a reclamation of kith and kin, for a return to values that you find across the world in places where modernisation has not managed to destroy the bonds of age within society.

These values are present in Britain too, of course, within many of the ethnic minority, communities. In 1997 I completed a book for Age Concern on the needs of ethnic minority elders and in the course of my) research I interviewed scores of older people from ten communities.

The respect I found, particularly among the Vietnamese and the Chinese communities, was deeply impressive. They did not necessarily like their older folk, many of whom were cantankerous and demanding. What they felt was that they were part of an important human chain between past and present and that the parents and grandparents were an embodiment of their ancestry as well as examples for future generations. As one Chinese businessman said to me: 'I look after my parents because I must. It is my duty and my history. It is also an investment because my children watch how seriously I take this responsibility and how much I value old age. This is now in their book. So when my turn comes, I hope the links continue.'

The way to re-establish value for older people, then, includes several strands. We need our politicians and others to be aware that talking about the future in terms only of shedding the 'old' ways will result in the further devaluing for our older citizens. Organisations campaigning for older people should not only promote the idea that the old too can be young, but that a society without respect for elderly people is a branch flying in the wind, without a trunk or roots. Inter-generational living and respect must be encouraged.

With young lone mothers, for example, why can't grandmothers be assisted financially by the government to help look after younger family members? We could educate our children to think of family obligations and continuity. My mother helped to bring up my son and his deep respect for elderly people grew out of that experience. At the heart of all this lies the knowledge that, as Somerset Maugham wrote: 'For the complete life, the perfect pattern includes old age as well as youth and maturity.'

How long do we put up with feminists behaving badly?

15 October 1998

A very dear male friend of mine phoned me in a state of some exasperation this Monday: 'Tell me, please. What do you women want? What will satisfy you?' He, as I, had just been listening to the well-known feminist writer Lynne Segal on Radio 4's *Start the Week*. She was describing a paper she is presenting in London this week to celebrate the F-word. Her theme was the real or imagined crisis that is afflicting the male identity.

In the course of the discussion, she dropped in the fact that there had been four hundred books written on the subject in the last decade. We were, I think, meant to supply scorn at this evidence of male over-indulgence and attention-seeking.

But why is it so wrong for men to talk and write about what is happening to them in the late twentieth century? Or to go out and beat drums with their mates in forests, for that matter? Why do we damn men whatever they do? I felt just as alienated by the tone of the discussion as my friend did.

Please don't get me wrong. Not only are some of my best friends feminists, I unabashedly describe myself as one too. But I increasingly despair of my sort, the well-heeled, well-placed metropolitan feminists who presume to tell women and men what they ought to be, and who are so uncompromising and relentlessly hard. I find many of the ideas and views that are propagated in the name of feminism unconvincing and infuriating, because they do not engage with the complexities or altering landscapes of real experiences. I would argue, too, that we have grown so accustomed to comfortable generalisations about men and women that we are now adding to the problems of sexism – real as they are – instead of finding ways of tackling them.

There is no need to go over the empirical evidence which shows us that gender inequalities persist in spite of decades of equal opportunity and equal pay legislation. Male violence against women is all too evident. Too much power still rests with an elite group of white men. But this does not mean that all men are essentially bad, or that men are almost all bad, or that women are, by definition, saints or saviours.

This is terribly difficult to write. I can already hear the accusations from the sisterhood. Another traitor, they will say, another soldier joining the backlash. This is why many women I know keep their silence. They, too, feel uneasy and, at times, angry about the dishonesty, the unfairness and the hypocrisy that have contaminated discourse about the status of men and women in this country.

Look clearly at the issues of the family, relationships, work and identity and you find just how much has been transformed for many people in this country. You find, too, that it is not as easy as it once was to categorise power, equality, access and values in terms of gender difference. And yet many of our feminist commentators insist on disregarding progress and turning away from uncomfortable realities.

Take the vocal women who have written off the New Man as a figment of our hopes. Some New Men do exist, and they make wonderful friends, lovers and fathers. You see it most of all in the way they parent their children. Watching many such fathers and their children – the openly displayed love and physical affection, the pride, the gentle conversations – it is hard to remember that even twenty years ago such intimacy between a father and a child would have been impossible. This week, an Asian man, Sumar Chakrabarti, became the first senior non-white appointee in the Cabinet Office. He has taken the job, but on condition that he can leave work at 5.15pm so that he can look after his three-year-old daughter in the evening.

Now, instead of due credit being given him for doing what so many of us have been asking for, all I have heard so far are gripes about how he gets these advantageous conditions because he is a man. This is nonsense. Men find it much harder to get time off work to look after children than women do. If they have female bosses, especially those who have had no children, the response to their requests is often hostile. Feminists never discuss how women bosses can and do bully workers and keep down other women. Just talk to black nurses in the National Health Service and listen to their stories of how many white senior nurses treat them.

At a personal level, too, we avoid the ugly side to the feminine character. When will we condemn women (including strident feminists) who encourage men to betray their long-term partners and walk out on their children? Monica and Gaynor were not simply objects to be manipulated. Will Carling didn't leave the mother of his infant child to go off on a drunken spree with Gazza. He went off with another woman.

Do these women have no responsibilities? Is part of the feminist rush to condemn the cads just to avoid that question? The discredited arguments of the personal not being the political can no longer be used. We, as women, need to stop debasing other women if our political principles have any meaning at all.

So do I not blame men at all any more? Of course I do. Too many men become wonderful new fathers but end up old bastards, rushing off with some nymphet who brings youth, red lips and endless promises of all night sex. Too many men with power are actively hostile to the progress of women. Too many violate the rights of women. But we cannot let these facts paralyse action or stifle optimism. It is absurd to insist that men must be perfect while we continue to deny the imperfections of women.

Nor is it helpful to keep looking for signs of regression. Yes, some young men are buying *Loaded* and tuning into Men Behaving Badly. But that is hardly proof that we are moving back into the caves.

Men are tired, too, of being told that they are not needed (except for DIY and sex, as another newspaper columnist put it), but that they must still live up to impossibly high standards. They are confused about whether they should be properly masculine or vaguely feminine and they are worried, too, that whatever choices they make, we will react only with contempt.

In the future – if there is to be a future here on Earth and not separately on Mars and Venus – we will have to be content that all that is possible is change; uneven, slow, difficult change in the way men and women behave towards one another. And that good things come out of small steps.

Spare me from more naked bodies

26 November 1998

Mary Whitehouse was right all along. There is far too much blaring, brazen sex on British television. And too much cookery too. There have been at least twenty programmes on these in the last two weeks including *Naked, Vice, Anatomy of Desire, Sex and Shopping*, not to mention cooking with virginal Delia and alluring Nigella.

Maybe middle-class white Britons feel an irrepressible need to show their disdainful European cousins that they are not repressed, inadequate or third-rate when it comes to the luscious things of life, but stuffing the channels with sex organs and offal dressed in frilly lettuce only reveals a pathetic sense of inferiority. What's more, these programmes are putting me off food and sex.

The first will probably do me no harm, but the second is ruining one of the main delights of my life. The problem with being mercilessly exposed to television 'pornography', as Mary describes it, is not that we will all become even more sex mad and have it off with customers at photocopying shops in broad daylight, but that we will simply give up on one of the most natural of human activities.

Most sex between consenting adults is not about having your bottom washed and powdered by a pretend mother who then pretends to breastfeed you (three programmes dwelt on this one) for £200 a session or, as four programmes suggested, having your balls crushed by a lady with long boots and sharp stilettos. Most couples who are happy with one another enjoy warm sex because it does not have to be a bloody performance.

You desire one another so much, so regularly that there is no need for satin nightgowns or purple spiky dildos. You can have unwaxed legs (bliss) and smelly feet as you collapse into that old bed at the end of an exhausting day; but for the blessed none of this matters because of the intimacy that time brings. You may no longer thrash about until dawn, but what you have instead is quality sex which comes out of knowing what turns you both on.

Perhaps I am being dangerously presumptuous here. Maybe as my partner watches these programmes he begins to yearn for that which he does not have and cannot have. Television is invading our retreat and manipulating our longings.

What makes us watch these programmes now – incredulity and a certain arrogance – may lead in some unquantifiable way to corrupt what has taken years to build up. And this must happen to some people. Suggestion and validation provided by the relentless obsessions with unusual sexual acts means the ordinary becomes unacceptable, an affront to our right to be on a sensual rollercoaster.

I am even more troubled by the way the essence of sexuality is killed off by such programmes. D. H. Lawrence understood this when he condemned pornography as 'an attempt to insult sex, to do dirt on it'. It does this by making us watch what should be intensely private.

Aphra Benn, the first professional woman writer in this country, said that love ceases to be a pleasure when it ceases to be a secret. I think this is even more true for sex. I love what I do with my loved one in my bed because what happens is unique to us and is inaccessible to anyone else. Even saying this is a kind of betrayal of that principle.

There is of course a need for information. There is no bliss in ignorance – and I speak as somebody who comes from a community where none of our languages have a word for the clitoris – but there is none either when your private parts become public property.

There is something very sexy too about modesty and restraint. I have just re-read John Berger's old, but wonderful book, *Ways of Seeing*, in which he says that a lack of modesty leads to a loss of mystery and shifts attention from the eyes, the mouth, the shoulders – all of which can convey many and complex messages – to the sexual parts 'whose formation suggests an utterly compelling but single process'.

The Horse Whisperer is an unforgettably sexy film because the ferocious desire between the lovers is only seen in their eyes and twitchy hands. Do you remember the perforated sheet in *Midnight's Children* which a young woman used to show bits of herself to the young doctor treating her 'ailments'? Seeing only parts of this woman drove him mad with physical longing.

Believe me, it works. Never strut around showing your all; cover yourself even in bed and choose the parts you would reveal. And remember to save your sex life by turning off that filth on the box. It is doing none of us any good.

Why do we still ignore the screams of abused children?

8 January 1999

Children are much better off than they were a century ago. They are seen and heard, especially when they have cuts and bruises on their bodies, and they scream with pain and confusion as the people they love and trust abuse them. Only, it seems, far too many of us prefer to ignore these sights and sounds, and carry on regardless.

It's time to sober up. Babies in Britain are more likely to be killed today than ten years ago. Those under the age of twelve months are five times more likely to end up murdered than those in other age groups. Between April 1997 and March 1998, eighty-two children were killed by adult abusers. They were beaten to death, starved, strangled, suffocated or tortured to death. This week Professor Sir Roy Meadows, of the Leeds Infirmary, said that, in his view, that number could be even higher because murdered babies are sometimes misdiagnosed as cot death cases. And, as general homicide rates continue to rise, the potential danger to children increases year by year.

The number of murders in Britain, according to newly released Home Office figures, has more than doubled since the mid-sixties, with 1995 being the worst year so far. These figures were released at the same time as a National Society for the Prevention of Cruelty to Children (NSPCC) research report indicating that too many people take no action for months, even years after they become aware of the possibility that a child they know may be at risk.

The research was carried out between 14 and 20 December when calls to the NSPCC helpline were analysed. Of the 173 calls which were considered serious by experts, only 25 per cent were made by people within twenty-four hours of the caller's first having concerns. Almost one in four of the callers had waited six months, and one in seven had waited a year, before making that vital call.

Asked why they had not reported their concerns earlier, fear of reprisal was the main reason given. Others said that they were unsure of how serious the situation was, or initially did not want to get involved. Evidence from inquiries into child killings shows clearly that there are always signs of cruelty and neglect suffered by victims before their death. As long as we have such 'silent witnesses', as the NSPCC calls them, frightened, suffering children will continue to be victims, and some will die as a result.

Those who do take action are not heroic. They are no different from you or me, except that they are social beings whose instincts to protect the next generation prevail more strongly over that other instinct for pure self-preservation. When people say that they are afraid of reprisals, what exactly are they scared of? Of not being able to borrow a cup of sugar? Of paint on the car? Of screams and insults across the well-maintained fences? Of physical attacks in dark corridors of housing estates? Some of these are real dangers, others are not. A realistic assessment, maybe with the help of the police or one of the child protection agencies, might release some people from their own sense of vulnerability. Most ordinary people remain unaware of the impressive standards of confidentiality and sensitivity that permeate child protection work.

But maybe the fears go deeper. One case in the NSPCC dossier is that of a mother who waited twelve months before talking about her suspicion that her ex-husband was sexually abusing her five-year-old daughter. She may have been afraid of him, but could it also be that, like so many of us, she was loath to accept how foul human beings can be towards their own children? We feel safer in a world where the only villains are strangers in the woods who spirit away our innocent young and deliver them back dead. We recoil from the reality that greater dangers lie not with those strangers we have taught the dears not to trust, but those from whom they happily and rightly expect sweets.

Over the years, the excitable public responses to the investigations of widespread abuse of children by their families indicate how unprepared we are to deal with the realities. The journalist Bea Campbell has written compellingly about the effects of this hysterical need not to know, and how the conspiracy of ignorance is maintained. The truth of what happened in Cleveland and other well-publicised cases of mass abuse has been buried away because such facts, properly acknowledged, would send us mad. Perhaps these are our own 20th-century sacrifices. We quietly allow a few children to be physically and psychologically destroyed in order to keep good all those myths, fairy tales and magic for the rest.

There are social impediments to getting involved, too, none of which have anything to do with people being selfish or indifferent. There is that tacit agreement among people that the home is a private kingdom and that parents have ownership rights over those they have brought into the world.

The privatisation of family life has probably been one of the most damaging effects of urbanisation and the break-up of communities that has occurred over the past three centuries. Children should belong to a society – by which I don't mean the confiscation policies once rife in communist countries, but in the sense that the wellbeing and development of every child should be an inescapable joint responsibility. In Africa they say it takes a village to raise a child. Hillary Clinton is so impressed with this simple truth that she has been promoting the idea all around the United States when she talks about health and welfare. If we learn to accept this idea, we shall more easily interfere with the way parents are treating their offspring.

It must be terrible to be falsely accused of hurting your children. But that is a price we should all agree to pay to safeguard the nation's children. I would feel better knowing that my children were protected from me if I ever maltreated them because there are strangers who would take the risk of offending me in order to protect my young. I am about to take that risk myself. There is a child we vaguely know who I feel is being abused. I have sat on my conscience for seven months. I will make that phone call today.

What's wrong with vindictive wives?

14 January 1999

I have read with incredulity the rubbish, mostly written by fortysomething men up to no good, I am sure, that has followed in the wake of the book by Margaret Cook (dump the surname – Margaret) about her marriage to Robin Cook, and the ignoble end at Heathrow airport of that period of her life. It is personal, they say – vindictive, vengeful and embittered.

Yes. What else is someone in her position supposed to feel? You may persuade yourself that you will try not to show these feelings, because the world will love and respect you less for this than if you pretend a saintly forgiveness, of the sort that Hillary Clinton has now made her own. But burning hurt and rage are what you feel, and revenge (preferably divine) is what you yearn for. Ask me – I know, and I wrote an emotional book about it.

What gets these commentators really foaming is not only that the partner of a famous or powerful person should be so weak as to respond in these human ways, but that she or he should then reveal this vulnerability. They have nothing to say about the public figure flaunting the new model in the media, thus further humiliating the ex-partner. But they do sanctimoniously ask whether it is right for someone as insignificant as a spouse to expose the private life of a politician, or whoever, and cause them damage.

Wrong question, sirs. You should instead ask whether the partner of a public figure has the same rights as you or me to say and write what they wish about their lives, especially when they have been maltreated. Or are they expected to render their pain invisible just to keep up appearances?

Writing, as the playwright David Edgar said this week, is a funda-mental and universal human right. It is also a 'vital part of being human to try to understand why other human beings – nasty as well as nice – behave as they do'. Other criticisms don't stand up, either.

If Dr Cook has said things that have alarmed her ex-husband's colleagues because of political implications, why should this be any more outlandish and unethical than the dirt-digging carried out by Paul Routledge and other unauthorised biographers? Maybe it is because she is not a seedy political chap hanging out with Charlie Whelan, but a fragrant wife, 'a slight and delicate creature' (the clever title of her book) who should be coping with her knowledge by devoting herself to nurturing a bonsai tree.

As for the ludicrous worries that if we scrutinise public figures in this way the best people will simply avoid public life, we should be more concerned that these ambitious and able people will fail to get the best partners in life – because anyone with personality, intellect and self-respect will refuse to sign away their rights and become trophies of compliance – thus leaving the selection pool bubbling with bland secretaries and too-eager-to-please personal assistants.

We used to laugh and cry at the appalling loyalty displayed by Tory wives and ex-wives in the inglorious past. Remember Mrs David Mellor as she was forced to smile for photographers after the dreadful revelations about her philandering husband – who then left her anyway for a rich woman with deadly red lipstick. Recall, too, the depressingly good behaviour of Mrs Tim Yeo and Mrs Alan Clark as they stood by their men, partly, I imagine, because they felt they had no other options.

You would have hoped that Labour men and women, although clearly not able to resist sexual temptation any more than the last lot, might be more democratic and fair in the way they dealt with those they betrayed and left after many years of good service. And if this is indeed 'new' Britain, which is more open and receptive to emotion, as everyone from Martin Jacques to Susie Orbach seems to be suggesting, we should rejoice that people like Margaret Cook are no longer hampered by the pressures of out-of-date, unjust social constraints.

Margaret is a thoroughly modern, bright, professional, emotionally honest woman, who has written a lively account of a survivor who saw it all her way, at least after Robin flew away. Like Diana, Princess of Wales, she refused to read out the part written for her by someone else. She wanted it put down as it happened, from her point of view.

If Robin Cook wants to do the right thing now and come out shining, all he has to do is praise his ex-wife for having the courage to do what she has done, say that he can understand how he has made her feel, tell his boys to respect their wonderful mother, and wish her well with all his heart.

Adoption might be good for parents, but what does it do for the child?

26 April 2000

It is good that the government is at last attempting to sort out our messy adoption system. The issue has, for far too long, been trapped in emotional fog, professional complicity and defensiveness. Credit is due to Paul Boateng, who first started peering into these concealed corridors when he was at the Department of Health and Social Services. He asked tough questions and was rightly dissatisfied with the answers he was given by those working in social services and the relevant agencies, who found such interrogations an affront.

A summit meeting at 10 Downing Street yesterday began the process of reform. The main focus is on parents who wish to adopt but who, at present, are being frustrated by bad rules and even worse practice. Tony Blair has set up a task force which aims to improve and increase adoption, using bright new ideas.

One inspired idea is to use the internet – through secure encrypted sites – to extend the numbers of adoptive families and to match children with suitable parents. (Though I do find the idea of matching a little strange. Nobody would ever think that my son and I make a good match. He is not the napkin to my tablecloth. What we have is commitment to a lifetime together, however hard.)

The initiative has been welcomed by adoption organisations who believe that the PM has thrown a lifeline to the 50,000 children in care in the UK. An impassioned Tony Blair says: 'I want to make it easier for children to be placed quickly. The most important thing is that children are in a loving family rather than a care home, however well it is run.'

But I wonder. Is this rush a little too enthusiastic? Should we not be a little more wary of bringing an excess of positive energy into play when we are dealing with one of the saddest and most difficult areas of human life? Adoption cannot be dislocated from social exclusion, family breakdowns and the other endemic problems that cause children to end up in the miserable care chain. Life for an enormous number of British children of all classes is immeasurably harder today than it used to be.

Just last week a compelling book, *Parent Problems!*, was published by Young Voice, a project funded by the Nuffield Foundation. In it, children spoke of divorce and separation. Most are never consulted when their parents decide to part, yet these children – increasing in number every day – have to handle the most complicated emotions and a painful network of relationships. We have yet to accept the emotional damage caused when families disintegrate. Many children from broken families end up in care.

Believing that you can magically procure bountiful parents for beautiful children is playing fairy tales with grim reality. For all the talk of joined-up government, this subject is being treated as a one-off blot on the landscape in a particularly dangerous way. There are wild assumptions being made about the sanctity and healing qualities of good family life. Yet many of these children are so damaged by time they end up in care that they are repelled by the very idea of a nuclear family.

In the last two years I have interviewed twenty-six articulate children in care. Only two said that they wanted to be adopted. The rest don't even want foster families because, as one of them said, 'I don't want a second-hand family who feel sorry for me.' Some wait in hope; others have become so hardened that they feel secure only with others like themselves. It is all much darker than I ever knew.

Take this harrowing story. Mary is a white woman from South Africa now living in Manchester. She married well and had a glorious house and, on the surface, all the trappings of an upper-middle-class life, with two clever birth children. But she had ideals beyond this. She was a member of the ANC and worked for an aid agency. They decided to adopt a young mixed-race boy, Rory, who had already been returned (like soiled goods) into local authority care by two sets of adoptive parents. This morning Mary told me that she has only now been told that social workers knew they were giving her a very disturbed young child, but that this was an 'experiment' to see if good parenting could cure him. It didn't.

Mary's love for him is absolute. She tried everything, including a specially tranquil boarding school where Rory became a tennis legend. But he carried on assaulting people, including Mary herself , burning things, getting into trouble and fathering a child. In the end he was framed and ended up in prison, from where he has just emerged into the arms of Mary. Rory's birth mother, herself a very damaged mixed-race woman, has resurfaced and abuses Mary almost daily. Mary's husband, meanwhile, has left, unable to cope. She has been suicidal and is furious about the sanguine way people talk about adoption being the fantasy answer to all our wishes.

As she says, children in care are a mirror reflecting back to us the society we have created. So perhaps we are a little too anxious to put them away behind net curtains. There is little ongoing help available to adoptive parents, even though we know that adoptive children can remain adolescents into their late twenties.

The Post-Adoptive Centre in London, Parents for Children, and other self-help groups do their best, and in many cases adoptions can result in happy endings. In my husband's family we have two such examples. But we do not know how many adoptions fail in the short or the long term, creating in a rejected child an even bigger wound than before.

And what happens when the adoptive parents split up (the likelihood of this happening must be very high) or if there are children who have such serious 'attachment disorder' that they can never be placed?

Tony Blair is wrong when he says that families are always better than even the best care homes. We need both. And yet nobody is talking about investing properly in making care homes into the kind of places they should be for the children whom nobody wants, or who will not thrive within any family, good or wonderful.

Family life is in crisis – and the left can no longer ignore this vital issue

21 June 2000

Family life is in crisis in Britain. And it is quite outrageous that this issue, central to all our futures, is being hijacked by the self-righteous right (they are at it again over football hooliganism) because the left lacks the moral substance and honesty to look at what is happening.

Most left-of-centre people I know recoil when I bring this up. I think they think I am turning into a right-wing prat, like Paul Johnson. But why is it right-wing to ask whether, in creating invaluable freedoms and rights, we have ended up with casualties, mostly children, without a voice or any influence to determine what is happening to them? Surely only the insanely complacent can continue to ignore the cumulative evidence that British children are suffering from unprecedented levels of emotional trauma and mental illness.

These ideological bun fights are, in any case, absurd. Both sides have contributed to the state we are in, though neither wants to accept responsibility. The sixties generation changed society immeasurably, often for the better. But it made self-gratification into the new religion and the new orthodoxy. The eighties Thatcherites changed the economic landscape of this country, but their economic libertarianism and consumerism also encouraged people to think in intensely individualistic and self-serving ways. The idea of choice, freedom and self-realisation entered the bloodstream of the nation, and every part of the body became infected. Marriage has become either just another stop on that bus ride to self-fulfilment or just another consumer item to be dispensed with when one is bored or when a new product presents itself.

Feminism was crucial to progress, because it helped to release the potential of more than half the population, but it, too, became excessively self-centred as it then developed. The influential feminist Jill Tweedie wrote just before her untimely death that she had advised her own children not to have children. 'They cause endless worry, and are now the greatest threat to women's equality.' Well, that kind of feminism, which so cruelly rejects nurturing, is not my feminism.

I went to a conference at the weekend on the future of families, where it became even more clear that this issue cannot be fudged any longer. There is a ground swell of people out there who are seriously concerned about family bonds and the stability they can bring. And by 'family' they don't just mean the narrow, nuclear model, but any formation in which there is a deep and permanent sense of obligation between individuals through hard and good times, and in which children's needs are prioritised. Even as I write this, all sorts of counter-arguments come to me. Family life can be brutal. It can crush and destroy; I would never want to deny that. But where there is a respect for both the individual and communal life, children especially do fare better.

The true left has always made a case for economic mutualities – the rich have an obligation to support those with less, because we are social beings. Why, then, does it fail to apply the theory to personal relationships? It is possible to be a feminist and a social democrat and be for a stable family life. We must embrace concepts of duty and nurturing as part of our humanity while continuing to fight for equality and individual freedoms.

Take childcare. The academic Carole Ulanowsky believes parental nurturing has become dangerously undervalued in our society: 'Increasingly, the lives of young and vulnerable family members are given over to the full-time management of others. This, in spite of a growing body of compelling evidence that full-time, paid-for services for babies and very young children rarely work to their benefit...' Such children can grow up with only paid-for people meeting most of their needs in life.

Their lives are completely structured. For pre-verbal children, biologically bonded to their parents, the experience must be terrifying. Children who were inadequately nurtured in the early years can have problems emerging as confident and autonomous human beings.

Employment is a necessity for most of us. But if we know that parents working all hours are destroying family life, should we not at least begin a discussion about that, instead of rushing out policies designed to get even more people on to the treadmill?

It is important to enable lone parents to work, because no child can be lifted out of poverty while living on benefits. But for very young children, surely it is more important for the state to provide properly for the child to be with its own parent.

We might all ponder, too, how we could spend more unstructured time with our children (not quality time – just time, much of it loose and unaccounted for) if we trimmed down our needs. It may not be possible for those in full-time, demanding jobs; but people can choose the part-time option, or self-employment, as my husband did. He had a secure and exciting job that he gave up to work at home to see more of our daughter. It is scary with both of us working as freelances, but she's worth it.

Divorces – now at an all-time high – are another destabilising factor. Even the free-living Martin Amis accepts that when he left his sons for his new partner, he diminished their ability to trust love. Vast numbers of children are coping with backpack living, trundling between parents and their reconstituted families. Which employer gives parents time off work to help their children adjust to their new way of life?

Ulanowsky and others have discovered that most people in prison come from homes where there was little security and continuity. A BBC survey for the series *The Soul of Britain* has found that 80 per cent of people think their parents have influenced them more than anything else. The survey has also found that substantially more people today than in 1981 believe parents need to be more dutiful towards their families and less self-obsessed. Those who believe parents should not sacrifice their own needs fell from 18 per cent in 1981 to 7 per cent in 2000. At least there is now an aspiration for something more humane. But is the left going to take up the challenge?

Victims of a culture that won't let our young people say no to sex

11 October 2000

My first sexual experience was with my ex-husband when I was twenty years old and he was twenty-one. We had been dating for two and a half years, during which time we held hands, hugged a lot and kissed each other with a bruising ferocity. Night after night we would carry on this petting, discharging the hot passion we felt for each other on a half broken bench outside Mary Stuart Hall, the women's residence at Makerere University in Kampala. Miss Stanton, the prim Englishwoman who was the warden, would make sure she walked by a couple of times, just in case.

The sixties culture had wafted into Uganda, but the old values fought back effectively. We loved the op art dresses, Jean Shrimpton eyelashes and the Beatles, but were fearful of the drugs and the free-for-all sex. I was, anyway, which is why I held out until after I was engaged. Fear of shame and gossip was a powerful deterrent, and I know that I only did what I did because I was absolutely sure that the young man was going to be my husband.

I described this eventual, longed-for surrender in my autobiography, which was published a few years ago. My mother phoned and summoned me over. She was furious, she said, ashamed that her daughter had no morals. Distraught too, that I had so little self-respect that I gave myself to a man before he had done the right thing and married me. What was the hurry? What would I have done if he had gone off with someone else? Men are men, she said through her tears, and they are only too happy to take. Why did I not say no and believe that I was worth waiting for? I felt like a young teenager again. I was forty-five a mother of two, and I stood there sweating and quaking in front of my eighty-year-old mum. I know most readers will think this quite ridiculous, but in my heart I think I believed she was right. Girls and young women should always be more cautious than they ever are about when they have sex, and with whom.

I look at my little seven-year-old daughter and I know that this is the lesson I want her to learn too. But she lives in a world where such caution is considered anachronistic, which is why most commentators have reacted with predictable derision to the new government campaign to encourage girls (and boys too) to think before they have sex. Obviously, those who think it is misguided for the government to give out this sensible and important message, think that it is perfectly OK for our children to be drawn consciously, and subliminally, into believing they must, must, must fornicate, as soon as and as often as possible. Girls are expected from the age of twelve (younger too) to be fully sexually aware, body-conscious, and to compete flagrantly in the marketplace for attention and sex. Our whole culture is driven by this obsession with youth sex and body image, from children's television programmes to the clothes girls buy in Top Shop.

Extraordinarily, the era that has produced unprecedented academic achievements among girls is also the period when we have the highest number of teenage pregnancies. Even if you allow for class difference, what this tells us is that large numbers of bright young girls feel they must be seen to be sexually desirable and active. The only difference between the middle classes and poorer groups is that the former have the wherewithal to 'manage' any unwanted pregnancies, while it is the children of the poor (as ever) who are ending up as child mothers. But most of our daughters are succumbing.

You can be brainy or exceptionally talented, but the only way to get recognition and respect is to be available and to look it. An item on *Woman's Hour* this week looked at how there is evidence of increasing violence among young girls and women. Some of the young schoolgirls interviewed said that their most vicious fights were often over young men. Pop videos reinforce these values relentlessly. Thrusting, semi-naked bodies have actually replaced the music now, and a large number of these videos feature bloody battles between hysterical young females all dying to screw the same cool guy.

Young people have become victims of a savagely 'free' culture which no longer gives them permission to say no.

Social disapprobation, once gone, can never be reinstated. And anyway, nobody is suggesting that we should return to the days when young women were damned for ever for having sex outside marriage. This is what still happens in some communities in Britain, and the pain and injustice is intolerable if one believes in gender equality. But these same communities – which include British Asians, Chinese, Turks – do seem to have children who are not ashamed of being virgins beyond the age of thirteen. I once interviewed a dozen Asian girls between the ages of fourteen and twenty who had run away from home and were in a refuge. They were all born here and they hated the strict restrictions imposed on them by their families. But only one said that she wanted the sexual freedom of her white peers. What would be the point, they said? It gives the boys what they want without giving any commitment in return. Wise words, I thought.

The writer and researcher Adrienne Katz, who has spent years studying the attitudes of young people, found in one recent study that the majority of girls interviewed not only wanted more information about sex, sexually transmitted diseases and sexual violence, but that 81 per cent wanted to know how to resist pressure to have sex. Interestingly, her research into the attitudes of 1,400 teenage boys revealed that when asked 'What makes a boy popular in another boy's opinion?', 'He's had sex' came at the bottom of the list. Only 8 per cent believed that this was important. Humour, trust and the capacity to be a good friend were the top three.

I know that my daughter will not be twenty and engaged before she has sex, and that she will just laugh if I behave like my formidable mother. But I do hope that she understands that during her teenage years, she can have boyfriends and even keep their attention without going to bed with them, and that she is more, much more, than a sex aid for grasping, growing boys.

How I became a surrendered wife

21 June 2001

It started with a smile, this experiment. In April an irritating new book by another American who presumed to tell us how to lead perfectly perfect lives was published in the UK. *The Surrendered Wife*, by Laura Doyle, blazed a trail of controversy like a firework, frizzling and frazzling and then dying away.

The book claims to be a step-by-step guide to finding peace with a man, essentially by giving him more control. You do this by making yourself pleasing in every way you can, never reading his mind or baiting or provoking him, letting him solve your problems, never showing him you are better than he is at doing things – essentially a sweet wee wifie like those stereotyped images from the 1950s.

None the less, as I watched the TV programme based on the book (which I later read), I thought I might try and live out these ideas for real. It would be fun; it would make good copy, and we would all have a laugh following the instructions and foolish homilies.

Now, eight weeks later, I am no longer laughing. I feel chastened, acutely alive to my own arrogance, to my inclination to control, and to my other terrible failings.

At the beginning, there were days when I couldn't bring myself to carry on with the experiment. But in fits and starts, like a struggling diet junkie, I stuck with it. And I have to say that something is beginning to change, and for the better. Personal re-engineering does work – just look at Michael Portillo's miraculous transformation into a man for all people.

Yes, yes, I know. The backlash is always round the corner (often led by the enemy within), determinedly forcing women into slavish servitude in order to deliver the world back into the greedy hands of men. The most girly anti-feminist would not have to walk far into the book to feel seized and imprisoned. Some nauseating bits I would gladly tear out and burn in a public place in Bradford. The title, to begin with. And Chapter 13, 'Abandon the Myth of Equality', which asks women to change hats when they come home from work and switch to acting all sweet and swooning helpless so that their male partners can feel like cowboys.

Actually, all the gender stuff is pretty trite and useless and potentially harmful, although at least there are warnings that if the cowboy starts kicking you or your children about or if he is 'chronically unfaithful' you must dump him.

But there are some sections and chapters which are startlingly revealing for anybody in a long-term relationship. Hidden mirrors placed around the pages which catch you out and make you look and see and think differently about how you are behaving and the effect of this on the people you most love in the world.

Falling in love or staying in love is not hard, says Doyle, but finding a way of being with somebody over a long time without forcing them to change into your idea of them is very difficult. To reclaim the relationship you had in your early years together, you need to push back the layers of exhaustion and habit which have settled over life and question the drift into spats that mean little but happen all too often.

People react in interesting ways when I tell them what I am attempting. A number of male friends and acquaintances are intrigued; some are even admiring. Although some of the latter are pleased because they think that yet another shovel of muck is being thrown over the dungaree-wearing Andrea Dworkin and her demented daughters.

Women laugh or despair. My son is unconvinced that I will go through with it, and my husband, Colin, who is likely to be the chief beneficiary of the sweet new me who will be emerging shortly, was at first appalled at the very thought that I would be offering him not demands and complaints (which he knows how to deal with) but contrition and generosity.

He said he feared that I would parade my virtue, like a Christian missionary in a heathen place, and that I would manipulate him: 'This is control, of the most insidious kind. I don't want to live with Mary Tyler Moore. You have not consulted me on whether you should do this, which breaks the first principle of a surrendered wife. How can you surrender if I ask you not to?'

He has a point, but I do so anyway – when I can keep it up. I have to confess that some situations are beyond redemption. There is a questionnaire early in the book which reveals that I tend to issue instructions and expect them to be followed, even when I know nothing about the matter in hand. Colin then will go to war to stop me getting my way.

One of the most idiotic encounters in recent weeks has been over the house gutters. I want to get them cleaned and he won't let me for no good reason. He stalls me by saying that we should maybe replace the whole lot. Nothing happens. I finally make a decision and present it to him as badly as I can, so that he feels at once tyrannical and indecisive.

This project remains blocked. But there are optimistic signs elsewhere. I come home from a tiring trip up north and go into the kitchen immediately. Why? Because I want to check up on my husband. I need to catch him failing so I can carp about it. I drive furiously down the road, fuming with self-righteousness and self-pity. 'You never cook. Men never think about anything else when they're working. I always make sure there is food for you when you come home . . .'

There is no sign of any culinary activity; and there is no turning back now. Colin watches me as I perform my rehearsed act, and then says: 'But there is enough food left over from yesterday. There was no point in cooking anything extra. And you told me this before you left.'

What follows is miserable defeat, bitter guilt, lots of apologies and promises, the force of which shocks him, I think, because normally these events (he can be unreasonable and nagging, too, of course) come and go. But now I see that each one scrapes off a little more of that shining paint, the colours that excited and drew you to each other in the first place.

I cook almost every night because I want to and because I think the kitchen is my space. Yet when we met he would cook wonderful meals and I loved watching him as he worked, wine glass in his hand, creating something for and with love. When did this stop? Why did I not notice? And why did I start to take over this activity and then blame him when he started feeling an interloper in the kitchen?

Questions such as this start small changes in behaviour which can lighten life immeasurably. I no longer start stupid rows over the best parking spaces or why he never asks for directions or who should phone our friends to invite them to dinner. I am teaching myself to notice the enormous amount he does instead of always alighting on the unfinished jobs and failures. I can't force him to do the same but he is trying and this too then makes my efforts easier.

We live in a place and time where men and women can have relationships based on equality, unimaginable intimacy and familiarity. You can still never really know another person, but in a loving modern relationship, you can come pretty close. My parents, in common with others of their generation, did not know each other. The men never discussed their work and the women lived most of their lives with their children, relatives and other women friends. They made fewer demands on each other, but hidden resentments, unhappiness, lack of fulfilment and loneliness choked many lives. But they understood better when to let things be and which blazing thoughts and words should be left to quietly cool down.

We still do have rows and arguments and some of them are more vicious than before because I am reminded that I am supposed to be a 'surrendered wife'. Once in a while, I need to binge on a spectacularly unnecessary argument. But these are getting less frequent and there is much greater closeness and intimacy once more. There is more tenderness too and vulnerability, which we feel able to reveal to each other again.

We are here for such a short time. The lucky among us find partners who are good and true. These two truths are too often lost in the baggage of our busy modern lives. The past few weeks have taught me this and much else. And I think that for all of us, my young daughter in particular, life is that much sweeter as a result. As Fay Weldon says of the book: 'Forget the rights and wrongs – it works. It's a miracle.'

Is feminism to blame for our dumbed-down, sex-now culture?

17 April 2001

So is this it then? Three decades of feminism and what do we have to show for it? An icon who struggles like a demented hamster on a wheel chasing weedy Hugh Grant, counting cals, drinks, and fags. And Carol Vorderman's video in Woolworths which shows you how one of the most intelligent women in the country went down two dress sizes to slip into thigh-revealing frocks.

Other reasons to be cheerless: fewer young women in Parliament next time round, intolerably high rates of teenage pregnancies, anorexic girl power. Yes, girls may be achieving higher grades than boys, but what most really, really want is to be laid by gyrating boy bands.

And so we whinge on, especially those of us who still call ourselves feminists. We positively wallow in this melodrama of lost hopes and shattered possibilities. All major campaigns have to dream beyond their means, and perhaps disappointment is just par for the course.

But I think that there are some especially restless demons that afflict traditional feminists (yes, even thunderbirds age and become 'traditional') because younger generations are not doing what we planned for them, and also because we, who were going to be green for ever, are getting resentful and closed off. This may also explain why every new young feminist writer – from Natasha Walter to Naomi Wolf – has been greeted with cruel derision by the established sisterhood, myself included.

Now comes a rush of books by liberated women describing their hellish teenage daughters. Awash with self-pity, they include *Hold Me Close, Let Me Go* by Adair Lara and *As Good as I Could Be* by Susan Cheever. These writers, who cannot forget the sixties and seventies, seem singularly ill-equipped to relate to young women, even their own daughters, whom they can only see as competitors.

The last few years have challenged this mean tendency in my own life. Through my twenty-three-year-old son and his many female friends, I have learnt how little we understand about both the failures and successes of old feminism. Not one of the women describes herself as a feminist; they fear the idea and what they think it means. It is an ugly word, says my son, conjuring up images of women who wear dirty dungarees and want to castrate men. Two of his girlfriends were frightened of me because they thought I was one. One was almost speechless when she found me cooking cheerfully, something I do almost every evening.

Adrienne Katz, who runs Young Voice, a unit specialising in surveys of young people, confirms this phobia. When testing questions for her study, Can Do Girls, respondents advised her to remove the word 'feminism' because they were uncomfortable with it. One young woman said bluntly: 'I am an egalitarian rather than a feminist. I think feminism is too much about how male domination has to be replaced by female domination.'

Female interviewees know all about gender inequality, but they approach this as a problem which is personal and not political. Research shows that 70 per cent of young women believe that girls have to be tougher than boys to survive; yet 87 per cent believe that there are opportunities for them out there. Most also think that diplomacy is better than relentless remonstration and castigation.

Debbie, now twenty-one, tells me: 'I don't want to appear ungrateful. We can be less bothered because you all had to do the hard stuff which came before. But I hated the way my mother never let anything go. She was a university lecturer, gender studies, and she made our lives hell. Everything was a big male conspiracy. My father was lazy but he was a great dad and tried his best. I am sure if she'd told him gently about what was bugging her, he would have changed. As a political gesture she would take me into her office, never my brother. It was all too loud. It turned people off.'

Bev adds her bit: 'I am not blaming the women. I don't want to go back to the fifties. But I think I am better at communicating with men about my needs and rights than my mum and aunt were. You know, I think we should worry that men feel so lost. Feminists just don't care about this.'

Some 80 per cent of young women interviewed by Katz said that women's equality had brought too much conflict into the world and their own lives. Many young people – the first generation to live in a world where divorce is commonplace – are conservative about family values. Roz's parents divorced when she was twelve: 'I won't marry until I know that I can keep the marriage for ever. I don't want my children to go through what I went through, keeping the peace, parenting my parents. You lot never thought about consequences. We never think about anything else.'

Hard though it may be to take such accusations, which are unfair, too, listen we must.

Which is not to say that I think that all is well with the lives of young women. Obviously not. Although teenage life was always a struggle for girls, who had to be pretty to get the boy, at university there was a time when brainy women could catch the best that was going. Just read the delightful descriptions of Iris Murdoch and the effect she had on men and boys at Oxford. Today, my son and his male friends only choose women with model looks. The young women are over-anxious, and some are already caught in unequal relationships with manipulative men.

But we didn't have to sell ourselves constantly in the marketplace. We listened to Mama Cass or Carole King or Janis Joplin – not to female singers who had to have a belly like the newly sculpted and starved Geri Halliwell. Although Twiggy pushed us into unsuitable stripey dresses, our role models were also the soft-quilt beauties – Marilyn and Liz. And, most important of all – for a while, at least – it was possible to have relationships with men which did not leave you feeling desperate.

But this did not last, and it was partly because, instead of dwelling on these real gains, we carried on being furious. Young people did not follow the path, and the empty road was soon occupied by the dumb-down, thin-down, sex-now, drink-now culture that has settled over all our lives. So, it may just be that Bridget Jones is the illegitimate daughter of Andrea Dworkin or Germaine Greer. Think on that, sisters, and sigh.

The powerful and immoral people who want to brainwash my lovely daughter

Daily Mail, 19 March 2002

My daughter turns nine next month and all I feel is foreboding. Not the usual sort that you always carry in you like another heartbeat from the minute your child is born, but a pulsating, loud panic which seems to be driving out hope and pleasure.

The awesome changes in her face, body, language and personality, the anticipation of a spring birthday and the relief that we have lived another year together – all reasons to be grateful – seem unable to divert me away from the persistent, thumping fear that my daughter, incredibly innocent still, is about to enter an increasingly sordid popular culture.

Powerful immoral people will manipulate her desires and appetites (even more than they have done already with their Barbies) and turn her into a needy, restless little soul who will be made to feel she is nothing unless she looks like Britney.

Not long after that, I imagine, she will be persuaded, by her also brainwashed peers that there is something wrong with her if she hasn't had sex or if lusty boys don't find her attractive enough meat.

Please don't tell me it was ever thus. That is a lie perpetrated by libertarians and merchants who profit massively from turning children into sex machines.

The majority of British children, boys and girls, have never before been under such relentless pressure to see themselves and others purely in terms of how sexually attractive they are.

And, no, I am not some highly strung prude who has problems with sexuality. Sex is precious, fantastic, for most people an expression of who they truly are.

But children forced into sexualising themselves by society are too immature and vulnerable to understand any of that.

301

In fact, a major *Lancet* survey last year found that although young people were having sex earlier, many of them regretted this when they got older.

We know already through research in the US and the UK that peer influence in most ethnic groups is now more significant than parental influence.

We know too that Britain continues to have the highest rate of teenage pregnancies in Europe and that sexually transmitted diseases are up.

A study by the National Centre for Social Research has revealed a sharp increase in drinking and drug-taking among children aged between eleven and fifteen, and Office of National Statistics figures showed that under-age abortions have risen by a fifth in the past ten years.

The real figure may be higher, because abortions on young teens are often kept hidden by private clinics. Now good old Tesco is about to sell the morning-after pill in Cornwall.

Experts are saying that sex education and the morning-after pill may actually be encouraging risky and uncontrolled sexual behaviour. Under-age promiscuity in Britain is now so widely spread that it is fast becoming just another teen norm, like bad tempers, slammed doors and smelly rooms.

Why teenagers and children in most of the rest of the world seem to be able to grow up without this level of fornication is not a question which anyone wants to ask. Policy-makers seem uninterested, too, in exploring why these 'norms' and statistics are not yet found among say, British Chinese people, British Hindus and others.

Of course, there are teenage pregnancies in these groups, but the levels are negligible perhaps because image-makers ignore them and because the family influence, though getting more fragile, is still strong and respected by young people.

I once interviewed twenty-three runaway Asian girls between the ages of, thirteen and seventeen. Only two said they wanted the sexual freedoms of their white and black peers. The rest had left because they were being denied basic autonomy and the right to carry on their education.

The problem is that most parents are told to accept the inevitable. It is one of those things which just happens, you know, like drugs, and semi-porn pop videos, and lapdance clothes for tots in respectable shops.

Just roll over. We don't want to come over all Victorian or like Mary Whitehouse, do we?

After all, we are modern parents who must learn to be friends with our children and encourage them to define their lives and values.

So what if ten-year-old girls now wear make-up to parties, or walk and talk in ways to make a seasoned tart blush? If you try to stop them they will only get more rebellious, and besides, they may face bullying in schools and find themselves isolated.

And like the best and the worst, I too feel lost about what one can or should do.

I abhor the violations and cruelties perpetrated by some Asian parents on their children, but I do understand that many of them are resorting to this because they, too, are shocked and agitated about the way this country's values have crumbled.

No, I am not about to dispatch my daughter to spend the next few years in the Convent of the Little Sisters of the Ayatollah in Isfahan. There is no such place of escape and no such plan to escape from my responsibilities or deepening anxieties.

The interesting news is that for the first time that I remember, some feminists are starting to worry about what has happened to girls. How come the brilliant self-empowerment they are acquiring about work and ambition is not making them less vulnerable to these other pressures?

The right to say no or when has not taken hold; instead, girls are being pushed into a position where, as Germaine Greer noted, they feel they must always say yes to sex, and look as if they are worth it.

At various events to mark International Women's Day this year, this topic kept bubbling up. There was much less of the usual glass ceilings, chauvinist pigs who still find ways to keep us down and out, home/work balance, tyrant women bosses, socially excluded women, feel-good speeches on the wonders of womanhood – and more introspection and shared worries about teenage promiscuity and what we should do.

Few seemed to believe that more sex education was the answer and fewer still that we wanted to promote the oppression of young people by their families. But almost everyone felt that to lie down and surrender to these brute forces is no longer an option.

I suggest the next major campaign for British feminism needs to be directed at those advertisers, broadcasters, celeb peddlers, newspapers, magazines, pop stars and others who have made this carnal hell for our young ones and who still insist that none of this is anything to do with them.

Isambard Kingdom Brunel

RSA Journal, October 2002

There are three excellent reasons why the extraordinary Victorian civil engineer Isambard Kingdom Brunel gets to be in my gallery of heroes and heroines, and the first of these means his place is assured for the foreseeable future, God willing

I met my husband in 1988, and all the key events in our life in that first year were connected in some way to Brunel's creations. By all accounts he was too busy ever to be a soppy romantic, except in the sense that he suffered for his talent. Yet I imagine him as a gentle ghost, smiling quietly as his creations became monuments to love.

My husband and I bumped into each other at Temple Meads station in Bristol, four months after my personal life had crashed. Later the same day we had our first drink together and fell in love at the Railway Hotel in Paddington Station. We decided to get married while on the Clifton suspension bridge, which Brunel started but could not finish because he ran out of money. Our wedding reception was at the Paddington Railway Hotel. We were staying at a hotel facing the suspension bridge when we discovered that I was pregnant.

The second reason for my admiration is that Brunel's work symbolises an optimism which, I fear, has all but gone now. The Victorians were hubristic and careless about the damaging effects of their imperialism, but they were also practical, versatile and imaginative. The infrastructures they built were meant to survive the ravages of lime and were among the best in the world.

At school in Uganda, which was a British protectorate, our heads were stuffed full with stories about these imperial heroes. These narratives made us succumb to the awe we had to feel in order to accept the sense of manifest destiny which defined the British national psyche at the time. Such powerful myths stay in your head, intact through the turbulence of decolonisation and rebellion; it is possible to admire our old masters and yet question their actions.

I remember the lessons about the Industrial Revolution, the Spinning Jenny, the Luddites and the great railway engineers. In fact, I believed that Brunel was a big company like Cadbury; only they made magnificent structures instead of delectable chocolate.

How did one man produce such wild ideas, and the conviction to see them through? Take the tunnel at Box Hill in Somerset. It was the longest tunnel ever to be built at the time, took two years and consumed a ton of gunpowder a week. It was perfectly straight so that on Brunei's birthday, 9 April, the sun shone through it from end to end at dawn. Ego or huge joke, it was a nice touch.

Brunel makes me think that this post-Enlightenment confidence in human progress was perhaps more productive than the more nervous postmodern times. Our designers are still brilliant, but maybe their faith in the future is shakier, so they give us wobbly bridges, glass edifices which shatter easily, and, these days, vulnerable, buckling railway tracks.

My final reason is that Brunel was the son of a French immigrant, Marc Isambard Brunel, also a brilliant engineer. We live in times of unprecedented hostility towards immigrants; our nation has yet to accept and appreciate the contributions of the groups and individuals who have swept in and, in small and big ways, transformed the country. For an immigrant who arrived a century on, Brunel, like Sir Isaiah Berlin, Claire Bloom, Lenny Henry, Zadie Smith and scores of others, represents an indisputable fact – that immigrants and their children give back more than they ever take from a country.

Manipulative as she was, Hindley didn't fool me

18 November 2002

Some years ago, after long negotiations with the Home Office, I was allowed to go into Cookham Wood prison to make a BBC film on Asian women prisoners. Many of them were in for twelve years for a first-time offence. They had been forced by the men in their families to become drug mules – and then abandoned by them because of the 'shame' they had brought; presumably by getting caught. I learnt much about women prisoners in general that week by listening to the hidden stories of these Asian women. One was nearly sixty. The most shocking discovery was that many of them felt freer in prison than they had felt as sisters, mothers, daughters or wives.

The other shock came in realising that the tall, commanding prisoner who watched over us with cold, staring eyes was Myra Hindley. I had not recognised her because she was nothing like the sinister blonde in the only picture I had seen of her, the picture which has been implanted into every adult brain in the UK. She had brown hair, well coiffed though very brittle – it had obviously been mercilessly over-dyed for years – and a painted face with lipstick the colour of baby-pink candyfloss. Her eyes fixed themselves on whomever she was scrutinising. When you met them, there was no flicker of discomfort. She spooked me the first time this happened, on the first morning of filming. It was only halfway through day two that one of my interviewees told me who she was.

I then watched her too. I remember her demeanour. It was like what you might expect of a Russian czarina, and since the prison allowed inmates exercise, jobs and hobbies, I was able to observe her relationships too. She had presence; she had status; she had power over people, including some officers who seemed not to mind what she did but were alert to the slightest lapse among other inmates, especially 'outsiders' – those who didn't belong to that culture and the hierarchy. Acolytes and hand-maidens were always around Hindley. Most of them were shorter than she was, as if she selected them so she could tower over them.

One afternoon, five of my interviewees were teasing our handsome, muscular cameraman, who blushed easily. He had been filming one of them holding up her erotic paintings of couplings. Hindley and her gang walked by and suddenly the laughter froze.

Deepa (not her real name), one of my interviewees, told me in Hindi – so that the white prisoners would not be able to understand – that this group tried to coerce newcomers into lesbianism, although she wasn't sure if Hindley participated. Deepa, a very lovely 29-year-old mother of one, had been physically accosted in the shower by two prisoners who were always with Hindley.

Others said that they all had to agree to request extra medication (which prisoners are allowed) if Hindley asked for it. I have no further proof than this, but I did believe the accounts and I felt the dominance of this murderer myself.

The campaigning journalist Yvonne Roberts, who has done so much over the years for better rights for female prisoners, met her in Cookham and she confirms that Hindley 'had charisma and status. She was articulate, coldly charming, [and there was] no empathy, no compassion; a slice of reason completely missing'. Roberts also found out, to her horror, that Hindley blamed the parents of Lesley Anne Downey for her being at a fairground alone late at night. It was from there that Hindley took her to Brady to be raped, tortured, beaten, audiotaped. Then the pair of them joyously killed her.

This is why I never trusted Lord Longford and others who campaigned for Hindley's freedom and why, in spite of strongly held beliefs in human rights and redemption, I would not have wanted to see her released. Life in this case had to be life just as it must in the case of Rosemary West and Harold Shipman. Liberal, good, reforming values should not easily be cast aside but they can be easily manipulated by the truly heartless, one of whom I think Hindley was. The good folk who were so readily convinced that Hindley had originally been under the influence of Brady, had repented and was contrite could only have met her under well-planned conditions, well planned and controlled by her. They could not have watched her as she was in the various prisons; otherwise they might have at least wondered what they were doing clamouring for her right to be free.

The core principles of reformists are only preserved and worth preserving if believers are prepared to examine those uniquely individual instances when these principles become a violation of all that they hold dear. Freedom from prison after an acceptable period and real evidence of growth and rehabilitation or after a miscarriage of justice is something that many of us passionately believe in and fight for. That we are heard and that we have remarkable lawyers and campaigners who keep this alive even in times when the hanging-and-flogging brigade seems to be gaining the upper hand (like now under the authoritarian Mr Blunkett) makes this country great in my view. But we are no better than the shrill right if we are never prepared to consider the exceptions which must be made; and Myra Hindley was one such exceptional case.

The same difficulties and challenges will arise with the double-jeopardy rule, which the government is planning to ease. I understand why this could seriously damage fairness in our criminal justice system, but I can also see that sometimes, rarely, injustice prevails unless this rule is waived.

I am not advocating some sort of brain-numbing relativism here. Some principles are more sacred than others, and compromises here are almost always impossible. Although I understand why so many people wanted her hanged, and I would too if it was my child who had been taken from me by such unforgivable sadists, I still think capital punishment is always wrong and I am glad we got rid of it a few months before Brady and Hindley were tried. To hang them would have been barbaric. Nowadays, punishment is not allowed to be as heinous as the crime committed.

We should also be wary in the days and weeks to come that the press does not begin to believe that it can decide the fate of criminals or people it has decided are irredeemable. They must feel thrilled that one sinner, damned by them, has been sent off to hell. They will be looking for a replacement. Some newspapers, for example, have started vilifying and hounding Winston Silcott, another iconic villain who has had a ferocious image of him branded into our subconscious by relentless pursuers. Venal though he was, he has done his time, and he was cleared on appeal of the murder of PC Blakelock for which he is still, nevertheless, blamed.

And no, I am not making excuses for him because he is black. The explosion of violent crime among black men is frightening. The causes are linked to racism and the lack of opportunities for these Britons, but this cannot be the whole explanation.

However, Silcott has served his sentence, and he now deserves the right to come out into society and live his life. It would be horrible if the final legacy of Hindley was to make life impossible for other lifers, even those who had tried to redeem themselves.

Celebrity meltdown

22 December 2002

I have had only the slightest taste of it, and it was unsettling and confusing. I was walking along the road in a pretty deprived area of London and three times in quick succession, people came up to me to say hello because they recognised me from my appearances on television. They were charming; I was hugely flattered yet the experience brought on a desperate panic too and a sudden loss of identity. It made me feel as if I was no longer my own person, able to disappear into the vastness of this city I love. I felt a failure because I looked like a laundry bag in an oversize sweatshirt and my hair was greasy. Within five minutes I was consumed by both the self-obsession and the vulnerability that fame – in my case fleeting and insignificant – brings in its wake to rattle even the most assured seekers of that fame.

Seasoned stars recoil from such mild and sweet moments of recognition and not always because they have become proud or irritated. It is the loss of control and the frequency of these spontaneous encounters which throws them. With their managers arranging their reputations through pre-set interviews and images, they are cut off profoundly from the world that adores them.

Modern celebs are also grappling with an enormous shift in British social behaviour and attitudes and the rules on what they must expect as people in the public eye. We have absorbed the American star-gazing, star-grazing culture but without the understanding, the deals and tools which come with that culture for better or worse.

Britain was a very different place not that long ago. I remember going to the Pit in the Barbican ten or so years back and there were many of the big names – Dame Judi Dench, Emma Thompson, Vanessa Redgrave and others – huddled on the benches. There were no stares, no requests for autographs, no unseemly violation of their space and time. Everyone there understood the actors had that right,

311

however excited the rest of us felt about their presence and talent. How cool is that?

Some of this 'normality' still exists if one is to believe the always delighted comments of American stars who have homes in Britain – Madonna, for example, says she can go to the pub or park here but couldn't do the same in the United States. This birthplace of modern idolatry has a history which until recently was not replicated here. I doubt whether Barbara Windsor and Sid James felt as manipulated and incessantly followed as Monroe did or Charlie Chaplin. Hugh Grant says most Brits are still admirably self-controlled, 'although they are excited to meet a star, they are not up your arse'. Most of our finest actors – Colin Firth, Sir Ian McKellen, Kathy Burke, Saffron Burrows, Helen Mirren – have few airs and pretensions. A number of them attended a vigil I organised with Corin Redgrave and his partner Kika Markham to remember the young Chinese men and women who suffocated to death in an airless truck a couple of years back, and it was great to see how easily they shed the trappings of fame.

But things are changing fast; this is no time for the modest or sensitive. False and true stories about actors, musicians, models, artists, film-makers, pop singers – genuine and manufactured – television personalities, comedians, politicians, satirists, rude cooks, gardeners, decorators, and frock experts, writers, criminals, it girls, people who are famous for attending parties, plus all their wives, lovers, cats, gurus, therapists, personal trainers, fixers, secretaries, emails, faxes and text messages, acquaintances, butlers, siblings overwhelm almost entirely the national conversations in our country, day in, day out. The pandemonium of parrots pecks and screeches to keep up with the ever-expanding pool of megastars who so want not to be ignored but so want to be left well alone too.

I hope never to be famous, to be the kind of person who would be watched, scrutinised, gossiped about by millions, commented on by journalists like myself. What a wretched life that would be, must be, especially these days when the beastly media never sleeps and is voraciously hungry for that story, that picture, that secret to blaze across the pages and airwaves to feed an addicted public. Together, these producers and consumers (I am both) make themselves the unwelcome shareholders who take over the lives of stars and public figures monitoring their every move.

As religious faith ebbs away from the mass of British people, the central fables and worship are transferred to celebrities who follow the same path as Christ or other archetypal narratives, says entertainment journalist David Gritten in his analytical exploration of the subject, *Fame: Stripping Celebrity Bare* (2002, Penguin). They arrive, they win millions over with their seemingly superhuman qualities – talent, beauty, unwavering determination – they fall, and some are reborn. Or as Bruce Willis described it in an interview: 'There's only four basic stories they can write about you. One: you hit the scene. Two: you peak. Three: you bomb. Four: you come back.'

Some also vanish such as the entire cast of the 1980 hit film *Fame*. Remember them belting out 'I'm gonna live for ever' with such conviction? Maybe they are happier than they will ever know. Some months ago we went to dinner with some friends and my husband talked animatedly to the very lovely woman next to him. They talked about politics, Palestine, and other non-showbiz subjects. He didn't realise it was Julie Christie and she didn't tell him. They both had a better time than they might have done if he had recognised her.

This week I met two women who are close relatives of famous people caught up in the maelstrom of scandals, one real, one mostly whipped up. They told me how this fame by association has destroyed their own lives. One was the sister of a star, her own husband had tried to sell invented stories to the papers and had then lied for months. They are going through a divorce. I also chatted to someone who knows the partner of Angus Deayton, a man I have myself mocked and criticised in public. It makes you think when you meet such people who know but can never tell (not that we would care) about the effects of our collective intrusions. That's the way it is, our sordid affair and fascination with fame – and it is pretty vile yet irresistible.

How many high-minded people truly turn away from What Ulrika did Next, or Edwina's sticky tales of romps, the gossipy snippets and star interviews now found in all the newspapers? Not me. You do feel wickedly excited to see Chris Evans and his childlike

Billie Piper looking unkempt and oddly dissatisfied with life, or the leprechaun Robin Cook stealing away from the house of his (then) lover.

Before she became the First Lady, Cherie Blair's hair, lips, body, friends, beauty treatments, business transactions, and small fiddles were no business of ours. From the first morning after the 1997 election victory when she opened the door looking an exhausted mess, she forsook the right to keep anything from us and we now regard anything she does as legitimately within our sphere of interference. We all pile in, some more crudely than others. Entirely proper enquiries about the role of the PM's wife get tangled with business that should be off-limits. Germaine Greer even thought she had the right to tell Mrs Blair off for being so Catholic and succumbing to motherhood four times. In return for this incessant meddling comes public admiration and affection. How the nation rejoiced (and was encouraged to do so by the Blairs) when they announced the last pregnancy; how they understood when Euan acted wild briefly. Diana was the emblem of this deal which in the end is always destructive to the protagonists.

There is a growing madness on both sides. Clark Gable once told David Niven: 'We all have a contract with the public. In us they see themselves or what they would like to be.' They are our fantasies, our best friends, possibly our nemesis in a godless universe.

None of it could happen unless almost everybody in society wanted it to carry on. The desire for fame is only growing. In living memory has there ever been a man like Jamie Oliver – talented all right – who is prepared to surrender, for the right price, all his privacy and that of his wife, baby, parents, friends, and granny? Yes some of this is a game, but when he wants to disappear and lead a life of essential anonymity how will he be able to argue his case? Or Nigella, who extended the performance even further. The daring is breathtaking. If you play out the drawn-out death of your husband, the next affair you have and the many children involved, all because you need the public infatuated with you, where do you stop?

Graham Greene once said in an interview for the *Radio Times* that fame was a 'powerful aphrodisiac', but even heightened lust must get tired and it is never in the power of the famous to make the exit when they wish, or to renegotiate their contracts with the public who put them where they are.

The stars exist in a palace of sycophancy (who dares tell Nigella that many of her recipes are dud?), only able to trust other stars equal in status and wealth – all others are potential enemies likely to shop or betray them, for their own small moments of fame and fortune.

These days novelists are required to be part of the circus too and while some loathe the demands, others love the attention and glitz, ignoring at their peril the warning given by Gabriel Garcia Marquez, 'a famous writer who wants to continue writing has to be constantly defending himself against fame'. Even Maya Angelou – who used to see herself as the voice of black America – now expects to be treated like a queen.

Some people will be destroyed by this ruthless game. Gritten rightly observes that modern fame has been extended, it has been democratised. Ordinary punters are now launched into that bizarre world because they are prepared to make themselves into exhibits. *Big Brother*'s Jade, crude and hopeless but game for many laughs, even those directed at her own flaws, is now as much part of the canon as the canny Ulrika. Perhaps it is because contemporary life crushes out the individual human spirit while professing to promote the idea of personal choice and freedom.

How do you gain the recognition you seek? By appearing on *Pop Idol* or *Fame Academy* where you will be affirmed, talked about, then buried.

But it would be a mistake to feel too sorry for our established stars. Too many of them seem to think they don't have to follow any rules of conduct or decency because they are so irreplaceable. Michael Barrymore and Deayton will be back, as will Jeffrey Archer. We do not condemn Billy Connolly for selling lottery tickets, there is no stopping the rise and rise of that irrepressible pair, the Hamiltons, who should send a bouquet to Mohamed Al Fayed for making them into the celebs they have become.

Unlike the US, we don't really pull people down to size. They don't ever have to apologise – have Margaret Thatcher or John Birt or Jeffrey Archer appeared contrite for the damage they caused? Like hell. In the US Clinton is admired but also held in scorn for all his weaknesses which may have led to the present Republican regime. Here they swoon when they see him, bow before him, treat him like he is the master of the universe.

We need to think about the popular culture we have made. Stars need to remember that celebrity is, as John Updike said, 'a mask which eats into the face' and that they do have choices even today. Bob Geldof survives but Paula Yates was destroyed by the fame game and all the distortions it brings. I am sure he gets riled when he is stopped by fans too often and when his privacy is invaded, but he has made his own life meaningful by using his fame for a greater good, something other attention-grabbing celebrities may try to emulate.

A generation now believes only thin is beautiful

13 January 2003

One day I may just want to take shelter within the secretive folds of a burka. At least under that cloak your body can turn, age, loosen up and relax. Maybe this is one reason why so many Muslim women (and droves of white women converts) are choosing the hijab to escape from our awful, oppressive 'world of slim'. The female body is under such grinding scrutiny – ordered to be ever thinner and tighter, mocked, scorned, rearranged, cut, filled, exposed, starved – and there is no end to it, as the misguided Kate Winslet has just discovered, poor lass. At school she was known as Blubber but she turned into an irresistible young actress with a beautiful, expressive face and a softly feminine body.

Then came a baby, more success, and the pressure was on: Winslet had to shed her pounds on the orders of Hollywood. She despises these injunctions: 'All the men I've ever spoken to say they like a girl to have an arse on them, so why is it that women think they have to be thin, very thin?'

But she obeys Hollywood's injunctions nevertheless. She got thin, very thin, and told us all (yawn, yawn) about her wonderful diet of buttered potatoes. Yet for GQ magazine, the thinking man's strumpet, her svelte form was still too corpulent. So they doctored her pictures admits Dylan Jones, the editor: 'Various parts have been improved [sic], including her stomach and legs' – a common practice apparently. Sophie Dahl too had to become very thin and even then they digitally drained more fat and blood out of her before showing her in a post-orgasmic trance on posters.

We have reached the point where only digitally produced images of perfection can be as perfect as male aesthetes want women to be. And women collude in this, says Felipe Fernandez-Armesto, the author of *Food: A History*: 'anti-fat propaganda is not gender-specific; female fashion editors and designers connive in its campaigns, and feminism has contributed to the hallowing of women's own bodily 'control', of which dieting is an aspect.'

What next for Kate then? Does she look at herself in the mirror now with shame? That is the point, of course: to make her and the rest of us believe that we are worthless gluttons. It is why the rare big birds, such as the morning-television presenter Fern Britton and the comedian Dawn French, are so adored by their public. They have guts.

The rest of us are not that strong. In January, the month designated by our media-wallahs for self-flagellation, self-disgust, self-deception and impossible forms of self-control, this message has been emitted ad nauseam. A sceptic, I somehow now know about the Pritikin and Zone diets, the Fat Flush Plan, the slimming pill Xenadrine, Jane Scrivner's Detox. Oh yes, and I confess that I am thinking, if not the burka, then maybe the tummy tuck.

They claim they are concerned about obesity and the terrible health problems that can result from this. This is a pernicious cover-up for their real intentions. It gives their obsessions a respectable face, another excuse to push their body fascism into every cell of our lives and those of our children. Winslet and Dahl were not obese but they were treated as though they were. Thousands of children and young people are not obese in any sense of the word and yet if they are not skinny, they are not only teased (which has always gone on) but panicked into thinking that soon they will be immobilised by fat and become fatally ill.

Worse, they know they are 'disgusting', a blot on our lovely landscape which should only have Kylie or Dannii floating across it. Tonight on Channel 4, the programme *Skinny Kids* shows how this is damaging to all children. Six-year-olds already hate their legs and tummies and want special medicines to keep them thin. Nine-year-olds talk like dissatisfied old bags.

Adults too suffer devastating low esteem brought on by any weight gain or continuous failures of endless diets: 88 per cent of British women have dieted; the majority of us hate parts of our bodies. Jobs and promotion are more easily given to slim enough people; most outspoken feminists are determinedly thin, perhaps because they never want to be accused of being like Andrea Dworkin.

Besides asylum-seekers, plump and fat people are the only other group in our society we are allowed to bully, reject and openly abuse. In a John Lewis shop before Christmas I saw a woman drop an expensive vase as she was bending to pick it up. It broke. I could see her hands were shaking involuntarily, as if she might have Parkinson's disease, but she was overweight and people quickly started expressing their contempt that she 'had allowed herself to get so fat'. She burst into tears and shuffled off. People such as her are now placed outside our moral universe, and that is what is truly disgusting. We blame them for being, and that is the worst discrimination of all.

The British Heart Foundation claims that two-thirds of the men and half the women in Britain are overweight, but what does this mean? Does it include me, probably 10 pounds above what I was in my twenties? If so, I reject these figures. According to Ellen Rupell Shell, whose book *The Hungry Gene* comes out soon, 1 billion adults in the world are clinically obese. Young obesity is up 70 per cent since the eighties. These are serious statistics. But being not thin is not the same thing. The NSPCC once produced figures showing absurdly high levels of child abuse by including actions which were harmless, thereby devaluing the damage. Obesity is a serious problem, but being a size 12 or 14 shouldn't be. And we are giving out dangerously mixed messages. Are we worried that people are fixated on diets or that too many are overweight? Is the persistent bulimic saner than the incurable flabby?

I also think there needs to be better scientific explanations about body size and food. Some people do eat too much, or the wrong foods and, yes, they could change their eating habits. But some plump people I know eat very little. It is iniquitous to accuse this group of indulgence. Developments in science are already giving us clues that there may be genetic differences between the naturally thin and the plump. An American doctor, Nikhil Dhurandhar, believes that a virus is causing the epidemic in obesity.

We criticise food manufacturers, yet free-market governments do not stop the ruthless advertising of sweets and other bad food to children. And why are the poor getting fat while the rich get thinner year on year? Could it be that the poor are making their own (and maybe even valuable) protest against the terrifying Trinnies who dictate how we may look? Or maybe we turn into over-eaters because the standards of what is normal are now so impossible that it hardly seems worth the bother?

Everything is distorted by the slim culture. I love Rembrandt's Danae – a young woman who, as Simon Schama says, is 'bathed in golden light, her breasts, belly and thighs turned hospitably to the beholder'. But like another of Rembrandt's women, Bathsheba, Danae has folds and soft flesh. I was showing these to some teenagers when I went to speak to them about the painter. 'Ugh', they all said.

Some of the loveliest images in the world are now only 'gross' for a generation made to believe that a woman is only beautiful if she is desperately thin and fading fast. How terribly sad.

Not all fathers deserve the right to be parents

20 October 2003

This week is Parents' Week, with events, pamphlets and campaigns planned across the country to help, however incrementally, to improve the way we 'do' family life in Britain. Today, Margaret Hodge, the Minister for Children, will launch an initiative to make this country a family-friendly one.

Not before time, I can almost hear millions of past and present harassed parents saying. These people know only too well how children, even the sweetest of sweet babies, are regarded by too many of their fellow citizens when they appear in public spaces. Have you noticed how smiles are often not returned, even in waiting -rooms of surgeries where parents are trying to comfort sick children. Huffy adults look this way and that and tut-tut their disapproval. It is as if they thought their taxes were meant to ensure that young Britons and their breeders would be kept in remote farms somewhere, anywhere in fact out of their sight. These are adults who either have no kids or were brought up to believe that society should only be expected to have a slight and uneasy tolerance of the young.

In media land, last week, yob children were the preoccupation, as was the delectable Michael Portillo, who warmed our cockles as he (childless himself) managed a household of several children. Watching Mr Portillo on the TV was like viewing the launch of a new sort of Center Parc concept – privileged ex-Cabinet ministers slumming it for seven whole days with mouthy children, an experience guaranteed to make them feel even more supermanly than they know they are. And then came Gordon Brown, who told the world with a wonderful smile that fatherhood now mattered more than anything. Anything.

Parenthood, motherhood, fatherhood, grandparent participation, divorce are now taken seriously by politicians and others who know that, although life is remarkably full of potential for increasing numbers of British children, there is also much social discord. Our divorce rates are now among the highest in the world, and many British children are coping with complicated allegiances and expectations and other influences which bear down on little lives – the impact of which we cannot know until it is too late.

We must rejoice that many British children are being nurtured and understood better than, say, a hundred years ago. The work/life balance is firmly on the agenda of big firms, violence against children is no longer sanctioned, and the voices of the young are listened to more. New fathers (they do exist, and in ever larger numbers, whatever some snide feminist may say) relate to their children with an intimacy which must flummox and irritate their own pops, who grew up believing that real men don't sing rhymes. We aren't there yet, and perhaps never will be, but enlightened child-rearing has been planted in our soil and the shoots are coming up nicely.

But some problems remain stubbornly in place, and new ones are shooting up fast, sometimes as a result of the good seeds that were sown. This week apparently, inspired by the biblical Bob Geldof, divorced fathers will be protesting, demanding that family courts bestow upon them a meaningful relationship with their children, a right to half the child, not unlike the dispute adjudicated by Solomon. For Geldof, a supporter of Fathers4Justice, the injustice is plain, and he has appeared in this paper ardently arguing his case. The current situation, where mothers on the whole are given custody with access rights for fathers, he believes, is a burning abuse of the rights of a father, who in modern times is an equal carer to the mother.

He is profoundly wrong, as are the other campaigners, mainly because they focus on their own rights, and not the needs or choices of the children. Now, Geldof has obviously suffered real torment with the painful custody battles he had with Paula Yates and all the mess that was left behind when she shacked up with Michael Hutchence. Hutchence, of course, was later found hanged and his death was followed by the miserable demise of Yates herself in the presence of their young daughter. That daughter now lives with her half-sisters and a doting Geldof.

But his personal experiences – powerful and Shakespearean though they are – may be pushing him to head a crusade he needs to think about much more honestly and dispassionately.

Custody and the best interests of the child are difficult judgements, and they go way beyond the battle of the sexes. A universal 'truth' has now been established that it is always fathers who are left out in the cold by manipulative mothers seeking to destroy their relationships with their children whilst emptying their pockets – often as revenge for the man seeking to go elsewhere. Another righteous belief is that divorced parents must be friends, and the third, growing fast, is that the only fair way is to split the lives of the children down the middle, with the offspring spending half their time with each parent.

Mothers leave too, of course, and women initiate divorces more than men do. The mothers whose children are looked after by the father believe that they too have an absolute right to be regarded as 'equal' parents and are forever complaining about what victims they are of an unfair world. Some departed parents are indeed denied fair access, and in too many cases there is an expectation of automatic alimony even if the caring parent can or does work. As it happens, I never asked for any maintenance for myself from my ex-husband – that is my kind of feminism. But we all know what caring mothers have had to go through to get pathetically small amounts of money from their spouses, and the lies that are told about incomes and bank balances to reduce the cash they should produce for their own children.

Manipulation happens on the other side too. Parents who have new lovers want their old children to agree that their mother/father was unworthy and that it is much more wonderful on the other side. I have a treasured fax from my own dear departed to his son going through wild adolescence days (which the father never had to cope with) in which he goes through all my defects and then reassures my son that one day he too will escape. There are people who can be friends after divorce, but to insist that this is the only way is emotional blackmail.

New research by Carol Smart at the Centre for Research on Family, Kinship and Childhood in the University of Leeds found that a large number of children hate the fifty-fifty lifestyle. They feel like possessions and they are not. As the writer Angela Phillips points out, they are not houses. And the best interests of the child are sometimes genuinely in conflict with the 'rights' of the absent parent, who must surely learn to give way.

Parenting is not a right but an obligation for life, a duty which we take on in the West as a choice. I hope that our children will learn that as adults they too have obligations to us, the parents. Banging on the doors of courts barking for more rights over children's lives and complaining incessantly about parental inconveniences shows that we are still unable to see that our own self-gratification has to take a back seat if we are to be the good parents we think we are. That is what our children need and deserve.